the little
PC book

By Lawrence J. Magid

Edited by Darcy DiNucci

Illustrations by John Grimes

Peachpit Press

to the point.
PUBLISHING

The Little PC Book
By Lawrence J. Magid
Edited by Darcy DiNucci
Illustrations by John Grimes
Cookbook by Harry Henderson
Copyedited by Tema Goodwin
Design by Chuck Ruthier, Earl Office
Cover by Ted Mader + Associates

Peachpit Press, Inc.
2414 Sixth St.
Berkeley, California 94710
800/283-9444
510/548-4393 (phone)
510/548-5991 (fax)

Trademarks

Many of the designations used by manufacturers and sellers to distinguish
their products are claimed as trademarks. Where those designations appear in
this book, and Peachpit Press was aware of a trademark claim, the designations have been printed in initial caps.

Notice of Liability

ISBN 0-938151-54-1
Printed and bound in the United States of America

To my mother, Fae Magid.
She taught me the value of asking questions.

Acknowledgments

It would have been impossible for me to take on this or any other large task without the constant support and patience of my wife, Patti. My children, Katherine and William, deserve credit for helping with the children's software section and for reminding me that there are things in life that are (a lot) more important than computers.

Ted Nace, the founder of Peachpit Press, has been a constant friend and a tremendous help during the process. I've worked with larger publishing companies, but never a better one. My editor, Darcy DiNucci, did an incredible job crafting, reshaping, and, at times, rewriting. Thanks also to Chuck Routhier for helping to make this book look as good as it does, and to John Grimes for his wonderful illustrations.

Don Sellers, author of the Peachpit book *Zap! 25 Ways Your Computer Can Hurt You and What You Can Do About Them*, reviewed the sections of this book having to do with computer safety. His extensive knowledge of the subject was a great help.

Beth Uyehara and Kate Korewick, who edit the material I write for Prodigy, helped with their patience and counsel. Thanks also to David Needle, editor of *Computer Currents*, in whose pages I've talked to novices and learned of their concerns; to Dan Akst, my editor at the *Los Angeles Times*, for his enthusiasm and gentle guidance; and to Diane and Dave Tyrrel, Lamont Shadowens, and Steven Klugman for reading the manuscript, pointing out its weak spots, and sharing the excitement.

Preface

The Little PC Book covers the absolute basics of using an IBM-compatible personal computer. It is meant to get you up and running with your PC, without bogging you down in technical details, and with a little fun along the way, too.

When you're done with this book, you should feel comfortable talking to a computer salesperson about how much "RAM" you need, using a new piece of software, or facing the C> prompt on your computer screen. You'll learn what the jargon that surrounds computers really means, and you'll find out where to get help when you need it.

Now, before you go any further, take note: This book covers IBM-compatible PCs, not Macintoshes. (If you want to know the difference, take a quick look at Chapter 3 of this book.) If you've gotten this book by accident and want to know about Macs instead, you can return this book to Peachpit Press or exchange it for a copy of *The Little Mac Book*. (Peachpit's address is on the copyright page of this book.)

The Little PC Book is divided into these parts:

Part 1, Getting Oriented, introduces you to the world of PCs. Here, you'll learn just what people mean when they say things like "MS-DOS," "IBM compatible," and "PC clone."

Part 2, Putting Together a System, describes the different parts that make up a PC, what each is for, and how to choose the one that's best for you.

Part 3, Rules of the Road, teaches what you need to know after you turn on your computer. You'll learn the rules of working with hard disks, creating and saving files, and getting help for problems.

Part 4, Stocking Up on Software, tells how to pick just the software you need. It sorts out the different categories of software and helps you choose exactly what's right for you.

The DOS Cookbook and **The Windows Cookbook,** on the gray pages at the back of the book, provide step-by-step instructions for common operations on your PC—running a program, finding out what you have on your disk, and all the other things you'll need to do.

This book is designed to make finding the information you need as easy as possible, and to make it easy to learn the jargon that populates the world of computers. I've boldfaced new terms as they're introduced, and anytime you see a boldface term, you can look it up in the glossary that's at the end of the book. I've also boldfaced the names of products and companies I mention. You can find their phone numbers in the accompanying Resource boxes.

Ready? OK, let's get started.

Table of Contents

Getting Oriented

Why Learn About Computers?

You've gotten along so far without learning about computers. Why start now?

I. Your job depends on it.

2. You've just bought a computer, and now you need to find out how to use it.

3. You've determined that computers aren't going to go away. In fact, they're becoming more and more common everywhere you look, and you just know that one day, one's going to land on your desk.

4. You're starting to feel like your life is a little bit out of control, and you've heard that a computer is a good way to get organized and get more done in less time.

5. You're using a computer at work and know your way around a program or two, but now you want to get to know a bit more about what the PC can do for you.

OKAY, POP, YOU TRY IT NOW!

ME?

6. You've decided to buy a computer for your home so that you and your kids can have access to all the useful and fun stuff you've heard is available for them. Now you need to know what to get, how to equip it, and what you can do with it once you've plugged it in.

7. You've decided to finally confront your fears. You've taken up bungee jumping, you're getting married, and you're learning about computers.

There are lots of reasons to learn about computers. Yours may not be listed here, but it's probably a good one. The truth is, computers aren't going to go away. And they can, in fact, help you organize your finances and work more efficiently. More than that, they're getting a lot easier to use than they used to be, and these days, they're surprisingly affordable.

I think you've made the right choice.

NOW HIT RETURN....

How Is a Computer Like a Record Player?

2

Learning how to use a PC isn't as difficult as you might think.

The first thing to remember is that you don't need to know how a computer works; you just need to know how to use it. It's like a radio, TV, VCR, movie projector, or any other piece of equipment. You can use it even if you don't know how it really works. When you turn on your TV, you don't think about picture tubes, vertical hold, or broadcast frequencies. What counts is the program: "60 Minutes," "The Simpsons," CNN. If you want to, you can learn about the technical workings of the TV, but you don't need to in order to enjoy the programs.

Like a stereo or TV, the PC itself is just the box that plays the programs. With a VCR, you play videotapes. With a stereo, you play CDs or audio tapes. With a PC, you play **application programs**, or **software**.

Just as some folks compose their own music, some people write their own software. But being able to create programs from scratch is not at all necessary. Instead, you'll simply buy the software you need, just as you buy the music you want to hear on your stereo.

With a computer, as with a stereo, you'll need to know just enough about your system—the **hardware**—so that you can buy one, set it up, turn it on and off, and play the software. You'll also want to become familiar with the different kinds of software you can get and how to buy them. This book will tell you all those things—and no more, because that's everything you'll really need in order to buy and use a computer.

Of course, if you'd like to find out more, great. This book will give you a good start and provide basic reference information that you can come back to down the line.

There Are Really Only Two Kinds of Personal Computers

CHOOSING A "PC" CAN BE LIKE CHOOSING A BREAKFAST CEREAL— TOO MANY CHOICES!

"MACS"

"PCs"

When you go into a computer store, you'll see computers of all sizes and shapes, from many different manufacturers. You'll see desktop machines and laptop machines, from Toshiba, IBM, Compaq, and countless other companies. Don't worry about it. There are really only two kinds of personal computers: IBM-compatible computers (or "PCs") and Macintosh computers (or "Macs").

Let's get back to the stereo metaphor we used in Chapter 2. Computers, like CD players, are classified by the type of software they play, not by who makes them. If you want to play standard CDs, you can get a CD player from Philips, Zenith, Sony—whichever has the features you want for the right price. If you want to play the new mini-CDs, however, you'll need a different kind of player. It's the same with computers. PCs and Macintoshes run different kinds of software.

About 90 percent of today's personal computers are **IBM compatibles** (some-

Technically, both Macintoshes and IBM-compatible computers are PCs—personal computers. When most people say "PC," though, they're referring to IBM compatibles (as I do in this book).

times called **PC compatibles**). That means that no matter who they're made by, they can run any software that's made for an IBM PC. All IBM-compatible computers, whether they're desktop computers or laptop computers, work the same way and can run the same software.

In order to run the same software, all these computers have two important things in common.

First, they're all based on the same type of **central processing unt (CPU)**. The CPU is the "brains" of the computer, the piece of equipment that actually does the computing. PCs are based on **processors** (or chips) made by Intel, which are called by names ending in "86." The oldest PCs have 8086 processors. AT-family PCs have 80286 processors. Newer computers have 80386 or 80486 processors. Generally, the higher the number before the 86, the faster the computer. Recently, Intel started naming rather than numbering its CPUs (the first one to get a name is called the Pentium processor). You'll find out more about what all that means to you in Chapter 10.

Computers that are IBM compatible but not made by IBM are sometimes called "clones" because they are identical to the IBM in every important way.

The second thing these computers have in common is that they all run an operating system called **DOS**. (Exactly what DOS is will be explained in the next chapter.)

The other 10 percent of today's personal computers are **Macintoshes**, made by Apple Computer. They use entirely different processors and require software made especially for them.

There are a few other types of computer, which run their own software, including Amiga, Atari, Apple II, and CP/M computers. Amiga and Atari machines are fine computers, with special features for some specialized tasks like game-playing, animation, and music-processing. Apple IIs and CP/M computers, once quite popular, are now largely obsolete. For general use, you're better off sticking to either PCs or Macintoshes. With well over 100 million PC users and 10 million Mac users, you can be sure that those computers are here to stay. There will always be plenty of software for both the PC and the Mac, and you'll have no trouble finding information and help for either of them.

Now, assuming you've settled on a PC and not a Macintosh, let's get on with the book.

A Little Bit About DOS and Windows

Almost any IBM-compatible computer you buy will come with a piece of software called DOS (rhymes with "sauce"). Usually, this will be the standard version, created by Microsoft, called MS-DOS ("em-ess-dos").

4

DOS is the computer's operating system, the foundation software that takes care of the basic functioning of the computer. DOS is required by almost all software that runs on a PC.

The other software, the kind that does a particular task, such as word processing, is the application software. Application software relies on DOS to take care of basic tasks that all programs use, like what happens when you press a key on the **keyboard**, or how your work will be stored on **disk**. With those basics taken care of, the application software can apply itself to the special tasks that it controls, like formatting text, drawing pictures, or filing information.

Like any other piece of software, DOS has a particular way of communicating with you, called its **interface**. In DOS's case, that interface is not very helpful. It consists merely of a **prompt** that usually looks like this:

```
C>_
```

A prompt is a message the computer sends you to let you know that it's your turn to do something. The blinking underline character following the prompt is called a **cursor**. It shows you where any characters you type will appear on screen.

The DOS Prompt

The DOS prompt is the signal that DOS gives when it's waiting for a command from you.

The DOS prompt usually looks like this:

```
C:>
```

But it might look like this:

```
C:\>
```

or this:

```
C:\WINDOWS>
```

or it might be an A: rather than a C:. Or it might show the date or have other characters. (There's a DOS command, called PROMPT, that lets you change it.)

In this book, we'll show the DOS prompt as C:>, its basic form.

Sometimes an IBM-compatible computer will come with an operating system called OS/2, rather than DOS. I won't cover OS/2 in this book, because it's not very popular, and even OS/2 computers can run like DOS machines.

The **DOS prompt** is also sometimes called the **DOS command line**, or even the **C prompt**. Anyway, whenever you see it, the computer is waiting for a **DOS command**.

In some cases, DOS commands are easy. To start a program, for example, you type the name of your program (or some abbreviation of it) and press the Enter key. To do other things, the commands may be more complex. Luckily, you don't need to know very many commands to do just about everything you'll ever need to do with DOS, and I've provided a cookbook for those commands at the end of this book.

Even more luckily, software makers have realized that DOS is too hard to work with, and they've supplied ways to make working with the operating system much easier. Starting with version 5.0 of DOS, you get an extra program called the **DOS Shell**, which provides a different interface. It looks like this:

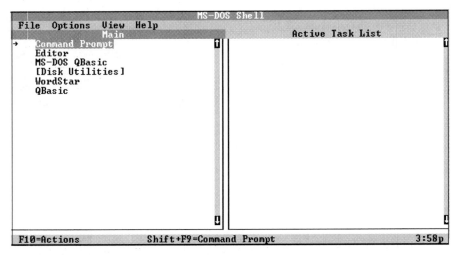

The DOS Shell makes it easier to give DOS commands.

With the DOS Shell, you don't have to remember all the DOS commands; you can just pick them from the screen or from **pull-down menus**.

An even more popular way of hiding DOS, though, is a program called **Microsoft Windows**. Windows provides a graphical user interface that looks like this:

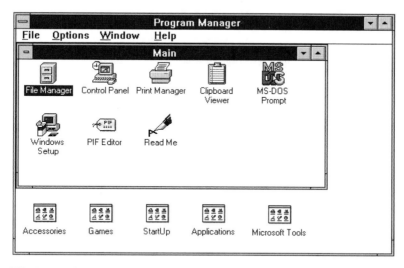

Windows isn't just an easier-to-use interface for DOS—it's a whole new way of working with PC applications that's based on interacting with **icons** and other on-screen controls.

Windows and the DOS Shell are designed to be used with a mouse, a device that lets you move the cursor freely around the screen so that you can easily choose among the items displayed there. If you're using Windows, you can also do a lot of things you can't do with DOS alone, like run more than one program at a time.

Many programs are designed to work especially with Windows. All those programs use an interface similar to the Windows interface; they also use the same commands for basic actions, so once you've learned a few basic commands, it's fairly easy to find your way around any Windows program.

Windows makes using the PC much easier than with DOS alone. Most PCs these days come supplied with Windows, and a lot of good new software is being written for it.

The next chapter describes what it's like to work in Windows.

Working With Windows

5

Like every Windows program, the **Program Manager** has a **menu bar** running across the top of the main window. The menu bar lists the menus available in this program.

Every item on screen is shown in a **window**, which you can open, close, and change the size of. You can have several windows open at once, with a different program in each.

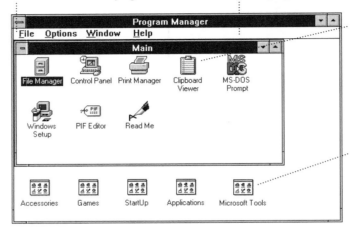

Icons represent **files** and programs in your system. To start a program, you just point at it with the **mouse** and **click** the **mouse button** twice.

These icons represent **program groups**. The Main group window is open on this screen. The others hold other groups of programs.

When you start Windows, you see the Windows Program Manager, shown here, instead of the DOS C:> prompt. From there, you can start programs and do everything else you need to do.

Most computers these days come with both Microsoft Windows and DOS. Windows not only gives DOS a more friendly interface, it also adds quite a few capabilities that DOS alone doesn't have:

- It lets you start programs by pointing at the one you want and clicking a mouse button.
- It lets you run two or more programs at the same time and keep them all on screen at once.
- It lets you pick commands from pull-down menus so you always know what commands are available and what they're called.
- It adds new graphics features so that you can view documents on screen just as they will be printed, typefaces, graphics, and all. (That's called **WYSIWYG**—"what you see is what you get.")

Windows' friendly capabilities go more than skin deep. Many application programs have been written especially for Windows and use the same methods of giving commands that you use in Windows itself—using the mouse to choose commands and move items around on screen.

Generally, all Windows programs also use the same basic commands for creating and storing documents and other standard procedures. That means that once you've mastered Windows or one Windows program, you've got down the basics for all of them.

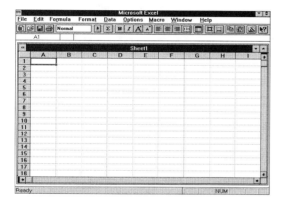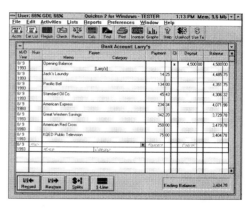

On the left is Microsoft Excel, a Windows **spreadsheet** program. On the right is Quicken, a Windows financial management program. As you can see here, even different kinds of Windows programs from different companies look similar and use similar kinds of commands.

Although Windows is really designed to be used with a mouse, you can also give commands from the keyboard, if that's more comfortable for you.

If you want Windows and it doesn't come with your computer, you can buy it at most software and computer stores. When I wrote this book, Windows' list price was $150. (See Chapter 35 for more on where to buy software.)

To run Windows you'll need a pretty fast machine. Part 2 of this book describes how to figure out how fast a computer is and how to know what kind of computer you'll need. The Windows Cookbook at the end of this book tells you how to carry out the most common operations in Windows.

Mouse Commands

Windows is designed to be used with a mouse, which provides an easy way of giving commands. As you move the mouse around on your desktop, a **pointer** on screen moves along with it, allowing you to point at the object on screen that you want to use. To select the object, you click the mouse button.

The mouse has its own vocabulary in Windows. One click means one thing, two clicks means another. The vocabulary is pretty simple, and it's the same in Windows and in any Windows program. It will soon become second nature. Here's a description of the basic mouse commands and some of the situations you'll use them in.

Clicking on an icon, menu, menu command, or file name on screen selects it. Clicking on a button activates it. Clicking on an arrow button next to a field in a dialog box displays other choices for that field. Clicking on it again makes the list disappear.

Double-clicking on a program icon opens the program. In a dialog box, double-clicking on a file name is the same as clicking on the file name and clicking OK.

You can **drag** to select text in a document, and you can drag to select commands from pull-down menus. In some programs you can drag selected text from one place to another in a document.

You don't need a lot of room to use a mouse. If you've reached the edge of your desk space before your on-screen pointer gets to where you want it to be, just pick up the mouse and move it to where it has more room.

For more on mice, see Chapter 17.

Ten Places to Get Help Learning About Your PC

6

The first thing you should know when you set out to learn about computers is that you're not on your own. There is something called the "computer community" out there, ready to give you help when you need it. Don't worry; it's a very informal group, and you don't need to sign up anywhere.

The computer community consists of all those people who, just like you, have learned about—or are just now learning about—computers. So they will understand your questions. This community has created a lot of publications and a lot of ways to get in touch with others who can help you. Here's a list of resources you can turn to at any time.

1. The manual and the help command
Every piece of hardware or software comes with a user's guide, which is designed to be your first resource when you need to find out something about your computer or a piece of software.

Most programs now also come with built-in **on-line help**, which calls up information about the program's commands when you issue a particular command from your keyboard. With most Windows programs you can press the F1 key any time and go directly into a help window. In most cases, you'll get help on whatever command you were using when you pressed F1. That's called **context-sensitive help**. Most Windows programs also have a Help menu.

2. Friends, relations, and gurus
You know who I'm talking about. That person down the hall who seems to know everything there is to know about computing. Your niece, your dad, your brother-in-law. Whoever it is, they're your best resource for helping you solve that little problem that's gotten you stuck. Most people are really glad to help. They're honored—flattered even—to be asked to show off their knowl-

edge, even if their level of accomplishment is only a month or two beyond your own. Trust me. It will be fun for both of you.

3. Tech support lines

Most hardware and software manufacturers have a support line you can call when you need help with their products. Some have toll-free lines, but others require you to make a long-distance call. Some companies have systems that tell you how long you'll be on hold. A few, though not many, have installed 900 lines that charge you a fee for the call—an inexcusable practice you should protest if you're as irate about it as I am.

Before you call tech support, make sure you know the version number of the program you have, as well as exactly what hardware you're using it on (especially how much **memory** your computer has and what **expansion boards**, if any, you have installed). Some technical support people will require that you tell them the serial number of the program

Tech Support Numbers

Aldus	206-628-4531
Borland International	408-438-5300
Broderbund Software	800-521-6263
	415-382-4400
Central Point Software	503-690-8080
Chipsoft	619-453-4842
Corel	613-728-1990
Electronic Arts	415-572-2787
Intuit	415-858-6050
Lotus Development	800-223-1662
Microsoft	206-454-2030
Software Publishing Corp.	800-447-7991
Spinnaker	617-494-1220
Symantec	800-441-7234
WordPerfect	800-541-5096

as a way to prevent "pirates" (people who didn't buy the program) from using the service. Most tech support operations, however, are pretty relaxed about such formalities.

The tech support provider will often try to walk you through a solution over the phone, so make sure you're sitting at your computer and your computer is turned on when you call.

And have a good book handy. Help support lines will often keep you on hold for a while.

4. User groups

User groups come in all shapes and sizes, from the internationally renowned, 20,000-member Boston Computer Society to the tiny groups that gather in the evenings at hundreds of companies, computer stores, high schools, and community colleges.

Most user groups have meetings and "special interest groups" aimed at novices. The typical group will meet once or twice a month and have a semiregular newsletter and perhaps an **on-line bulletin board**. Typically, user groups don't charge for their help, but

A Quick Guide to Software Manuals

Over time, most manuals have evolved to a standard organization that has been proven to work. Look for these sections:

System requirements The minimum hardware and software you'll need to use the program are listed right up front in the user's guide, often in the installation instructions. Sometimes this information is also on the outside of the box.

Installation instructions These are usually near the front of the user's guide, or in a separate booklet, and lead you step by step through installing the software.

Tutorial Also generally near the front of the user's guide, the tutorial leads you through a practice session with the software. Usually, practice files for use with the tutorial are included on the program disk.

Reference guide An alphabetical listing of commands. Use this when you want to know how a particular command works.

Troubleshooting A list of problems you might run up against and how to solve them. Of course, no troubleshooting section lists every possible problem, but it's the first place to look.

if you want to get the newsletter, you might be asked to pay a small fee to join.

Many user groups offer a library of free or low-cost software. Often, belonging to the group gives you access to special discounts on software, books, and other products. Many groups publish the phone numbers of people who can be called with questions on a particular software product, and groups often invite speakers from computer companies to demonstrate their new products.

You can find a local user group by calling the User Group Locator hotline at 914-876-6678. (Call from a touch-tone phone.)

Perhaps the best part about being involved in a user group is the informal opportunity it provides to ask the sort of questions that you just can't ask anywhere else, such as: "I've taken my broken **printer** back to the local Fix-a-Computer three times, and they just can't seem to get it right. Is there another store someone can recommend?"

As in most volunteer groups, a handful of stalwart souls ends up doing most of the work. If you have the time to pitch in for some of the chores, your efforts will be heartily appreciated. (You volunteer to bring refreshments one week, and the next week you find out you've been nominated for a two-year term as group secretary.) Pitching in is more than courteous, though. If you get involved, you'll find you're on the inside track for all sorts of information.

5. Your local computer store

Chances are that you live within driving distance of a computer store. One would hope that computer stores would be staffed by people who know a lot about computers and are willing to share that knowledge.

Maybe yes, maybe no. While some computer and software salespeople are very knowledgeable, others just act as if they are. People who sell computers certainly know more than the average novice, but they just can't know everything there is to know about what they sell.

With these caveats in mind, it's still a good idea to become friends with the folks who work at the computer store. Once you've latched on to one or two of these people, milk them for all they're worth. Call them up with questions. Ask their advice. Flatter their ego. And when you need some hardware or software, make sure you buy stuff from them, too. I'm encouraging you to use these people—not exploit them.

6. Magazines and newsletters

There are hundreds of magazines devoted to personal computing, and many of them can be understood by beginners. All of these publications carry software reviews that are written by professional computer journalists who usually give their educated opinions. In any case, the magazines are a good place to start when you want to find out about a particular program. They are all available at any good newsstand and by subscription.

Peed Publishing company has an interesting offer. You can start by subscribing to *PC Novice* and, as you become more advanced, switch to its sister publication, *PC Today*. Both are excellent magazines.

PC/Computing is one of my favorite computer magazines for relative newcomers to computers. It's well written but not condescending. *PC World* is also well written but a little more advanced. *PC Magazine* is a great place to turn for encyclopedic data on anything you might consider buying. Its product reviews cover all the bases and then some. *Windows* magazine and *Windows Sources* offer advice and product information for people who are interested only in Windows products.

Computer Shopper is mostly a compendium of advertisements for computer hardware and software. It's a good place to find bargains. It's also a good way to build up your muscles—it's a huge publication.

If you use your computer to work at home, you might enjoy a subscription to *Home Office Computing*. It gives tips on running a business as well as a computer.

Some communities have free computer newspapers like *Computer Currents* (editions in San Francisco, Boston, Dallas, Atlanta, and

Resources

Computer Currents
800-365-7773, 510-547-6800.

Computer Shopper
212-503-3500.

Home Office Computing
212-505-3662.

PC/Computing
212-503-3500.

PC Magazine
800-365-2770.

PC Novice, PC Today
800-424-7900.

PC World
415-546-7722.

Windows
800-284-3584, 303-447-9330.

Windows Sources
800-365-3414.

other cities). These papers often have some very good articles, including reviews and tips. They often bring you a local angle, and they're a good place for notices of user group meetings, training classes, and other local resources. (Some editions of *Computer Currents* carry a column by yours truly. That, of course, doesn't blind me to its true worth.)

Some software companies also publish newsletters that provide tips and current information on their software. You can call the company that makes the software to find out if a newsletter is available.

7. On-line services

Another great way to get in touch with the world of computers is to log on to one of the on-line information services. This is where you use a device called a **modem** to have your computer dial up another computer. **On-line services** such as Prodigy, CompuServe, and America Online have special-interest areas where beginners can ask questions. (For more details, see the box "On-Line Services" in Chapter 19.)

8. Books

Computer books can be a great aid for learning about computers in general or about a particular piece of software. If you're confused by the array of computer books at the bookstore, just ask the clerk for a recommendation.

A quick way to get a particular book is to call Computer Literacy, a bookstore that prides itself on carrying practically every computer book ever published. You can even get the book mailed Next Day or Second Day Air. Even if you know the topic but not the title, such as "A tutorial about Microsoft Works," the people at the store will be able to make a knowledgeable recommendation. They'll also refund your money if you don't like what you get.

Resources

Computer Literacy
408-435-0744.

A Pocket Guide to Computer Books

Any trip to the computer section of a bookstore will overwhelm you with choices. The books will range from beginning through advanced information, and from general topics to very specific. You can narrow down your search with these guidelines.

Beginner books These are generally slimmer, under-$20 volumes with titles like *ABCs of...*, *Introduction to...*, *...Made Easy*, *...For Dummies*, and so on.

Quick-reference books These generally cost less than $10 and just provide very brief explanations of the various commands or menu options of a program. They're better for looking up an occasional piece of information than for learning a program.

Tutorials These books walk you through exercises classroom-style.

Interactive tutorials These books come with a disk that leads you through lessons on your own computer.

Advanced books Titles such as *Tips & Tricks* or *Supercharging* make it clear that these books are for those who already know a program and want to get better at it.

Reference books These tend to be the super-fat books, sold by the pound. Once you know the basics of a program, they're useful for looking up features.

Dictionaries The first thing anyone who is new to personal computers needs is a nice, easy dictionary of common computer terms. The glossary at the back of this book is a good start. If you're interested, you can get dictionaries (thick ones) that have nothing but computer terms. With a few terms like "kilobyte," "coprocessor," and "asynchronous communications" under your belt, you too can soon be wowing the masses around the water cooler, at cocktail parties, and at your next family reunion.

9. Courses

Of course, for personalized help, there's no substitute for a live instructor. Computer courses are available everywhere. Start by checking out the course offerings at a local community college. There are also many private companies that offer computer training. Check your local Yellow Pages under "training" or "computer training."

10. Experiment

Last but not least, don't be afraid to experiment. You should know that no matter what you do on a computer, it's very difficult, if not impossible (unless you directly assault the machine), to actually damage the hardware. The worst you can possibly do is lose some data and waste some time. Look through the menus to see what's there. In any program, try out any commands you don't know about. Watch what happens and you'll learn your software in no time.

Part 1 introduced you to your new partner, an IBM-compatible personal computer running DOS alone or DOS with Windows. Now that you know you want one, and you're convinced you can get any help you need to use it, you're ready for a computer of your own.

Part 2 will help you make sense of all the different pieces that go into a complete system.

What Do You Call That Thing Anyway?

7

The **monitor** (sometimes called the **display**, the screen, or the **CRT**) is the main way your computer communicates with you. This is where the computer shows you what your system is doing and what your files contain.

See Chapter 15 for more on monitors.

The **floppy disk drive** holds disks on which you can store programs and data that you want to get into or out of your computer.

For more about floppy drives, see Chapter 13.

A **modem** lets you connect your PC to other computers over a phone line. A modem can be external to the computer or it can be added as an expansion board inside the main system unit. Some modems, called **fax modems,** can also be used to send and/or receive faxes.

For more about modems, see Chapter 19.

MONITOR ("THE SCREEN")

SYSTEM UNIT

MODEM

KEYBOARD

This box, called the **system unit**, contains the guts of your computer. It holds the central processing unit), the memory (**RAM**, or **random access memory**) chips, and all the other electronic components that make your computer do what it does.

For more about CPUs and memory, see Chapters 10 and 11.

The **hard disk** (which is usually inside the system unit) stores most of your data. Most of today's hard disks store 80 or more **megabytes** of data (1 megabyte equals just over a million characters).

For more about hard disks, see Chapter 12.

The **expansion slots,** at the back of the system unit, are where you can add expansion boards that enhance what the machine can do. Expansion boards (sometimes known as **cards** or **adapters**) can increase speed or add features such as fax, extra disk drives, and other capabilities.

For more on expansion slots and expansion boards, see Chapter 14.

A PC system is made up of many parts. When you buy a PC, you can buy only the system unit or you can buy a system that includes a keyboard, a monitor, a mouse, and even basic software. Buying a complete system, of course, makes it easy, but buying separate components makes it possible to get exactly what you want. In any case, here are the basic parts that make up a full system. Each one is explained in detail in the chapters that follow.

GUY

PRINTER

MOUSE

The printer puts the documents you create onto paper.

For more on printers, see Chapter 18.

The keyboard is one way you communicate with the computer. You use it to issue commands and enter words and numbers. Its layout is similar to that of a standard typewriter keyboard.

For more on keyboards, see Chapter 16.

The mouse can be used with some programs to do some of the work of the keyboard. You use it to move a pointer around your monitor's screen to show the program where you want your next action to apply.

For more on mice, see Chapter 17.

Laptop and Notebook PCs

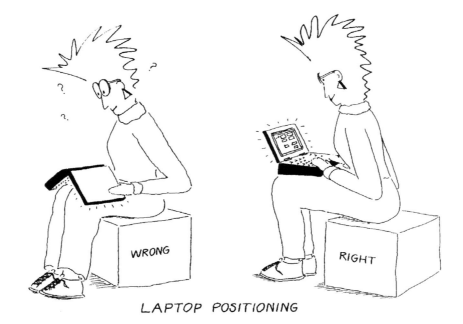

LAPTOP POSITIONING

Laptop and **notebook PCs** combine all of a system's components into a single, portable unit. They look different, but they have essentially the same kind of components as desktop machines have—just smaller. The term "notebook PC" generally refers to the smallest portable PCs (those weighing less than 7 pounds). The slightly larger ones are called "laptops." On portable PCs, the screen and the keyboard are built into the main unit. Many portable PCs also have built-in modems. If they have expansion slots at all, they usually use special, credit-card-size expansion devices called **PCMCIA cards**. Portable PCs can usually run either from a wall socket or from batteries.

Where to Buy a PC

When it comes to figuring out where to buy a PC, there are plenty of options. You can go to a computer store, you can buy it at a discount or warehouse-type store, you can buy it mail order, you can even find a small computer shop that will custom-build you a PC clone. You can also find PCs at some home electronics and stereo shops. I'll try to describe the advantages and drawbacks of each option here.

8

Computer Stores

Computer retail stores tend to be the most expensive option, but the advantage is that the good stores offer a great deal of customer support. If you buy from one of those stores, you can ask their service people to preinstall your operating system and software and check to see that everything works together before you take it home. You could even ask them to deliver the computer and set it up for you, and you have the right to expect someone to answer all your questions.

Not all computer specialty stores have the time or inclination to offer that kind of service, however. It depends in part on how competitive the market is in your area.

Discount Stores

If you know exactly what you want, and if you have such stores in your area, you can get a great deal by buying your computer at buyers' clubs like Price Club and Costco or even department stores like Sears. You're not going to get any hand-holding at those places, but most computers these days come preconfigured with DOS, Windows, and one or more application programs, so the lack of support might not be as much of a problem as you might think.

Stereo and Home Electronics Stores

An increasing number of stereo and home electronics stores are carrying computers right along with CD players, TV sets, and boom boxes. You may find a good deal at one of those stores, but if you decide to buy from a stereo store, make sure you get a brand name with a national warranty. The guy or gal who knows all about hi-fidelity isn't likely to be all that helpful if you have a problem running Windows.

Mail Order

Buying computers by mail order used to rank on the spectrum of foolishness somewhere up there with buying desert real estate by phone. But companies like **Compaq**, **CompAdd**, **Dell**, **PC Brand**, **Zeos**, and **Gateway 2000** have proven that quality and value can coexist at a single 800 number. Look for the glossy mail-order ads in the major computer magazines. These companies will build a machine to your specifications and send via UPS, generally within a couple of weeks. Some offer attractive service contracts with 24-hour on-site repairs.

The best way to be sure you're dealing with a reputable company is by word of mouth. Ask other people where they bought their computer and whether they were satisfied. Also look at the ads. If a company advertises for several months (or years) in a row, chances are it's a reasonably substantial business. At least it has stayed in business and paid its advertising bills.

One disadvantage of mail order is that you can't walk in to return items, get repairs, or ask questions. However, most of the major mail-order firms now offer toll-free telephone technical support. This is critical. Test them before you buy. Your first call shouldn't be to the sales department but to the technical support group. Ask some questions and see how responsive they are. Did you get through on the first call? Were you kept on hold? If they had to call you back, did they get back to you quickly? Are the people patient and friendly?

If you do buy mail order, it's a good idea to

Resources

Compaq Computer
800-345-1518.

CompuAdd
800-925-5515.

Dell Computer
800-545-1567.

Gateway 2000
800-846-2000.

PC Brand
800-722-7263.

Zeos
800-554-5230.

When to Buy: Now or Later?

One frequently asked question is, "Should I buy a PC now, or should I wait till the prices come down or the technology improves?" It doesn't matter when you ask the question, the answer is always the same. If you need or really want a computer now, buy it now, assuming you can afford what you want. And, yes, if you wait, you'll get a better and faster machine for less money. The technology is continually evolving. Whatever you buy today will be outclassed by what comes on the market tomorrow. And what you buy tomorrow will be superseded by something introduced after that.

The thing about PCs is that they never really become obsolete. There are still tens of thousands of original, vintage 1981 IBM PCs in use. You can upgrade any desktop PC as new technology becomes available. I have one of the first batches of PCs, a machine that I've upgraded over the years. It works great. And some of those original PCs out there continue to function with the original equipment they came with in the early 1980s.

Unlike a car, a PC isn't likely to break down just because it's old. Quite the contrary. A PC is far more likely to succumb to infant mortality than to die of old age. Five years from now, the PC you buy today should be just as good as the day you bought it.

If you wait a year or two, you'll save some money or wind up with a more powerful system, but think of the opportunities you'll have missed. Isn't it better to get started right away, even if it costs you more? Besides, even though prices are likely to keep dropping, I believe we've reached a point where the price drops will start to level off. That's because the technology is no longer so new that you're also paying for the research and development. So long as you stay away from the ultra–high end (which you don't need anyway), you can get some very good values. Go ahead. Take the plunge.

use a credit card such as Visa, MasterCard, Discover, or American Express. The credit card companies offer you an extra layer of protection against fraud or mistreatment. If you have a beef against the PC vendor, you can withhold payment and send a detailed letter to the credit card company describing your problem. The credit card company will suspend the bill while it investigates.

New or Used?

Most people buy new computers, but if you're looking for a bargain, consider buying a used one. Unlike buying a used car, buying a used PC has relatively few risks. If electronic components are going to break, they're likely to do so during a machine's early days. If you know what you want, don't need the latest model, don't need a guarantee, and can

When shopping for a used system, be sure to check the ads for comparable new machines. Prices on new systems are constantly dropping, so what may seem like a bargain to the seller may be overpriced in today's market.

spend the time calling around, you might consider a used machine.

The *American Computer Exchange*, a broker that matches buyers and sellers of used PCs, regularly updates an index of used computer prices. I've also seen various "blue book"-type publications that list prices, but prices change so quickly that I wouldn't rely on anything that's more than a few weeks old. The best way to find out what a certain kind of computer goes for is to watch the ads. You'll find that the market sets pretty standard prices.

One last thing: If you're paying extra for software on a used machine, make sure you're getting legal copies that you can register in your own name. Insist on documentation and original disks.

Resources

American Computer Exchange
800-786-0717, 404-250-0050.

How Do You Choose a Computer?

There are three major things to consider when buying a PC. The first is the machine's central processing unit (CPU). The second is the hard disk. And the third is the amount of memory it has.

9

Once you've figured out what you need from those three areas, your selection will still be wide. That's when you start thinking about the "extras," such as the number of expansion slots the system has, and, if it comes with a monitor and keyboard, the quality of those components. Other considerations might be the quality of the case, whether the controls and switches are in convenient positions, and how much energy it uses (some "green PCs" are designed to use less). Does the computer fit into your work environment? Will it fit on (or under) your desk? Is it quiet? (Some PCs have very noisy fans.)

You Don't Need a Brand Name

Does the brand name make a difference? There was once a time when I would have told you to stay away from "no-name brands," but those days are over. It's now possible for a neighborhood PC dealer to assemble a quality computer that stands up against the likes of those from IBM, Compaq, AST, or other big-name companies.

A PC company doesn't have to be big to be good. The trick is selecting and integrating the right components and backing the unit up with service and support.

The advantages to dealing with well-established companies usually (but don't always) include a nationwide guarantee, telephone support, and the peace of mind of that comes from knowing that you're dealing with a stable company. But while the big-name companies usually deliver quality systems, they sometimes cut corners by limiting the number of available expansion slots or by going with less memory, smaller disk capacity, or slower CPUs than comparably priced clones. My advice is to forget the name; just judge each computer by its qualities and how well its manufacturer backs it up.

It's the Components That Count

While the name of the PC itself doesn't make much difference, the companies that make the components do. One critical chip, called the **BIOS** (it stands for "basic input/output system") helps determine whether the machine will be compatible with all your software and add-on hardware. You want to be sure your computer has a BIOS chip from a company that's shipped lots of them, because the popular ones have been field-tested. The most popular BIOS makers for PCs are AMI (American Megatrends) and Phoenix Technology. Name-brand PC makers, such as Compaq and IBM create their own BIOS chips, which are also fine.

Name-brand hard disk makers include Quantum, Seagate, Rodime, Micronics, Conner Peripherals, Maxtor, Toshiba, Fujitsu, and Micropolis, among others.

The box below is a summary of what you should look for in a computer. In the next chapters, I'll explain what this all means.

Buyer's Guide to the Perfect PC

1. CPU: 386SX or better. If you're running Windows, you're better off with a 386DX or a 486.

2. Memory: At least 4 MB if you're running Windows. At least 1 MB if you're just running DOS.

3. Name-brand BIOS and hard disk.

4. Hard disk space: At least 80 MB.

5. Expansion slots: At least three empty, ISA-compatible slots (for a desktop PC).

6. Monitor: Super VGA with .28 (or lower) dot pitch, comfortable for you.

7. Keyboard: Anything that's comfortable.

The CPU: The Real Brains of the Computer

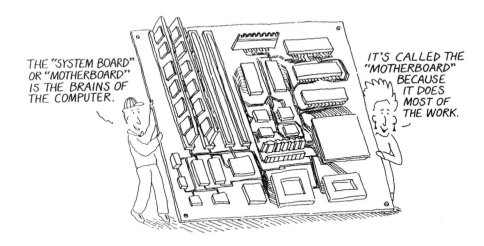

10

THE "SYSTEM BOARD" OR "MOTHERBOARD" IS THE BRAINS OF THE COMPUTER.

IT'S CALLED THE "MOTHERBOARD" BECAUSE IT DOES MOST OF THE WORK.

The central processing unit, or CPU, is the part of the computer that does the main computing work. It's usually less than an inch square, but when you talk about the computer, that's what you're talking about. The rest of the machinery is just a way of getting data to and from that chip.

The CPU is just one chip on the computer's system board (sometimes called the "motherboard"). Other components include system memory and all sorts of other circuits that get the data to and from the central processor.

PC processors are based on CPUs created by Intel. In the past, PC processors have been in the Intel 80X86 series (where the X stands for a number from 2 to 4): the 80286, the 80386, and the 80486, often referred to by the shortened "286,"

"386," and "486." The higher the number, the faster the computer. The very oldest PCs had a chip called the 8086. The newest Intel processor, though, has a different name. It's called the Pentium processor.

There are also variations called the 386SX and the 486SX. The 386SX is a bit slower than the regular 386 (which is sometimes called the 386DX). The 486SX is the same as the 486DX, except that it has no **math coprocessor** (an extra circuit specially designed for math work), so it is slower than the regular 486 for math functions, but just as fast for other operations.

To make things even more complicated, computers with the same processor can run at different CPU speeds, measured in **megahertz** (MHz). The higher the number, the better, but you can't compare speeds from different kinds of CPUs. A 486 running at 25 MHz is faster than a 386 running at 33 MHz. The CPU speed rating is only useful for comparing machines with the same kind of CPU.

While most CPUs in PCs are made by Intel, other companies, such as Cyrix and Advanced Micro Devices (AMD), also supply CPUs for IBM compatibles. These chips work just like Intel chips, use the same numbering system, and can run all the same software.

Another factor that affects your computer's speed is whether or not it has **cache memory**. A cache is a bank of high-speed memory on the system board that runs up to five times as fast as the regular memory. Cache memory speeds up the operation of some programs by storing the most recently used information in this faster bank of memory. All 486 CPUs have a built-in 8 **kilobytes** (K) of cache, and many offer larger external caches to supplement the built-in one.

One advantage to getting a 486 is that you can upgrade the chip if you decide later that you need more speed. You can add a math coprocessor to a 486SX machine, and you can upgrade to even faster CPUs as they become available.

Here's the bottom line: If you're buying a PC today, you should almost certainly get a system with either a 386 or 486 processor— especially if you plan to run

Two Kinds of Cache

Don't confuse cache memory with **disk cache**. The concept is similar, but cache memory requires special hardware, whereas you can always create your own disk caching using software that comes with DOS and Windows. A disk cache uses your computer's memory to speed up hard disk performance by copying recently used data from the disk to memory. The computer can get information from memory quicker than it can from disk, so this speeds up the computer. (See the box "The Difference Between Memory and Storage" on page 42 for an explanation of the two concepts.)

Windows. If you're running DOS programs or occasional Windows programs, you can get away with a 386SX, minimum. If you're running Windows a lot, get a system with at least a 486SX. If you plan to run software that uses a lot of math functions, such as complex spreadsheet or 3-D modeling programs, you'll probably want the better performance of a 486DX. The simple rule is: Get the fastest processor you can afford.

How Fast Is Fast?

Speed is relative, so we've put together this very scientific chart to give you an exact idea of the kind of performance you can expect from different CPUs running at different speeds. As you can see, you'll get good performance from any 386SX or better if you're running DOS alone, but if you're running Windows, you'll probably want a stronger machine. These ratings also assume you're running with enough memory, a concept explained in the next chapter.

Chip	Speed	DOS Performance	Windows Performance
386SX	25 MHz	very good	fair
	33 MHz	very good	fair
386DX	25 MHz	great	pretty good
	33 MHz	great	good
	50 MHz	fantastic	very good
486SX	33 MHz	fantastic	good
	50 MHz	fantastic	great
486DX	33 MHz	unbelievable	very good
	50 MHz	unbelievable	great
	66 MHz	unbelievable	great

Memory: The Electronic Workspace

The computer's RAM (random access memory) is where it keeps programs and data that are in use. The more memory you have, the more programs and files you can keep open at once.

More memory also makes your computer run faster. Many programs work with limited RAM by keeping only the most often-used parts of the program in memory. When you want to use a less often-used part, it loads in the data it needs to perform that function, which takes a bit of time. If you have more memory, the computer can load more of the data at one time so that it's right there when you need it.

If you plan to run Windows, don't even think about using a computer with less than 4 MB of RAM. Windows will run in 2 MB, but then a family of four could live in a one-bedroom apartment if it really had to. Windows performs much better with 4 MB, and a lot of people find they need 8 MB to get all the speed they want.

Most DOS programs, on the other hand, do fine with just 1 MB of RAM, although some perform better with additional memory.

Memory comes in units called **SIMMs**. (It stands for "single in-line memory module.") SIMMs are small bars with preinstalled memory chips that plug into your computer. To add memory to your computer, you plug in one or more SIMMs.

Units of Measurement: Bits and Bytes

Computer data is measured in special units called bits and bytes. These terms (and the variations on them described below) are used to describe the size of files, memory, hard disks, and the speed with which data is transferred—any measurement of computer data. Here's what the terms mean.

A **bit**, the smallest unit, is one-eighth of a byte.

A **byte**, the next unit up on the ladder, is made up of 8 bits. It takes 8 bits to store a single character, such as the numeral *1* or the letter *J*. The word *THE* is 3 bytes long, for example.

A **kilobyte** is approximately 1,000 bytes (1,024 to be exact). It's equivalent to about a page of double-spaced text.

A **megabyte** is just over one million bytes (OK, 1,048,576)—about as much text as in the average novel.

A **gigabyte** (GB) is a billion bytes—a thousand novels. Already there are hard disks that can store a gigabyte of data, and they'll become common very quickly.

SIMMs come in different sizes. A single SIMM can hold 1 MB, 4 MB, or 16 MB of memory.

When you buy a system, the salesperson will say something like, "It has 2 MB, expandable to 64 MB." That means it has two 1-MB SIMMs installed in it, and, probably, four SIMM slots total (that's pretty standard).

In that kind of setup, you have lots of options for adding more memory. For example, you could add two more 1-MB SIMMs, for a total of 4 MB (1 MB x 4). Or you could take out the two 1-MB SIMMs that are in there and replace them with two 4-MB SIMMs for a total of 8 MB (2 MB x 4). If you fill all the SIMM slots with 16-MB SIMMs, you'll have 64 MB of memory (16 MB x 4). See? Simple math.

The price of SIMMs changes all the time. The last time I checked they cost about $40 per megabyte. In any case, they're easy to install and relatively affordable. Ask your dealer to preinstall as much memory as you think you'll need to start with. Later, if you find you need more memory, you can easily buy more SIMMs.

The Hard Disk: The Computer's Filing Cabinet

12

INSIDE YOUR COMPUTER IS A HARD DRIVE, LIKE THIS ONE. ANY QUESTIONS?

TOUR GUIDE (PLEASE TIP HEAVILY)

Disk storage is your computer's filing cabinet, where it keeps all the programs you use and the files you create. Unlike RAM, disks hold their information even when the computer is turned off; the information is physically recorded on the disk's magnetic surface. You probably won't ever see your hard disk; it's buried in the system unit of your computer. What you will see is a blinking light on the front of the system unit that indicates when the hard disk is in use.

How much storage do you need? The rule of thumb is simple. Estimate what you think you'll need, double it, then go for the next higher size.

Hard disks are like closets. You think you have plenty of room until you've lived with them awhile.

Some of today's systems come with 40-MB hard disks, but that's getting rare. Many start off with 80 MB and go up to 200 MB and more. Windows is a real storage hog. It will take about 10 MB, and each major application will take up another 4 to 15 MB. And that's just the software; don't forget the room you'll need for your files. If you get into graphics or multimedia, you'll need an enormous amount of storage space, because each graphics file can easily take up 2 to 20 MB.

After capacity, speed is the most important thing to look for in a hard disk. The speed at which a drive stores and retrieves data can have a big impact on your machine's overall performance. In some situations, a slow hard disk can slow you down even more than a slow CPU can.

There are several ways to report the speed of a hard disk, but the most common number is the average time it takes for the disk's head to move from one random spot on the disk to another. That time, measured in milliseconds, can be anywhere from 9 ms to over 100 ms. (A millisecond is $1/1,000$ of a second.) The lower the number, the faster the drive. As with everything else in computing, faster is better and, naturally, more expensive.

If you run out of room on your internal hard disk, you can replace it with a larger-capacity disk or add another hard disk drive. You can also get programs, called compression programs, that let you squeeze more files onto your existing hard drive. (Compression programs are described in Chapter 42.) These programs accomplish this seemingly miraculous trick by removing redundant information from your files. It's like squeezing the air out of your data, and it's perfectly safe. In fact, DOS 6.0 includes its own built-in compression program, called DoubleSpace.

A hard disk is the primary type of disk storage for most computers, but it's not the only kind. In the next chapter I'll describe **floppy disks** and some other kinds of removable storage, which work on the same principle but are used for different purposes.

The Difference Between Memory and Storage

THINK OF "STORAGE" AS A FILING CABINET FOR LONG-TERM INFORMATION....

....WHILE "RAM" IS LIKE THE DESK WHERE YOU KEEP JUST THE STUFF YOU'RE WORKING ON.

A lot of people—OK, most people—have trouble keeping the difference between memory (RAM) and storage (the hard disk) straight, probably because memory and storage are both usually measured in megabytes. Maybe it will help to remember it this way. Storage (the hard disk) is your computer's filing cabinet, where you keep everything you may ever need to use again; memory (RAM) is like a desktop, where you keep just the programs and documents you're working on at the time.

Your computer's hard disk and RAM are physically different and have different size requirements. Your filing cabinet (hard disk) needs to be able to hold a lot more than your desktop (RAM). Also, you need to be able to clear the desktop of things that you're not using at the time, to make room for things you are.

Information stays in RAM (on the desktop) as long as the computer stays on, but once you turn off the power, that information is erased. In order to hang on to that data when the computer is off, you need to store that information on disk, where it is physically written to magnetic platters that keep the information intact until it's needed again.

Floppy Disk Drives: The Computer's Front Door

13

THE SLOTS IN THE FRONT OF THE SYSTEM UNIT ARE FOR "FLOPPIES" ONLY.... *NEVER* STUFF FOOD IN HERE.

Floppy disks are small, removable disks that you can use to transfer data to and from your computer. Like hard disks (described in Chapter 12), they store information even after the computer is turned off. A floppy disk, however, stores much less data than a hard drive—from 360 K to 1.4 MB. Your computer's floppy drive lets you open files from other sources on your computer, and it lets you transport files you want to share with others.

Unlike hard drives, which include the **disk drive** (the mechanism that reads the data) and the storage medium (the disk itself) in the same unit, floppy drives separate the two. Floppy disks are very inexpensive—generally less than $1 each—and so can be used to distribute software or share data among co-workers.

Floppy disks—and floppy drives—come in two sizes: 5.25 inches and 3.5 inches.

THE BLACK MYLAR YOU SEE PARTIALLY EXPOSED IS WHERE DATA IS STORED.

THE MYLAR IS TOTALLY COVERED ON THIS MODEL.

5.25"

3.5"

The two kinds of floppy disks are different in more than size. The 5.25-inch variety is in a flexible plastic case, and the 3.5-inch floppies are in a hard plastic case. Why do they call them "floppies"? The answer lies inside the case, which contains a round, thin piece of flexible mylar that does, indeed, flop around. This disk is coated with metal oxide, which holds magnetically encoded data.

Both sizes of floppy (5.25-inch and 3.5-inch) are in broad use, although the 3.5-inch format, introduced just a few years ago, is becoming more and more popular.

Variety is good, right? Well, the bad news is that your computer will need different disk drives to read 5.25- and 3.5-inch floppies.

Ideally, you should have two floppy drives: one for 5.25-inch floppies and one for 3.5-inch floppies. Having both kinds of drives means you'll never have to worry about disk compatibility. Many of today's programs come in both formats, but some packages include disks in only one size or the other.

If you wind up with just one floppy disk drive, I recommend you get a 3.5-inch drive. The 3.5-inch disks are easier to work with, more durable, and they hold a little more data. And having a 3.5-inch disk makes it easier to exchange data disks with Macintosh computers or laptop PCs, both of which use only 3.5-inch disks.

When a Floppy Isn't Big Enough

Floppy disks are the most common method of distributing software and transporting data from computer to computer, but people who use a lot of graphics files or large **databases** will probably find that the relatively small capacity of floppy drives is too limiting.

To get around this problem, you could buy an external hard drive to move your files, but that would be pretty expensive. Instead, the computer industry has come up with other kinds of storage media that, like floppies, are separate from the drive itself. That means you can buy just one drive (the most expensive component of a storage system), and then just buy many removable disks that you insert into the drive for saving or reading files. Common forms of removable media include **CD-ROM**, **cartridge drives**, **optical discs**, and **tape cartridges**, which are described below.

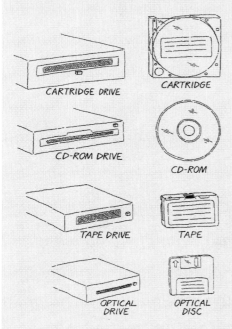

CARTRIDGE DRIVE

CARTRIDGE

CD-ROM DRIVE

CD-ROM

TAPE DRIVE

TAPE

OPTICAL DRIVE

OPTICAL DISC

Cartridges are removable hard disks that are enclosed in a plastic case. Sometimes people just call them "Bernoulli drives" or "Syquest drives," after the two major vendors. Cartridges can hold up to 105 MB and cost about $75 to $100 each. It's not a good idea to use cartridges as your primary storage medium because they're quite a bit slower than a regular hard drive.

CD-ROM discs look just like audio CDs. CD-ROM stands for "compact disc, read-only memory," and, as the name suggests, can be used only for data that you don't need to change. CD-ROM discs are used to distribute graphics libraries, multimedia programs, large databases, and other data that takes up a lot of space. They can hold up to 680 MB of data.

Tape cartridges look like cassette tapes, and, in fact, work in pretty much the same way. You can't use a tape as a primary storage medium because, just as with the cassettes you play in your stereo system, you can't go quickly to just the track you need. For backups and archives, though, they're a good solution because they're cheap: about $20 for a 220-MB cartridge. In fact, tape drives are so popular for backups that some computers come with a tape drive built in. (For more on **backing up**, see Chapter 30.)

Optical discs are similar to cartridges, but they store even more information—up to a gigabyte (1,000 megabytes), depending on the model. Like cartridges, they're somewhat slower than hard drives or floppies.

Expansion Slots: Room to Grow

14 *If you think your hardware buying spree is over once you buy a computer, then you haven't heard about peripherals. Peripherals are those wonderful things that can increase the performance of your machine or add functions. Many peripherals require a card that plugs into an expansion slot on your PC. Watch out: If you run out of slots, you've run out of your ability to expand the machine.*

Some PCs have as many as eight slots, and others have as few as three. More to the point, some computers use up most of their slots just adding the basic functions: controllers that handle the hard disk and monitor, **parallel ports** and **serial ports** for modems and printers. The real question, then, is how many slots the computer has free once it's set up with the basics. All things being equal, of course, the more slots you have, the better.

Anything you plug into a PC's expansion slots plugs right into the system board, adding capabilities to the basic system setup.

The next thing to remember is that not all expansion slots are the same. What kind you need depends on the kind of **bus** your computer uses. A computer's bus is the method it uses to move information through its circuits. There are several bus standards in use, and you should make sure your computer uses a common one. If it doesn't, you might have trouble getting expansion cards for it later, or you might end up paying more for the cards you get.

The vast majority of PCs use what is called **ISA**, for "industry-standard architecture." Unless otherwise advertised, most expansion boards are designed for ISA slots.

To complicate things, though, IBM came along with a faster and, in theory, better type of slot called **MCA**, for "micro channel architecture." But because MCA isn't as popular as ISA, there are not as many MCA expansion boards. The result is you have fewer options and may wind up paying a premium for your peripherals.

Some manufacturers offer a more powerful version of ISA, called **EISA** (the *E* stands for extended.) The same problem applies here: Most peripheral makers haven't developed EISA boards. Regular ISA boards work on EISA machines, but you're not getting any special advantage for the extra cost.

The newest type of expansion slot is called **Local Bus**. Local Bus has the potential of being dramatically faster than other models, but so far,

Expansion cards are sometimes called adapter cards or adapter boards, or just adapters.

it is being used primarily with fast video cards and disk controllers. Eventually, it may be used for other devices, and it is also compatible with standard ISA boards.

When you buy a PC, make sure you have plenty of slots free for add-ons. If you want the fastest possible performance, you might consider getting Local Bus slots. Otherwise, stick with ISA.

Monitors: The Face of the Computer

15 *Computer monitors (sometimes called "displays") come in color or monochrome, in many different resolutions, and in many sizes.*

A computer monitor is actually a two-part system:

- The monitor itself
- The **display adapter**, which the monitor plugs into, and which generates the video information for the monitor. The display adapter itself plugs into one of your computer's expansion slots.

If you buy a system complete with a monitor, the display adapter will be preinstalled. In some cases, the display adapter is built into the system board so there's no need for an expansion board. Be aware, though, that if you change monitors, you may need to buy a new display adapter as well. Your dealer will tell you if a new monitor is compatible with your existing display adapter.

Multiscan monitors are able to work with different kinds of display adapters. Their advantage is that they don't become obsolete if you get a new display adapter. Their disadvantage is that they are generally more expensive. If you stick with **Super VGA (SVGA)**, you're probably in good shape for at least a couple of years.

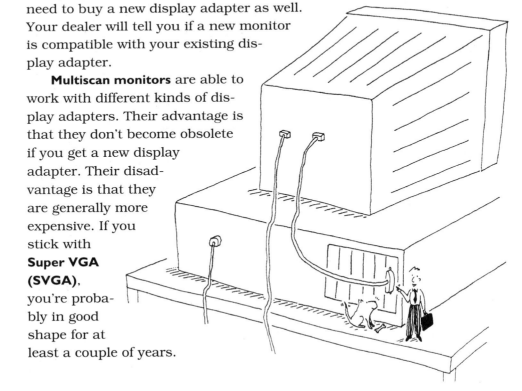

Color

Do you need color? Well, who cares? My advice is, get it. Even if you spend your time working with words and numbers and other things that will ultimately be printed in black and white, work is just more fun in color. And most of today's programs display color in ways that make your work easier to do. For example, **word processors** might display selected text in color to make it easier to see, and a spreadsheet might show negative numbers in red.

Resolution

Display resolution is the number of dots of light (they call them **pixels**, for "picture elements") that a monitor can display. The higher the resolution, the easier the monitor will be on your eyes and the more detail you'll be able to see.

Today, the minimum standard for IBM-compatible systems is **VGA** (for Video Graphics Adapter), which displays 640 pixels horizontally across the screen and 480 pixels vertically down the screen. These days, most systems come with Super VGA (SVGA), which displays 800-by-600 pixels or 1024-by-768 pixels, depending on the software. Super VGA monitors usually operate in standard VGA mode, unless you load special software, called **drivers**, to provide the extra resolution. (Most Super VGA adapters and Windows versions after 3.1 come with the necessary drivers.) Super VGA is only a little more expensive than standard VGA.

Sometimes you'll hear display adapters referred to as graphics adapters (or graphics boards) or even video adapters (or video boards). Don't get confused: All these terms mean the same thing.

Size

The standard size for monitors is 14 inches (measured diagonally, like a television set), but if you can afford it, you might want to opt for a 15-inch or 16-inch monitor, especially if you're using Microsoft Windows.

Still larger monitors are available, measuring 20 inches and even 24 inches diagonally. These ultra-large monitors cost about $2,000, and they have their pluses and minuses. On the plus side, they're quite useful for desktop publishers who need to see a full page of text at a time, or even two pages side by side. They're also handy for people who work on very large spreadsheets.

Can Your Monitor Be Harmful to Your Health?

MONITORS ARE LIKE BILL COLLECTORS: KEEP 'EM AT ARM'S LENGTH.

In the last couple of years, there has been a lot of attention given to reports that the radiation put out by computer monitors may be hazardous to your health. Although studies on the topic haven't really been conclusive, there may be good reason to be careful about what kind of monitor you buy, how you set it up, and how you use it.

The type of radiation of greatest concern is extremely low frequency (ELF) radiation. It is now generally conceded in the scientific community that ELF radiation does have biological effects, but the jury is still out on the circumstances in which these biological effects may translate into health effects. For example, are small amounts of radiation over a long period of time something to be concerned about, or should you worry more about brief exposure to larger amounts? Or should you worry at all? Although no studies have yet proven that computer monitors have caused specific health problems, other sources of ELF radiation, such as electrical transmission and distribution lines, have been associated with an increased incidence of childhood cancer.

Under the circumstances, the best strategy seems to be "prudent avoidance." Recent articles in *Macworld* magazine and *PC Magazine*, which included measurements of ELF radiation, revealed some interesting facts:

- The greatest intensity of radiation is found not in front of the monitor but behind it and on either side (due to the elliptical shape of the electromagnetic field created by the deflection coils at the rear of the monitor).

- Color monitors usually generate a lot more radiation than monochrome monitors do.

- With all monitors, the intensity of radiation falls off very rapidly with distance and it is a good rule of thumb to stay an arm's length from the front of the monitor.

- Screen shields block the electrical component but not the magnetic component, of ELF radiation.

- The liquid crystal display (LCD) technology used in most notebook and laptop computers does not generate ELF radiation.

The upshot of these findings is that the best thing you can do to minimize the risks of ELF radiation is simply to sit at arm's length from the monitor and also avoid having someone else sit close to the back or sides of your monitor.

These basic precautions should be sufficient to protect you, but if you want to go further, you can switch from a color to a monochrome monitor, or from a desktop PC to a laptop. Yet another alternative is to buy a monitor specifically designed to meet the radiation standards published by the Swedish government, referred to as the MPR-II Very Low Frequency and Extremely Low Frequency emission standards.

The biggest drawback to mega-monitors is that they require a special driver to work with Windows and with each non-Windows program you want to use. I've loaded up large spreadsheets on several ultra-large monitors and have been impressed with how many rows and columns I could see on the screen, only to be disappointed to find out that scrolling to another part of the spreadsheet was painfully slow.

Another drawback to these large monitors is that looking at a light source that big can be hard on your eyes, and if you're concerned about radiation (see the box "Can Your Monitor Be Harmful to Your Health?" on pages 50 and 51), they do generate more of it than regular monitors do.

An advantage of a large-screen monitor is that you can have more than one program showing at the same time—a word processor here, a communications program there, and so on. But if you want to use several programs at the same time, you can accomplish the same thing with a normal-size monitor by using the capabilities built into both Windows and the DOS Shell—a single keystroke will switch you from one program to another. (See the Cookbook section at the back of the book for details.)

Image Quality

A lot of different factors go into how good the image displayed by a monitor will be. The most important things to consider are **dot pitch**, **vertical refresh rate**, **interlacing**, and, last but not least, your personal preferences.

Dot pitch, a measurement that applies only to color monitors, describes the resolution of each individual pixel on the screen. The lower the dot pitch, the better the image. Look for a dot pitch of .28 or lower.

Personal taste is perhaps the most important consideration when choosing a monitor. I'd gladly order a computer from a catalog, but I wouldn't buy a monitor that I've never seen working.

Vertical refresh rate describes the number of times per second that the screen is repainted from top to bottom. The higher the number the better. A refresh rate of about 60 refreshes per second (referred to as 60 Hertz, or 60 Hz) is OK for text but can cause annoying flicker in Windows or graphics applications. For Super VGA, 72 Hz is considered good.

Interlaced monitors refresh every other line of the picture with each pass, and therefore require two complete passes of the electron beam to refresh the display. (Televisions use this method.) A noninterlaced monitor updates the entire display in a single pass and is less likely to flicker, so you're better off with this type of monitor.

Finally, and perhaps most important, is personal taste. Don't let a salesperson dazzle you with impressive color graphics. Ask the dealer to show the monitor displaying both text and graphics in real-life applications such as a word processor, a spreadsheet, and a graphics program. Viewing small black type against a white background (in Microsoft Windows, for example) is an excellent way to judge overall resolution and quality.

The Bottom Line

Confused yet? I'll make it simple. If you want a quality display system without having to sweat the details, get a noninterlaced Super VGA monitor and display adapter. If you get a color monitor, get one with a dot pitch of .28 or lower.

The Keyboard: Not Exactly a Typewriter

16 *A computer keyboard is a lot like a typewriter keyboard. But there are some important differences. Surrounding the alphabetic keys are a lot of keys you won't see on*

The keys labeled F1 through F12 (there are more on some keyboards) are called the **function keys**. These keys can be programmed, either by you with a **macro** program, or by a piece of application software, to carry out special functions. Usually, F1 means "give me some help."

You might think that the Backspace key would move you back one character, but that's what the backward-pointing arrow on the cursor pad is for. The Backspace key deletes the character to the left of the cursor.

The Esc (Escape) key can often be used to get out of trouble. It backs you out of whatever situation you're in.

The Shift and CapsLock keys work just like they do on a typewriter. On a computer, though, presing Caps Lock has no impact on number keys.

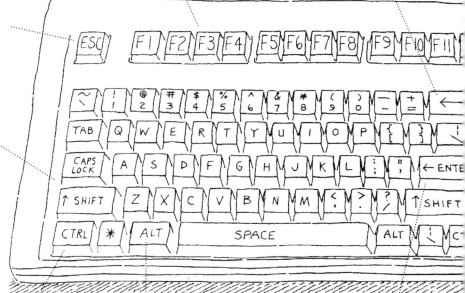

You usually hold the Ctrl (Control) key down while you press some other key to perform a special command.

As with the Ctrl key, you hold the Alt (Alternate) key down while pressing some other key to perform a special command. In Windows, the Alt key activates the menu bar.

When you're typing, you use the Enter (or Return) key to start a new paragraph. When you're in DOS, you press Enter to execute a command.

your old Smith-Corona. Keyboards vary a lot in their layout, but the one shown here is a pretty standard one.

The Print Screen key usually causes your printer to print out a snapshot of what you see on the screen, but it doesn't work with all programs. Watch out: If you press Print Screen when no printer is attached, your computer might freeze up.

Usually, the Scroll Lock key doesn't do anything, but in some programs it might.

When you're working in DOS, the Pause/Break key causes the screen to freeze, until you press it again. Pressing Shift and Pause at the same time activates the Break key, which interrupts and discontinues some programs.

In many programs, when Ins (Insert) is on (that's usually the default), the cursor pushes characters to the right as you type. When it's off, you type over (erase) existing characters as you type.

The numeric keypad has two uses; you toggle between the two with the Num Lock key. When Num Lock is on, you can use this keypad to enter numbers as with a 10-key calculator. When Num Lock is off, this keypad can be used to navigate around your document. The numbers become inactive and the arrows, Home, End, PgUp, and PgDn keys become active.

C'MON UP HERE. IT'S TIME YOU LEARNED TO TYPE.

The Del (Delete) key generally deletes characters. Depending on the program, it may also delete entire words, lines, or even files.

The arrow keys, also known as **cursor keys**, move the cursor around on the screen.

SORRY— OLD DOG, NEW TRICK.

Choosing a Keyboard

Keyboards vary in feel as well as layout. Some are virtually silent. Others click every time you press a key. Some keyboards are mushy; others provide a slight amount of resistance. You'll have to experiment to see which kind is best for you.

Preferences for keyboard layout are also subjective. The illustration on the previous pages shows just one possible configuration for a PC keyboard. Another keyboard might have the function keys on the left, or at both the left and the top. Some keyboards have no separate cursor keypad, since the numeric keypad does double duty as a cursor pad.

You should be a fanatic about getting the right keyboard.

You don't have to blindly accept whatever keyboard your system comes with (unless it's a laptop computer, of course). Make sure you try a keyboard out before you buy it. After all, if you're a touch typist, you probably enter two or three thousand keystrokes per hour. A poorly designed keyboard can slow you down, increase your mistakes, and cause wrist strain. You should be a fanatic about getting a keyboard that's right for you.

Most PC keyboards work with just about any PC, so a mismatch isn't likely. There are, however, two types of keyboard plugs. The little round ones, designed for IBM PS/2 computers, are used by several companies, while the larger round ones are used by many others. If your keyboard and keyboard plug don't match up, you can buy an adapter for about $5.

Mice: Making Quick Moves

mouse buttons

Moving the mouse on your desk causes a pointer on screen to move in the same direction. Clicking the mouse button selects the item on screen that you're pointing to.

There's a good chance that your PC came with a mouse, and if it didn't, you can get one for less than $50. It'll be worth it, because the easiest-to-use programs, including all Windows programs, are designed to work with a mouse. The mouse lets you quickly move around a file to make selections and activate commands.

There is a particular vocabulary for using a mouse to communicate with Microsoft Windows, consisting of clicking, double-clicking, and dragging. The language is described in Chapter 5, in the box titled "Mouse Commands."

Mice are palm-size contraptions that sit on your desk. Once you see one, you'll immediately understand how they got their name: They're about the size of a little rodent, and their cord resembles a tail. A small ball on the bottom of the mouse tracks the mouse's movement on the desktop and communicates that information to the computer, which then moves an on-screen pointer in the same direction. A button on the top of the mouse allows you to signal the computer when you want to choose the item the cursor is pointing to. In most cases, the kind of sweeping movements you can make with a mouse are much quicker than what you can accomplish using the keyboard's arrow keys, which is the alternate method for moving around the screen. Programs that are specially designed to be used with a mouse allow you to carry out almost every action with the mouse except actually typing text.

Mice connect to the computer in one of three ways. Some mice, referred to as "bus mice," come with an adapter board, which plugs into an expansion slot in your PC. Others, which are more common these days, are called "serial mice." They plug into a serial port on your computer. (For more on serial ports, see Chapter 21.) Some PCs have a built-in socket, called a **mouse port**, that you plug the mouse into.

Keeping Your Mouse Squeaky Clean

As you move your mouse about the mouse pad, it may pick up lint, eraser shavings, and other such common desktop detritus. If this happens you'll notice that the mouse just doesn't work as well as it should.

Periodically, you'll have to turn the mouse over and inspect the ball for debris. Remove what you see with a soft cloth, brush, or clean fingers. Every few months it may be necessary to remove the ball completely to clean the rollers inside with an alcohol-soaked Q-tip. If you study the bottom of the mouse, you should be able to figure out how to remove the ball.

The most common mouse for PCs is made by Microsoft and is called, appropriately, the **Microsoft Mouse**. The Microsoft Mouse, like many other mice, has two buttons, although most programs use only the left one. Another mouse maker, **Logitech**, typically designs mice with three buttons and also designs mice especially for people who are left-handed.

Resources

Logitech
800-231-7717, 510-795-8500.

Microsoft Mouse
Microsoft, 800-426-9400,
206-882-8080.

Another device, called a **trackball**, does the same thing as a mouse, but in a slightly different way. A trackball is sort of an upside-down mouse, with the ball on top. You move the on-screen cursor by rolling the ball with your hand. Some people find trackballs easier to use than mice, and because they stay in one place, trackballs work well where desk space is limited. (That trait also makes them popular on notebook and laptop computers.) You can get a trackball at any computer store for about $50 to $75, and they work with any program that works with a mouse.

DON'T TRY THIS AT HOME.

TRACKBALL

Printers: Putting Your Work on Paper

18

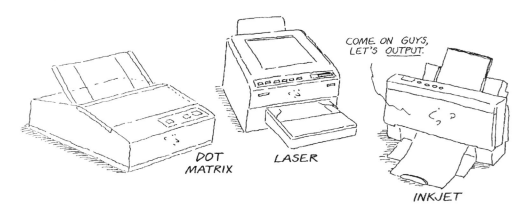

A GANG OF PRINTERS

COME ON GUYS, LET'S OUTPUT.

DOT MATRIX

LASER

INKJET

Almost everyone needs some kind of printer. Fortunately, there's a wide variety to choose from, ranging from dot matrix printers, which start at about $200; to laser printers, which start at about $600 and go (way) up from there; to high-end color printers, which can set you back around $10,000.

Basically, there are three types of printers. Laser printers, popular in offices, are the fastest and most expensive printers, and, generally, they print the best-looking pages. A document printed on a laser printer can look almost as if it were professionally typeset. Ink jet printers are slower than laser printers and a little more expensive to use, but they offer print quality that's almost indistinguishable from most laser printers, at a much lower price. **Dot matrix printers** are usually the least expensive option. The print quality isn't as good, but they can be fast if you print mostly text, and they are generally reliable and inexpensive to use. All three kinds can print both text and graphics.

Printing Fonts and Graphics

Fonts are what determine how type looks on screen and printed out in documents. In the old days, the number, style, and size of the fonts you could print were determined by the printer. Now, however, the creation of different fonts and graphics is mostly handled by software in the computer itself. If you have Windows, you have something called **TrueType**, which takes care of sizing (or scaling) and styling fonts. DOS software sometimes also comes with TrueType or other font-handling software.

Having the capability to print many fonts is one thing. The other part of the equation is getting the fonts themselves—the actual alphabets in different styles. Windows comes with 14 fonts (see the box "Windows Fonts" on the next page.), which you might find is enough for your needs. If you get interested in experimenting with different designs, though, you can buy extra fonts, often quite reasonably. Many font vendors, such as FontHaus and Microsoft, sell font packs that include hundreds of fonts for a price that comes to less than $1 per typeface. (You can buy fonts in TrueType format or **PostScript** format. Unless you do desktop publishing and have a PostScript printer, you'll probably want TrueType fonts. (For more on PostScript, see "PostScript and PCL" on page 63.)

Often, printers will have built-in fonts. That means those fonts are stored in the printer itself, where they can be gotten to quicker and therefore output faster than fonts that need to be sent to the printer from the computer.

Graphics—which includes rules, artwork, photos, and anything else besides text on the page—are handled in much the same way fonts are. In the old days, when some computer printers worked a lot like typewriters, most printers couldn't print graphics. Now, however, the computer processes the image and sends the information for the page to the printer, using the same process to create type or graphics.

Laser Printers

If you decide to go for a laser printer, you'll base your choice mostly on three factors: how fast it is, its **resolution**, and what language it speaks: PostScript or **PCL**.

Speed. Laser printers vary in speed from 4 pages per minute for the less expensive models, to 8, 9, or even 12 pages per minute for high-end office models. The speed rating is based on the maximum speed that the printer can operate. Your actual speed will be a bit slower, and documents that have a lot of graphics will take longer than those with text. Also, it will usually take longer to generate the first page of a document than subsequent pages. This is important to keep in mind when

Windows Fonts

A basic set of TrueType fonts comes with Windows. If you have Windows, you can use these fonts on any text, in any size, on any printer.

Times New Roman
Times New Roman Italic
Times New Roman Bold
Times New Roman Bold Italic

Times New Roman is a classic serif typeface that is easy to read in long passages of text . ("Serifs" are those little lines at the ends of the letters that seem to connect one letter to another.)

Arial
Arial Italic
Arial Bold
Arial Bold Italic

Sans serif fonts such as Arial are often used for headings and other display type in documents. Sans serif means "without serifs."

```
Courier New
Courier New Italic
Courier New Bold
Courier New Bold Italic
```

```
You can use Courier whenever (if ever)
you want your page to look typewritten.
```

Symbol (γ, ι, α, σ, ο, υ)
Wingdings (✏,✂,☺,✿,✒)

These fonts are full of useful and not so useful (but fun) characters you might want to use in your documents.

choosing between a laser printer and an ink jet printer, because it means that if you print a lot of one- or two-page documents, an ink jet printer can be almost as fast as a laser printer.

Resolution. A laser printer's print quality is a function of its resolution, which is a measure of how many dots per inch (dpi) it prints. The higher the resolution, the better the text and graphics will look. The standard for laser printers is 300 dpi, which is all you'll ever need for such things as correspondence or spreadsheets. A resolution of 300 dpi will also do quite a respectable job with different typefaces.

Laser printers that print 600 dpi are now becoming more common, especially now that Hewlett-Packard has introduced its 600-dpi LaserJet 4. The extra resolution is only necessary if you're actually printing copy that will reproduced for publication. If you want exceptional quality, resembling what you're used to seeing in glossy magazines, you can take your disk to a publishing service bureau that will run out your files on machines, called "imagesetters, that print up to 2,500 dpi.

PostScript and PCL. If you shop for a laser printer, you're going to hear the terms "PostScript" and "PCL." These terms refer to the language that's built into the printer. Don't worry. You don't have to learn these languages. Your software knows how to "speak" to both PostScript and PCL printers.

PostScript printers are slower than PCL printers, and they tend to cost about $500 more. The only people who really need PostScript are graphic artists and desktop publishers. The reason PostScript is necessary for those people is that it provides more power for working with graphics, color, and fonts than PCL offers.

If you're looking for a laser printer, look for a PCL printer. PCL (sometimes called "HP-compatible") printers are cheaper than PostScript printers and generally a lot faster, too.

PCL stands for "Printer Control Language." It's the language built into the popular Hewlett-Packard LaserJet series of laser printers and most other laser printers designed for the PC market. Note that there are different levels of PCL, but the differences between them aren't worth paying attention to.

Brand Names. Hewlett-Packard's *LaserJet* series of printers are the most popular and have excellent quality. Other companies that make good laser printers include Panasonic, Epson, and Texas Instruments, but HP's prices are not much higher than those of the competition. For home use, HP's LaserJet 4L is fine. It's designed for light duty, with an output of four pages per minute. Texas Instruments' *Microlaser* series, starting at under $1,000, is also excellent. If you plan to do a lot of printing and want great quality, you can't do much better than the HP LaserJet 4. Last time I checked it was selling for just over $1,300, but, as prices go in this industry, it could be a lot cheaper by now. HP and its competitors are constantly coming out with better and less expensive printers, so shop around.

Resources

LaserJet series
Hewlett-Packard,
800-752-0900, 415-857-1501.

Microlaser series
Texas Instruments,
800-527-3500, 214-995-2011.

Ink Jet

An ink jet printer works by spraying ink onto the page through tiny nozzles in the print head. To the naked eye, the print quality from an ink jet can be indistinguishable from that of a laser printer.

Ink jet printers can give you high resolution at a low price.

Most ink jet printers, including HP's popular *DeskJet* line, print at the same 300-dpi resolution that laser printers use. At that resolution, the quality is close, but not quite as good as, a laser printer's. Canon *BubbleJet* printers operate at 360 dpi for output that can actually be better than that of many laser printers.

Ink jet printers are virtually silent, use almost no electricity in standby mode, don't take up much space, and are lightweight, easy to move, highly reliable, and pretty inexpensive (around $300). For home offices, students, and others on a tight budget, they're a great option. Ink jet printers are slower than laser printers but, remember, for short jobs the actual time it takes to print may be pretty close.

You can also get color ink jet printers (described under "Color Printers," on page 66.)

Resources

BubbleJet series
Canon, 800-848-4123,
714-438-3000.

DeskJet series
Hewlett-Packard,
800-752-0900, 415-857-1501.

Dot Matrix Printers

For a long time, dot matrix printers were the only game in town if you couldn't afford a laser printer. The original ones produced the kind of type most people think of as computer printing: very low resolution characters in which you can see each separate dot. They are still popular because they are so inexpensive (as little as $200) and they are usually very reliable. The cheaper ones have a resolution of only 9 dots per character; the more expensive ones, called "near letter quality," have a resolution of 24 dots. If you're on a tight budget, look at the 9-pin printers before you settle on a 24-pin unit. The technology has come a long way, and some of the 9-pin printers are actually quite good.

While some dot matrix printers use regular, cut-sheet paper (the type that you put in copy machines), most have "tractor feeds" that require continuous form paper. That's the kind of paper most people think of as "computer paper," the kind with the holes running down the sides, with the sheets attached end to end. Theoretically, pins in the printer use those holes to feed the paper neatly through the printer. Inevitably, however, the paper slips out of the feed mechanism and you have a mess on your hands.

Dot matrix printers are not a good idea if you intend to print a lot of fonts and graphics. They usually have built-in fonts, and with Windows' TrueType, you can get a full gamut of fonts (see the box "Printing Fonts and Graphics" on page 61). They can also print graphics, just like any other kind of printer. However, the quality of the fonts and graphics won't be nearly as good as the only slightly more expensive ink jet printers, and the printing time will be very slow.

Epson is the longtime leader in the dot matrix printer field, so to assure compatibility with virtually all software, it's important to get a printer that's Epson compatible. (Fortunately, most are.) Other brands to look for include **Citizen**, **Panasonic**, **Lexmark**, and **Okidata**.

Dot matrix printers are typically given speed ratings in terms of characters per second (cps). That's how long the printer takes to print in draft mode with built-in fonts. Draft mode gives you the lowest quality but the highest speed. There is also a rating for "near letter quality." Near letter quality gives you text that looks as if were typed on a typewriter. Look for a printer with a rating of at least 200 cps in draft mode. Remember, though, the cps rating only applies to printing text in the printer's native font. It will be much slower if you plan to use Windows' TrueType. Frankly, if you're looking for fancy print quality, you're much better off spending a little more money for an ink jet printer.

Resources

Citizen America
800-477-4683, 310-453-0614.

Epson
800-922-8911, 310-782-0770.

Lexmark International
800-358-5835, 606-232-2000.

Okidata
800-654-3282, 609-235-2600.

Panasonic
800-742-8086, 201-348-7000.

Color Printers

Color printers are not only more expensive to buy than black-and-white printers, they're more expensive to print with. They need special inks or color sheets and often require special paper—all bought at a premium. Unless you're regularly doing business presentations on your computer, you probably won't need one. If you do, though, here's a rundown of what's available.

The least expensive color printers are dot matrix color printers, which start at less than $400. In general, these use multicolored ribbons that move up and down, depending on what color the printer is working on at the time (making for a pretty limited range of colors). The ribbon has a band of black ink for regular printing.

Color printers are not only expensive to buy, they're expensive to print with.

When quality counts, you're better off going with color ink jet printers. Color ink jet printers use red, green, and blue, or cyan, magenta, yellow, and black ink cartridges to generate a full spectrum of colors. They start at about $500. One excellent choice is the affordable **Hewlett-Packard DeskJet 550C** color ink jet printer. You can load the printer with as many as 100 sheets of paper or 20 envelopes, and it does a good job in black as well as in color. If you need even better quality, HP's **PaintJet XL** series offers 300-dpi color at prices starting around $3,000. One model uses a special version of HP's PCL language, and another offers color PostScript. These printers provide richer colors than the less-expensive DeskJet models yet cost far less than other top-of-the-line color printers.

For high-quality color, the most common technology is called "thermal wax" printing. These printers use sheets of red, green, and blue, or magenta, yellow, and cyan, which the printer fuses to the paper in combinations to create any color. These printers generally print at 300 dpi and come with PostScript. The drawback to thermal wax is that while the colors these printers create are very bright and snappy looking, they won't necessarily match the true colors in your file. Also, although prices have started to come down quickly, they'll probably set you back at least a couple thousand dollars.

Resources

DeskJet 550C
Hewlett-Packard,
800-752-0900, 415-857-1501.

PaintJet XL series
Hewlett-Packard,
800-752-0900, 415-857-1501.

The Bottom Line

Now that you've heard me describe all the options, you've probably guessed my recommendation. If you're on a really tight budget, get a dot matrix, but if you can afford a little more, treat yourself to the Canon BubbleJet 200. If you're going to be printing fairly long documents on a regular basis, go for a laser printer that supports PCL. And if you need color, grab an HP DeskJet 550C.

Printers at a Glance

	Scalable Type?	Prints Graphics?	Plain Paper?	Speed (ppm)	Resolution	Color Available?
Dot Matrix	yes	very slowly	tractor feed	<1	9 or 24 dots per character	yes
Ink Jet	yes	yes	yes	1–4	300–360 dpi	yes
Laser	yes	yes	yes	4–12	300–1,200 dpi	for very high prices

Modems: Dialing for Data

19

A modem is a device that translates a computer's data into sounds that can be transmitted over phone lines. You don't really need a modem, but having one gives you access to a lot of information and services you can't get to without one.

Perhaps the most important use for a modem is that it lets you hook into on-line services, such as GEnie, Prodigy, CompuServe, and America Online. On-line services are sources of loads of information about a variety of topics, from job listings and airline flight schedules to discussion groups for senior citizens, skydivers, investors, and every other interest group imaginable. These services now offer time-saving, do-it-from-home services that let you shop for anything from coffee to major appliances from brand-name vendors. They even let you pay your utility and credit card bills from your keyboard.

On-line services are also a good place to get **shareware** or **public domain software** (also called **freeware**), which is software you can get for little or no money. (For more on shareware and public domain software, see Chapter 35.)

On-line services also supply **electronic mail** (usually called **e-mail**). When you sign up for a subscription to an on-line service, the service generally gives you a mailbox to which other users can post mail. You, in turn, can mail files to other users on the service. If you exchange computer-generated information with anyone, this feature alone could save you the cost of the service in what you save on FedEx—and it's faster. Most on-line services are now connected to the Internet, a world-wide "network of networks" that lets you exchange e-mail with people virtually anywhere in the world.

The last big reason to get a modem is that certain modems, called fax modems, also supply the services of a fax machine. If you have a fax modem, anyone with a fax machine can send images of text or graphics to your computer, and you can send any file on your computer to any-one with a fax machine.

If you get a modem, you'll also need communications software, which runs your modem for you. You may not need to actually buy it yourself; often, the modem manufacturer will supply communications software along with the modem, and a simple communications program comes with Windows. (For more on communications software, see Chapter 40.)

Some fax software comes with an optical character recognition (OCR) feature. This software, in theory, can turn an incoming fax into a file that can be edited by your word processor. Trouble is, the incoming fax has to be very clean. My experience with OCR fax software has not been satisfactory. It's a good idea, but it needs some work.

How to Choose a Modem

Of the hundreds of modem makers, the leading vendors include *Hayes*, *Intel*, *Practical Peripherals*, and *U.S. Robotics*. You should also check around for bargain brands, which are often very reliable.

Resources

Hayes Microcomputer Products
404-840-9200.

Intel
800-538-3373, 408-765-8080.

Practical Peripherals
800-442-4774.

U.S. Robotics
800-342-5877, 708-982-5010.

There are four factors that go into choosing the modem that's right for you:

- modem speed
- what **communication standards** it supports
- whether it's internal or external
- whether it has fax capability

I'll describe each consideration in turn.

Speed

At any one time, there are usually two modem speeds available—one that is in common use, and a higher speed that is just beginning to be used. The difference in price can be significant. As I write this, the common speed is 2,400 **bits per second (bps)**, and you can get a good 2,400-bps modem for well under $100. The up-and-coming speeds are 9,600 bps and 14,400 bps. When I wrote this, those higher-speed modems cost from about $150 to about $350.

If you plan to use a modem primarily to read information from on-line services, then 2,400 is fast enough. However, if you plan to transfer large data files or programs, you can benefit from the faster speed. If you wanted to get a 500-K file from an on-line service's bulletin board, for example, it would take about 28 minutes at 2,400 bps. At 9,600 bps it would take only 7 minutes. Because on-line services often charge by the minute, and

Sometimes modem speeds are referred to by the term "baud," as in "2,400 baud." The term is pretty much interchangeable with bps (bits per second) now.

you also have to pay any toll charges on your phone service if the call is long-distance, buying a faster modem could actually save you money in the long run if you use it a lot.

Remember, though, the modems at both ends of a connection need to be working at the same speed. On-line services are just starting to support 9,600 bps, and they may charge you a higher fee for the faster service. Higher-speed modems can work at lower speeds, too, if the modem they are communicating with only works at the slower speed.

Communications Standards

Just like people, modems need to be talking the same language in order to communicate with one another. For that reason, international committees have been set up to create communication standards, or **protocols**, for modems. Unfortunately, whether or not any one modem uses them is up to the modem manufacturer, and it's up to the buyers to make sure they have the communication standards they need. Even

If you don't need a high-speed modem, get a 2,400-baud modem with V.22bis. If you want a high-speed modem, go for 14,400 with V.32bis.

worse, the standards are called by names that are a confusing mixture of letters and numbers that all sound alike. Don't try to understand them all—I'll spare you the gory details and give you the bottom line. If you're getting a 2,400-bps modem, look for one that conforms to V.22bis ("vee-dot-22-biss"). If you're getting a 14,400-bps modem, look for V.32bis. Those are the only really important standards.

Internal or External

If you're buying a modem, you'll have to choose between internal and external modems. An internal modem is an expansion board that plugs into one of the PC's expansion slots. An external modem sits on your desk and is connected by a cable to a serial port on your computer.

The advantages of internal modems are that they are generally cheaper, they don't take up any desk space, and they don't require any cables. However, I prefer external modems for a number of reasons. You don't have to take the PC apart to install them, they don't take up an expansion slot, and you can easily move them from machine to machine. What's more, most external modems have lights or displays that provide a visual indication of what they're doing.

The Handshake

In order to communicate with one another, two modems must be working at the same speed and using the same communications standards. Luckily, you shouldn't have to worry about this; the communications software takes care of making sure everything matches. At the beginning of the transmission, the modems perform a **handshake**, in which they compare available speeds and communications standards and settle on the ones they'll use for that session.

Fax

As long as you're getting a modem, I suggest you go the extra mile and get one with fax capabilities. Fax—once a luxury for all but the biggest companies—is rapidly becoming a necessity even for the home office. If you're sharing information with colleagues, clients, or customers, it's a good investment. On a modem, fax capability lets people send you faxes from any regular fax machine or fax modem, and it lets you send any file from your computer as a fax to any other fax machine or fax modem. Fax capability on a modem isn't exactly the same as having a stand-alone fax machine (I'll explain why later), but it's a great convenience. And since fax modems cost very little more than modems without fax capability, I'd say go for it. (Of course, all fax modems are also fully functional as regular data modems.)

Whether or not a fax modem can fulfill all your faxing needs, I suggest you get fax capability if you're getting a modem anyway.

When you have a fax modem and good fax software (fax software usually comes with the fax modem), sending a fax is as easy as printing; you give the Fax command, and voilà, it has gone to its destination. Faxing from the computer saves you the step of printing out the file and sticking the document into a separate fax machine. Computer-generated outgoing faxes are also generally more readable than ones sent via regular fax machine, because the image doesn't have to go through the translation of the fax machine's reader. When you receive a fax, it is stored on your disk, waiting for you to print it out or view it on screen. Since you print the faxes on your regular printer, the faxes are printed on plain paper, which won't fade and curl like normal fax paper. That's a feature you would pay a lot extra for on a stand-alone fax machine.

Faxing Without a Fax Modem

As it turns out, you don't even need a special fax modem to send text messages from your PC. If you have a regular data modem, you can connect to MCI Mail, CompuServe, America Online, or AT&T Mail and use those services to send out faxes. It's relatively inexpensive. MCI Mail, for example, charges 50 cents for the first half-page plus 30 cents for each additional half-page, within the United States. Of course, if you send more than a few faxes, that quickly adds up to the cost of a fax feature on your own modem.

But there are some disadvantages. First, using a fax modem is more work than using a fax machine. You have to fool around with cables, software, and configuration files. And you can't receive a fax unless your PC is turned on and the fax software is running. And if you want to send a copy of a brochure, newspaper article, or other document that's not in your computer, you'll have to get something called a **scanner**, which turns hard-copy information into graphics information for the computer. Add one more piece of equipment (a pretty expensive one) and one more step.

Most fax and fax/data modems come with fax software. In some cases, they come with DOS programs that are functional but not very easy or fun to use. If you have Windows, I recommend that you get a modem that comes with Windows-based fax software. *WinFax Lite*, which comes with some fax modems, is very good. You can also buy fax software programs such as *WinFax Pro*, *UltraFax*, and *Eclipse Fax*. All these Windows fax programs give you WYSIWYG ("what you see is what you get") results: What you see on the screen is what the other person gets on his or her fax machine. And faxing is as easy as printing.

Resources

Eclipse Fax
Eclipse, 800-452-0120,
312-541-0260.

UltraFax
Z-Soft, 800-444-4780,
800-227-5609.

WinFax Lite, WinFax Pro
Delrina Technology,
800-268-6082, 416-441-3676.

Sharing Your Phone With a PC

Before you buy a modem, consider its effect on your phone service. If you're using your computer and modem a lot, you may need at least one extra line. This is especially true if you have a fax modem.

If you plan to use your modem for short periods of time, you can probably get away with a single line. Remember, however, that when you're "on line," your phone is busy. If you have a call-waiting feature on your phone line and someone calls when you're receiving a fax, your fax transmission will be terminated. (In most areas, you can turn off call waiting for the duration of outgoing calls or faxes.)

If you plan to use your modem often, or if you have a fax modem that you use for incoming fax messages, you are better off adding another phone line. Depending on where you live, they cost as little as $8 per month, after the initial installation charge. In most situations, you don't even need any toll-call service, since most on-line services can be accessed by a local call from most areas.

If you do plan to use a single line for voice and fax, you'll need some kind of intelligent device to "answer" that line. Prometheus Products' **Fax Line Manager** is one of several products on the market that answers the phone, determines whether it is a voice or fax call, and routes it to the appropriate device. Such devices are not foolproof, however, and they don't necessarily work with all fax machines. If the sender has an incompatible machine, you could have a problem.

Resources

Fax Line Manager
Prometheus Products,
800-477-3473, 503-692-9600.

On-Line Services

When you buy a modem, you will usually find invitations to subscribe to a few different on-line services in the box. Most will offer you a free month or two when you sign up.

Choosing an on-line service can be daunting; there are several options, each with its pros and cons. My best advice is to forge ahead. Any on-line service will offer you electronic mail, bulletin boards, forums (which let you "chat " with other users about all kinds of topics, using your keyboard), and plenty of news services. The initial cost of signing up for a service is somewhere between free and reasonable. Monthly charges run around $10 a month, and there are also per-hour usage charges in some cases, usually well under $10 an hour. Here's a chart of the main services and their characteristics.

Service	Description
America Online 800-827-6364	Provides news, information, e-mail, and libraries of shareware and other software. Comes with Windows and DOS software that allows you to copy and paste from the service to your word processing program.
CompuServe *Information Service* 800-848-8199	The most in-depth of the on-line services, it has extensive research information along with standard on-line features. It also has libraries of shareware and other software.
GEnie 800-638-9636	A good place for people interested in games and entertainment. Also has basic e-mail, news, libraries of shareware and other software, and other features.
MCI Mail 800-444-6245	Specializes in electronic mail.
Prodigy 800-PRODIGY	Provides news, e-mail, an encyclopedia, shareware, and other services.

Accessories: Making Yourself Comfortable

20 *Now that we've run through the parts of the computer itself, it's time to turn to the accessories, those inexpensive but important pieces of equipment that will keep you and your computer in working order. Accessories such as mouse pads and surge protectors are just as important to your work as a good keyboard. Luckily, they're also very inexpensive.*

Surge Protectors

Surge protectors are designed to insulate your computer from electrical surges that can happen during lightning storms, when your refrigerator's motor kicks in, or for no reason at all. Some electrical engineers I've spoken with claim that surge protectors are not necessary because

Plugging computer equipment into a surge protector shields it from irregularities in your power supply.

circuits inside your PC's power supply will automatically protect your system in case of an electrical surge; others claim that they're very important. I'd certainly get one if I lived in an area where the power was unsteady. In any case, I like to err on the side of caution. You can get surge protectors for as little as about $20, but the more expensive ones can offer better protection. Look for a surge protector with a UL (Underwriters Laboratory) 1449 rating, which means that it will prevent more than 500 volts from reaching your equipment.

Wrist Rest

Pound at the keyboard for a full hour and, if you type 50 words per minute, and you'll enter 18,000 keystrokes. Keep that up for a full workday and that's a lot of keystrokes. It's no wonder that tens of thousands of computer users have complained about hand and wrist pain.

The repetitive motion of typing and clicking the mouse can lead to stiffness and minor pain in the hands and wrists. Beware: These symptoms, if ignored, can turn into major disabling injuries. Since computers have come into wide use, doctors have seen a burgeoning number of cases of Carpal Tunnel Syndrome, a sometimes crippling disease caused by inflammation of the wrist tendons.

The best way to avoid the trouble is to make sure your wrists are in the proper relation to your keyboard. The keyboard needs to be lower than your elbows, and your wrists should be higher than your fingers. In addition to

Carpal Tunnel Syndrome

Carpal Tunnel Syndrome is a serious kind of wrist injury linked to computer use. It results from inflammation of the tendons or the synovial sheaths that surround and protect the tendons.

The symptoms of Carpal Tunnel Syndrome vary, but they often include numbness, tingling, or a burning sensation in the palms, fingers, or wrists. Over time, the condition can lead to a weakening of the muscles. You could also experience loss of sensation, pain, or weakness in the arm or other parts of your body.

If you're experiencing pain or weakness in your wrist, hand, or arm, see a medical doctor or a chiropractor. It may not be a full-fledged case of Carpal Tunnel Syndrome, but it's a good idea to give any pain early attention. It's also a good idea to look for a doctor who has experience with diagnosing and treating Carpal Tunnel and other stress-related injuries. The complaint has only recently become more common, and many doctors may be unfamiliar with it.

making sure your desk is the proper height, a good way to ensure the best posture is with a **wrist rest**, a simple device that elevates your hands so that your wrists remain straight while typing.

Wrist rests keep your wrists elevated and cut down the strain that can cause Carpal Tunnel Syndrome and other painful wrist conditions.

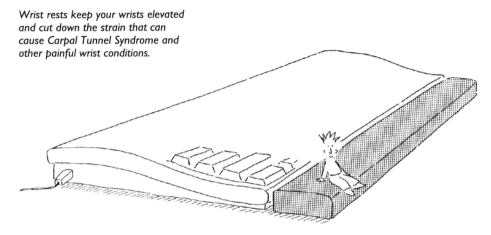

You can get a foam wrist rest at any computer store or business supply store for around $10. Fancier ones go up from there. One person I know uses a rolled-up towel to serve the same purpose.

Mouse Pad

A **mouse pad** is a small pad of soft material that sits under your mouse to give it better traction. It costs just a few dollars ($3 to $10 at office supply and computer stores) and makes a big difference.

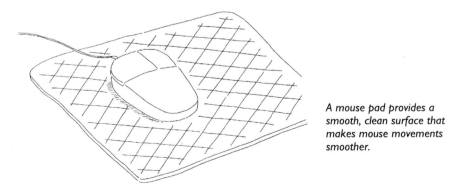

A mouse pad provides a smooth, clean surface that makes mouse movements smoother.

Screen Shield

Screen shields can block the electronic component, but not the magnetic component, of monitor radiation. Some models can save your eyes as well, by sharpening the screen image.

A less crucial accessory, but one that makes a big difference to some people, is a **screen shield**. These devices slip over your monitor screen to help eliminate glare. Screen shields that include grounding wires can also shield you from the electronic component (but not the magnetic component) of the ELF radiation associated with some monitors. (More on the risks of radiation from monitors can be found in the box "Can Your Monitor Be Harmful to Your Health?" in Chapter 15). If you get a screen shield, try it out before you buy it to make sure that it actually helps your ability to read the screen. Some shields can block the screen's brightness and reduce contrast as well as reduce glare, offsetting the benefits with other eye-straining drawbacks.

Putting It All Together

21 *OK, you've brought your PC home. Now it's time to plug it all together. That's not as difficult as it may seem. If you have a desktop PC, you just plug your various components into the plugs on the back of the PC that fit them. If you have a laptop or notebook PC, you don't even have to put it together—just install and charge up the battery.*

Here's how to set up a desktop PC, step by step.

1. The first thing you should do is plug the keyboard into the system unit. The keyboard usually has a circular plug that goes into a round plug at the back of the system unit. Some machines use other arrangements, such as a phone-type jack. Whichever it is, there should be just one place that it fits.

2. Next, plug in the monitor. There are two cords coming from the monitor. One provides power; the other—the funny-looking one with nine little pins—handles the video signals.

TURN YOUR SYSTEM'S POWER OFF BEFORE YOU START MESSING AROUND BACK HERE.

PLUG YOUR MONITOR'S POWER CORD INTO THE OUTLET ON THE BACK OF YOUR COMPUTER.

PLUG THE COMPUTER INTO THE WALL *LAST.*

ON

THE KEYBOARD "PORT" IS USUALLY ROUND.

Remember: Don't plug the PC into the wall until everything else is connected.

Be careful with the video wire. Monitor plugs typically have fairly wimpy pins. It's easy to try to plug them in upside down, and if you exert too much pressure trying to do that, you'll bend the pins. Since most monitor cords are hard-wired to the monitor, you'll encounter a hefty service charge if you have to have the plug replaced. So before you start, look very closely at the plug and at the receptacle in the back of the machine. Don't exert pressure until you have aligned the plug with the receptacle. Now, insert the plug slowly.

Some computers have an outlet on the back of the system unit where you can plug in your monitor's power cord. If your computer doesn't have one, just plug the monitor's power cord into any electrical outlet (but not yet). Plugging the monitor into the system unit makes it easier to turn on the computer for day-to-day use. You can leave the monitor power switch on at all times and start the whole system by turning on the computer's power switch.

THE MONITOR PLUG HAS 15 PINS IN THREE ROWS AND GOES HERE.

IF YOU HAVE AN INTERNAL MODEM, THE PHONE JACK WILL BE HERE.

SERIAL PORTS HAVE 9 OR 25 PINS.

THE PRINTER USUALLY PLUGS INTO THE ONE WITH 25 HOLES.

....THE MOUSE USUALLY PLUGS INTO ONE.

3. Next comes the printer, if you have one. Most printers use a cable with a large connector that goes into the parallel port of your PC. One side of the cable plugs into the printer and the other into the PC. The side of the cable that plugs into the PC is the "male" connector, which plugs into the "female" connector on the back of the PC. (The male connector is the end with the pins; the female connector has the holes.)

Some, though not very many, printers attach to your system's serial ports. These are the small, male connectors on the back of the system unit. Older-style machines use 25-pin connectors. Some newer machines use 9-pin connectors, some stick with the old style, and some have one of each. If your connector isn't right for your cables, you can always get new cables, or cable adapters, at the computer store.

4. If you have an external modem, it will plug into one of your computer's serial ports. (If it's an internal modem, it will be inside the PC.) It will usually have two phone jacks: one to connect the modem to the wall, and the other to connect the modem to your phone.

5. The final step, after you have everything else connected, is to plug your PC, monitor, and printer into the wall or a power strip. If you are in an area that has uncertain electrical power, you might consider a surge protector as well. (See Chapter 20 for more on surge protectors.)

That should do it. You now have a working system.

Use the Proper Plugs

You should plug your PC, printer, and other peripherals into a three-prong, grounded electrical outlet only. Connecting one of those three-prong cheater plugs to a two-prong outlet is not a good idea unless you also run a ground wire to a furnace, pipe, or other grounded device. Radio Shack and hardware stores sell an inexpensive device that determines whether an outlet is properly grounded.

Your computer is all set up and ready to go. Now what are you going to do?

Well, you could just turn it on and see what happens, but as with any powerful gadget, you'll get a lot more out of it if you learn the few basic rules that will help you get the lay of the land and maneuver around roadblocks.

In Part 3, I'll take you through those basic rules. Don't worry, there aren't too many.

Rules of the Road

Setting Up Your Workplace

22 *One of the most important things to think about before you sit down at your computer is just how you're going to sit down at your computer.*

You can get away with plopping a PC on a table or desk, plugging it into the wall, and sitting down any which way to type. But making things pleasant and comfortable takes some thought. And it's more important than you might think. You can actually hurt yourself if you don't have your computer set up correctly. Typing for hours in an uncomfortable hunch over the keyboard can cause neck and back pains, eyestrain, and a painful injury to your wrists. Here's a guide to how to set up a workspace that's safe and comfortable for both you and your computer.

A Comfortable Chair

Don't skimp on your chair. A dining room chair is designed for the length of a meal, not a workday; you need something that will allow you to work comfortably at a desk for several hours at a time. The chair should let you adjust the seat height and the position of the backrest. It should be comfortable and offer you plenty of lower-back support. Check with an office supply dealer for a chair designed to be used with a computer, and test it out before you buy.

The Desk

You don't have to spend a lot of money for a custom-made computer desk. The main thing is to be sure that your keyboard is at the right height. The keyboard should be about 26 inches from the floor—or low enough that your elbows are higher than your wrists while you type. A desk that is too high can result in repetitive stress injuries to your arms and wrists (Chapter 20 has more info on Carpal Tunnel Syndrome and other injuries that can result from typing all day at a badly positioned keyboard.) Most office desks and dining room tables are too high. The computer desks that you see at K-Mart and most other discount stores don't look great and may fall apart after a few years, but if they're the right height and depth, they'll do the job just as well as the fancy ones you get from office supply dealers. It's better to sit at a cheap computer desk than at an expensive office desk that's too high for your keyboard.

If you don't want to invest in a new desk, there's another option. Most office supply stores sell special keyboard holders that attach to your desk and let you adjust your keyboard to a comfortable height. Providing a shelf for the keyboard also adds some extra desk space.

Lighting

Your workspace should have plenty of light, but the light should be diffused so that it doesn't create glare on your screen and strain your eyes. Adjustable lamps and lamps that let the light bounce off the ceiling work well for that purpose.

Choosing an Area

Plan your work area from the floor up. A carpeted area will be quieter than wood or linoleum floors, but if you can, stay away from plush carpets. They generate too much static electricity, which can be dangerous for your equipment.

The Monitor

OK, you've got a low desk so that your keyboard is below your elbow level, and now your monitor is so low that you've got to bend over to see what's on the screen. That can't be good.

You're right, it's not. Your monitor should be up around eye level—when you're sitting up straight. Most monitors these days come on tilt-and-swivel bases, but in many cases they don't offer a wide enough choice of adjustments. You can buy many different kinds of gadgets to take care of this problem, ranging from simple monitor platforms to elaborate adjustable arms that enable you to set your monitor in almost any position and height. If you don't want to spring for one of those solutions, however, try propping last year's Yellow Pages under the screen.

Remember, too, that if you're using a standard color monitor, it's best to keep it at arm's length to avoid the risks of radiation. (See the box "Can Your Monitor Be Harmful to Your Health?" in Chapter 15 for more details.)

Turning Your Computer On

23 *OK, it's finally time to turn on your PC.*

- If you have all your equipment plugged into a power strip, just flip the power strip switch and your whole system will spring to life.
- If you have your monitor plugged into your system unit, just flip the switch on the PC. (I'm assuming you are leaving the monitor switch in the on position at all times.) Your system unit and monitor should both start up.
- If everything is plugged in separately, you'll have to find the switches on your system unit, monitor, and printer. They're at a different place on each brand, so you're on your own here.

Turning on a PC is often called "booting" it. The term comes from the expression "pulling oneself up by the bootstraps," because the machine gives itself all the instructions it needs for its startup process, using intelligence built into its chips and stored on disk.

While you're waiting for the DOS prompt or the Windows opening screen, the computer will be flashing all sorts of messages on the screen and flashing some lights on the system unit. For the most part, you can ignore all that. When your system beeps at you, though, it wants something from you. When you hear a beep, look on the screen for a message that tells you what to do.

On some systems, somewhere in the middle of this startup process, your system will beep and display the message:

```
Please enter new system date:
C:\>
```

When you see this, just press the Enter key twice. The computer will continue its work. Pressing Enter twice tells the computer to use the default for the system date and for the next request it will make, which is for a new system time. The clock on your computer keeps correct time even when the system is turned off, so you need to reset the time only if you move and change time zones, for daylight savings time, or if the internal battery fails for some reason.

If your system doesn't ask you for the date, don't worry. It just means that whoever set up your system thought ahead and decided to save you the trouble of this step. (If you want to know how, read about the **AUTOEXEC.BAT** file in Chapter 25.)

At the end of the startup process, you'll see one of these three things:

If you see this, the DOS prompt, you're running DOS.

If you see this, you're running DOS with the DOS Shell.

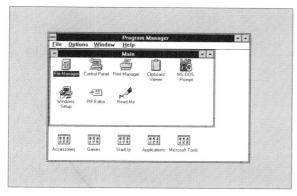

If you see this, you're running Windows.

Whichever screen you see, it indicates that your computer has successfully started. Congratulations!

What do you do now? Most likely, the next thing you'll want to do is run a program, though you can also take care of some computer housekeeping by working directly with DOS or Windows. The DOS and Windows cookbooks at the end of this book supply recipes for most of the operations you'll want to carry out from the DOS prompt or from the Windows **Program Manager**, including how to run a program. The next chapters will fill you in on all the things you'll need to know why and when you should use all those recipes.

How to Fix Things That Might Go Wrong During Startup

Disk Error

Sometimes during startup your computer may beep at you and display the message

```
A:>
Non-System disk or disk error.
Replace and strike any key when ready
```

Don't worry—there's probably nothing wrong with the computer. Chances are you have a floppy disk in the floppy drive—the drive that DOS looks in first for its system files. Just remove the floppy disk and press any key on the keyboard. Your computer will continue its startup process.

Things Seem to Be Happening, but Nothing Shows Up on Screen

If you turn your monitor on and the screen stays dark, don't panic until you've checked the brightness control. (You should find brightness and contrast controls at the side, rear, or bottom of the monitor.) A lot of service calls to fix "broken" monitors turn out to be false alarms—the brightness is just turned all the way down.

You Get the DOS Prompt, but You Know You Have Windows

If you get the DOS prompt, but you know you have Windows, type WIN and press Enter. If you have Windows, this should start it.

All About Files

WHATSUP.DOC

FILE NAME

FILE EXTENSION

Files are what hold the information your computer works with.

24

A file might contain a program; your yearly budget; a letter to your Aunt Hilda; the price, location, and inventory number of every stamp in your valuable collection—in short, any information entered into the computer and saved there.

A file is simply a bunch of data with a name attached. The name is there so you can find that information again once it's stored on disk.

Naming Files

The rules for naming files are set by DOS and are the same no matter what program you use.

DOS's rules for naming files are strict, but pretty simple:

- The **file name** can have up to eight characters.
- It can also have a **file extension**, consisting of a period and three more characters.
- There are a few characters you can't use in file names, mostly punctuation characters. (Those characters are listed in the box at right.)

Forbidden Characters

You can use any characters on your keyboard in file names, except these:

< >	angle brackets		,	comma
\	backslash		=	equal sign
|	bar		+	plus sign
[ ]	brackets		" "	quotation marks
:	colon		;	semicolon

These are all fine file names:

CHAPTER3.DOC	A word processing file
93BUDGET.WKS	A spreadsheet file
AUTOEXEC.BAT	A batch file

These aren't:

CHAP.3.DOC	Uses a period other than the one before the file extension
CHAP/3.DOC	Uses a slash
CHAPTER10.DOC	Has too many characters

If you break these rules, DOS will let you know with an **error message**. If the file name is too long, the program you're in may just shorten it to an acceptable length.

You can use any characters for the extension that you can use in the first eight characters of the file name. Most programs automatically place their own extension on the file name of every file you save with the program. The box below shows some common extensions.

Most programs let you override the application's default file extension and give a file any extension you'd like. Usually, however, it's better not to. I'll explain why in the next section.

File Formats

As you will notice very quickly once you start working with application programs, you can't open just any file with any program. Programs can only work with files that are in a **file format** they recognize.

Files include a few different types of information. Of course, they include the contents of the document —the text you type in a word processing or database document, the pic-

Get to Know Your File Extensions

These are some file extensions used by common PC programs.

Extension	Program	File Type
.BMP	Windows Paintbrush	graphics
.DBF	dBase	database
.DOC	Microsoft Word	word processor
.WKS	Lotus 1-2-3 or Microsoft Works	spreadsheet
.WRI	Windows Write	word processor
.XLS	Microsoft Excel	spreadsheet
.WP	WordPerfect	word processor

ture you draw in a graphics program. They also include information for the application program to use, which tells it how those contents are formatted—how they will look on screen or on paper. That information is different for every program, because the scheme is dreamed up by the programmers who wrote the application. And that extra information in the file is what makes it specifically that program's own.

The three-character file extension at the end of the file name usually indicates what format the file is in. For example, the extension .DOC means that it is a Microsoft Word document, .WKS means that it is a 1-2-3 or Microsoft Works spreadsheet file. The box "Get to Know Your File Extensions" on the previous page shows the extensions used by some common programs.

Exchanging Information Between Programs

The fact that every program has its own format can make sharing information between programs a complicated affair. What happens, for instance, if you want to hand over a word processing file to someone who uses a different word processing program than you do, or if you want to move some information from your database into your word processor?

Often, it won't be a problem. As a special feature, most programs these days will open the files of the leading word processors and other popular programs. In many cases, the second program will accept the file with no problems.

Sometimes, however, that won't be the case. Sometimes your program won't be able to open another program's files at all, and sometimes it will open it, but the file will look different in the new program. The formatting might be messed up, or it might not even be readable, with a lot of strange characters scattered throughout.

ASCII stands for "American Standard Code for Information Interchange." ASCII files can be created and read by almost any application program.

There's an answer to that, too. If you want to share files between incompatible programs, you can always save the file in **plain text**, also called **ASCII**, format. Almost every text-based program can save and read files in plain text format, in addition to its own application format. Plain text files include just the content information, and not the formatting.

These files can be opened by almost any program, so this is used as the standard format for exchanging files between programs, and your friend's word processing program will almost certainly be able to read it. You will lose all your formatting—boldface text, paragraph indents, and all other design information—but the contents should come across fine.

Program Files

Like other programs, DOS has certain file formats that it recognizes as its own. These are DOS program files, and they end with these three extensions:

- .BAT
- .COM
- .EXE

Files ending in .BAT are **batch files**. These files consist of a list of DOS commands that DOS runs as a group when you execute the batch file. **AUTOEXEC.BAT** is a special batch file that DOS runs automatically when you start up your computer (for more on AUTOEXEC.BAT, see Chapter 25).

Files ending in .COM and .EXE are **program files**. All your application program file names will end with one of these extensions. When you type the name of the file at the DOS prompt, DOS executes the program.

The **AUTOEXEC.BAT** and **CONFIG.SYS** Files

When DOS is installed on your computer, it creates two
special files: AUTOEXEC.BAT and CONFIG.SYS. Every
time you start your computer, DOS takes a look at
both those files to see exactly how your system should
be set up.

25

The **AUTOEXEC.BAT** File

AUTOEXEC.BAT is a special batch file, a type of simple program that contains DOS commands. DOS runs the whole batch of commands when you type the name of the batch file on the DOS command line.

DOS runs the AUTOEXEC.BAT file every time you start up the computer, so it's the place to put any commands that you want run every time you start up. For example, if you want to start Windows every time you turn on your computer, you include the command WIN in the AUTOEXEC.BAT file. The AUTOEXEC.BAT file often contains other commands that tell DOS to use the default date and time, set the DOS prompt to include extra information, and otherwise set up the system just the way you like it.

Any command you can type on the DOS command line can be run from the AUTOEXEC.BAT file.

The **CONFIG.SYS** File

The CONFIG.SYS file contains information that DOS needs in order to set up—or "configure"—your system to work properly with your particular combination of hardware and software. Commands in this file often tell DOS how to configure its memory to work best with your software, for example. Another common use of CONFIG.SYS is to tell DOS to load up driver software that runs extra hardware such as a CD-ROM drive. As with AUTOEXEC.BAT, DOS reads CONFIG.SYS every time it starts up your computer and follows the instructions written there.

Changing **AUTOEXEC.BAT** or **CONFIG.SYS**

The AUTOEXEC.BAT file is easy to change, and once you get the hang of using DOS commands, it's pretty easy to work with.

The CONFIG.SYS file is a bit more complicated to work with than AUTOEXEC.BAT, and you probably won't want to mess with it. When you install new hardware, though, some manuals may instruct you to change CONFIG.SYS as part of the installation process. In that case, the hardware manual will give you explicit instructions about what to change in the file. If you're lucky, though, the hardware manufacturer will include an installation program that makes the necessary changes for you, and you won't need to worry about it at all.

If you do need to edit your AUTOEXEC.BAT or CONFIG.SYS file, you can find instructions for what to do in the Cookbook section at the end of this book.

Managing Your Hard Disk

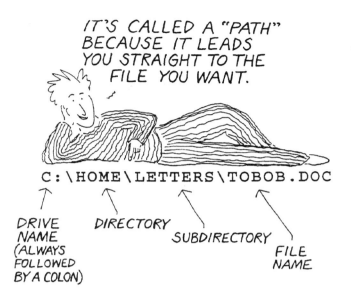

IT'S CALLED A "PATH" BECAUSE IT LEADS YOU STRAIGHT TO THE FILE YOU WANT.

26

C:\HOME\LETTERS\TOBOB.DOC

DRIVE NAME (ALWAYS FOLLOWED BY A COLON)

DIRECTORY

SUBDIRECTORY

FILE NAME

Your hard disk is like a giant warehouse that may hold thousands of files. When you first buy your computer, that space is almost empty, except for a few things the dealer has preinstalled on the disk, such as DOS, Windows, and perhaps a few programs. Watch what happens, though, as you fill your hard disk with hundreds of program files, text files, picture files, and font files—all the information you're going to store there. To keep this warehouse from turning into a total mess, you need to learn some basic rules for saving, finding, and retrieving files. DOS has a system, called "directories," just for that purpose.

To get a feel for this system, let's start by imagining that you are moving to a new town and you have to give the moving company a precise list of where you want all your belongings to go. You have a tool shed, a garage, and a main house, and in your instructions to the moving company you refer to them as A, B, and C, respectively. If you gave the movers a list like this one, they could easily figure out where all of your possessions go:

```
A:\SAW
A:\RAKE
A:\HOSE
B:\BICYCLE
B:\LAWNMOWER
B:\OILPAN
B:\RAG
C:\KITCHEN\TABLE
C:\KITCHEN\CHAIR1
C:\KITCHEN\CHAIR2
C:\KITCHEN\FRIDGE\MILK
C:\KITCHEN\FRIDGE\JUICE
C:\KITCHEN\FRIDGE\APPLES
C:\KITCHEN\CUPBOARD\SOUPCAN
C:\KITCHEN\CUPBOARD\PASTA
C:\BEDROOM\BED
C:\BEDROOM\CLOSET\REDSHIRT
C:\BEDROOM\CLOSET\BLUESHIRT
```

Now let's apply this to your computer's filing system. Instead of different buildings, your computer has different disk drives. Instead of rooms, it has directories, and instead of soup cans and red shirts, it has files. The directions that tell DOS exactly where a file is stored are called **paths**.

You can create any number of "rooms" (directories) on your hard disk, and just as rooms in a house can contain yet smaller storage units such as cupboards and closets, directories can contain other directories. You probably won't need directories at all on floppies, which, like the tool shed and the garage in the example, are so small they don't really need to be subdivided.

You can nest directories in as many levels as you want, but for practical purposes, just a few levels should be sufficient for your hard disk.

Sometimes a directory that is within another directory is called a **subdirectory**, but calling it a directory is also correct.

The names of the rooms, or directories, are up to you. You could actually have a directory system on your hard disk that matches the one shown here, with directories called Kitchen and Bedroom. More likely, though, you'll set up a system with names that are more descriptive of how you use your hard disk. Your system might look more like this:

C:\BUSINESS\PROJECT1\BUDGET.WKS
C:\BUSINESS\PROJECT1\PROPOSAL.DOC
C:\HOME\CHKBOOK.WKS
C:\HOME\LETTERS\TOBOB.DOC

In DOS, A: refers to your first floppy drive, and B: refers to your second, if you happen to have two. C: is your computer's hard disk. If you have more than one hard drive, they are named, D:, E:, and so on.

Naming directories is a lot like naming files. A directory name can have up to eight characters, and the same characters that are forbidden in file names are forbidden in directory names. (See the box "Forbidden Characters" in Chapter 24.) Generally, you wouldn't use a three-character extension on a directory name, though you could if you wanted to. (The Cookbook section of this book includes instructions for creating and deleting directories in DOS and Windows.)

The directory structure of a disk is called the **directory tree**, because it starts from a single root and grows into many branches. The main directory, which holds all the other directories you create, is called the **root directory**.

In Windows, you can see the directory structure, in the form shown here, in Windows' File Manager. In DOS, you can see your directory structure by using the TREE command.

Using Paths

When will you use paths?

- When you're saving a new file.
- When you're opening a file that's saved on disk.
- When you're using a DOS command to operate on a file.

In short, you will use paths anytime you need to specify a file's location in DOS or in an application program.

Moving Around the Directory Tree: The Concept of the Current Directory

Once you get the hang of it, directories and paths are pretty easy to use, but you can see how using paths often would call for a lot of typing. DOS and Windows both provide a way around this.

Let's say you had a bunch of tasks to do in the living room of the house I just described. The sensible thing to do would be to just go to the living room and start working. In DOS, you can move to a certain directory in the same way. The directory you move to is called the **current directory**. Once you're there, DOS just assumes that any files you work on will be in that directory until you give it a new path.

Moving to a certain directory is clearly a useful thing to do when you want to operate on a number of files in a single directory. It saves you the trouble of typing long paths in front of every file name. It also reduces the possibility for mistakes that might happen if you typed the wrong path or forgot it altogether.

You can find out how to create directories and how to move between them in the Cookbook section at the end of this book.

Hard Disk Smarts

Now that you know what directories are and what   **27**
they're for, I'm going to give you some advice on how
to use them.

How you use directories depends on how organized a person you are. Some people organize and reorganize their directories all the time, whenever they start thinking about their work in a different way. Others build a very basic structure and work with it as long as they own their computer. Either way is fine; the beauty of directories is that you can set them up in any way that suits your working style.

That said, here are a few rules to keep in mind as you create new directories.

1. Keep document files in a different directory from application files.

The natural instinct of novice computer users is generally to save Microsoft Word files in the Microsoft Word directory, for instance, but that's not a good idea. You should create new, special directories for the documents you create yourself.

The reason is this: Your hard disk will basically include two types of files, ones you can edit and others you should never touch. The first group includes your document files. The second group—the ones you shouldn't touch—include all the files that come with an application, including the program file itself and any associated files, such as dictionaries and help files. Keeping the files you shouldn't touch in their own directories keeps them out of harm's way. It also makes it easier to find the document files you need.

2. Don't mess with the directories that software or hardware installation programs create.

When you install a program, the installation program will generally create a directory specifically for the application's files. You should leave those directories just as the program created them: Don't delete any files, rename the directory, or move that directory inside another directory. The application will need to use files that are in that directory, and it makes certain assumptions about the directory's name and whereabouts. For example, your word processor will look for its dictionary file to perform a spelling check. If you've moved the application directory to a new location, you're out of luck. It's possible to fix, but make it easy on yourself and stick with the default organization.

3. Keep only one copy of each file on your hard disk.

If you save a file in a directory that already includes a file of the same name, the program will generally ask you if you want to replace the old file with the new one. If you save the new file, or a new version of the file, in a different directory, DOS will just save it, no questions asked. This means that it's possible to have several versions of a file on your hard disk. This is a bad idea. Always keep just the latest version on the hard disk, with a backup copy on another disk entirely. Or, if you want to keep a backup copy on your hard disk, give it another name or another file extension (such as .BAK). You'll soon find out that nothing is worse than working on—or actually distributing—a document that you think is the latest version, but in fact isn't. (For more on backups, see Chapter 30.)

4. Keep your directory structure simple.

If you're a hyper-organized type, you can get really carried away creating directories inside of directories so that practically every file has its own classification. My advice is, don't. If you create a directory structure more than three levels deep, you'll find yourself spending an awful lot of extra time typing serpentine paths (if you're in DOS), or clicking away at directory folders (if you're in Windows or the DOS Shell). You can probably create all the divisions you need with no more than three levels, if you plan it right.

To find out how to create and delete directories, see the Cookbook section at the end of this book.

Opening, Saving, and Closing Files

When you open a file, whether you're creating a new one or opening one that already exists, it creates a space on the electronic desktop—your computer's memory—in which that file is stored while you work with it. This is important to remember: It means that any work you do exists only in the computer's memory. It's not saved permanently until you save the file to disk.

28

It's important to save your work every few minutes, or whenever you stop for a break, whichever comes first.

Common sense might suggest that you save your file to disk once you've finished working on it. Wrong. You need to save your file EVERY CHANCE YOU GET: when you get up to stretch, when you stop work for a minute to think about what you're going to do next, when you switch between programs. It should become an automatic gesture. When you create a new file, it's a good idea to give it a name and save it right away, before you even start to work on it. Once it's saved the first time, you can save it easily at short intervals.

Why? Because more often than you might expect, something goes wrong. If your cat trips over the power cord, if a three-car pileup a mile away takes out a power line, or if your computer just freezes up (which it sometimes will, believe me) and you need to restart it, you will lose everything that isn't saved to disk. Perhaps the most important time to save is just before you print a document, since printer problems are probably the most frequent reasons a computer freezes up.

Invariably, thanks to Murphy's law, foul-ups become almost inevitable just before a deadline, or when you've just created something that will win you international fame—and you haven't saved. Don't worry about saving too often. That's impossible.

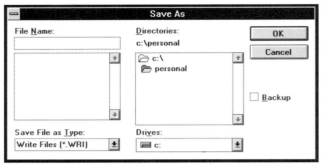

The first time you save a document, you must give it a name and choose the directory you want it in. (If you're using Windows, you'll see a dialog box like this one from Windows Write.) Every time you save after that, the program will save your changes in the same document.

Many programs have a feature that lets you tell your computer to automatically save at regular intervals. Look in your user's manual index under Save to find out how to activate it. I never choose an interval longer than five minutes.

Many programs also help you out with a "double backup" system that gives you extra protection by preserving the last version of the file on disk in addition to the current version. The backup version has the extension .BAK. This is a lifesaver on those occasions when you do something bad to your file (like delete most of it) and then absentmindedly save the messed-up version. You can then go to DOS, delete the messed-up version, and rename the version with the .BAK extension, giving it the extension used by your program. You can then open that up and resume work.

When you close a file, the computer removes the file from its memory. This is a different from saving it, and if you don't save your work before you close the file, any work you've done since the last save will be lost. If you haven't saved all your changes when you give the Close command, the program will usually notify you of that and ask you if you would like to save your changes before closing.

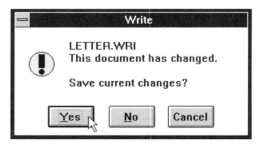

If you try to close a program without saving your work, most programs will ask you if you want to save changes before you leave the program.

Working With Floppies

If the hard disk is where you save all your programs **29**

and information, what are floppy disks for?

In Chapter 13, I called
floppy drives the front door
to your computer—the way
data comes in and goes out.
You'll use floppy disks in a
lot of different ways:

- When you buy a new
  piece of software or when
  a friend or co-worker
  gives you a file, it usually
  comes on floppy disk.
- When you want to share
  files with other people,
  you can give them the
  files on a floppy.
- When you want to remove
  files from your hard disk
  but keep an archive copy
  elsewhere, or when you
  just want to have extra,
  backup copies of files, you
  save them to floppy disks.

You can open files and
save them on a floppy disk in
your floppy drive just as you
would use them if they were
on your hard disk. (The only
difference is that it takes a
little longer to open and save
files to a floppy than it does
to a hard disk.)

TO INSERT A 5¼"
DISK, GENTLY PUSH
IT INTO THE WIDER
SLOT. WHEN THE
DISK STOPS, PUSH
THE LATCH DOWN.

HERE.

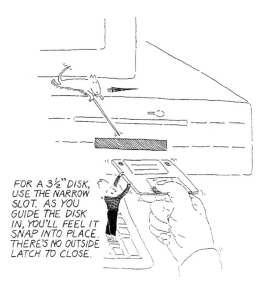

FOR A 3½" DISK,
USE THE NARROW
SLOT. AS YOU
GUIDE THE DISK
IN, YOU'LL FEEL IT
SNAP INTO PLACE.
THERE'S NO OUTSIDE
LATCH TO CLOSE.

Make Sure You Get the Right Kind

As I described in Chapter 13, PCs can use two different sizes of floppies, 3.5-inch and 5.25-inch. Whether or not your PC can use both sizes depends on how many disk drives you have, and in what sizes. These days, most computers come with 3.5-inch drives, though if you're lucky, you'll have one drive in each size.

What I didn't tell you in Chapter 13 was that the trouble doesn't stop there. Each size of disk comes in two different densities: **double-density** and **high-density**. High-density disks hold more information than double-density disks. To make it even more confusing, the smaller 3.5-inch disks hold more data than the 5.25-inch disks.

Make sure you get the right density when you're shopping for disks. Disk drives are generally referred to by the capacity of the disks they can read. If your computer has a 1.4-MB (3.5-inch) or 1.2-MB (5.25-inch) drive, you can use either high-density or double-density disks. If your computer has a 720-K (3.5-inch) or 360-K (5.25-inch) disk, you can only use double-density disks.

How Much Data Can You Fit on a Floppy?

	3.5-inch	5.25-inch
double-sided/ double-density	720 K	360 K
high-density	1.4 MB	1.2 MB

Formatting Floppies

If you insert a floppy disk fresh from the store in your disk drive and try to save a file to it, DOS will display an error message. What exactly it will say depends on what program you're in. It might be something as scary as "General failure reading drive A." There's nothing wrong with your disk drive or with the floppy disk; it's just that before you use a floppy disk, you have to first perform an operation on it called **formatting**.

A 3.5-inch disk that you buy at the store can be formatted for DOS or for Macintoshes. Formatting a floppy disk is DOS's way of personalizing the disk so that it will be ready to receive information in the form that DOS writes it.

As you've probably noticed by now, you'll run across this word "format" a lot when you're using computers. Here it means readying a disk to save information.

DOS includes a special command, called FORMAT, especially for this operation. Windows includes a Format command, in the **File Manager**'s Disk menu, that does the same thing. Instructions for formatting floppy disks are included in the Cookbook section at the end of this book.

Formatting disks is easy, but it takes some time. If you want to avoid the operation altogether, you can buy preformatted floppies for a little extra money.

Locking a Disk

It's easy to save information on a floppy—sometimes too easy. In some cases, you won't want the information on a floppy disk to be altered—you'll want it to stay in just the condition you saved it in. Take, for example, the original program files of some software that you bought, or important copies of business transactions that you've archived to floppy disk. How do you keep them from being changed once they're opened on the computer?

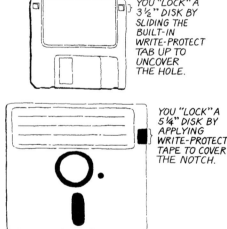

YOU "LOCK" A 3½" DISK BY SLIDING THE BUILT-IN WRITE-PROTECT TAB UP TO UNCOVER THE HOLE.

YOU "LOCK" A 5¼" DISK BY APPLYING WRITE-PROTECT TAPE TO COVER THE NOTCH.

Floppy disks have a built-in mechanism for keeping files safe from accidental changes. It's called "locking" a disk or **write-protecting** it. When a disk is locked, your computer can read files from the disk, but it can't write (that is, save files) to it.

Locking a disk is totally reversible. You can lock and unlock a disk over and over again.

Storing Floppies

Floppies, especially 5.25-inch floppies, are fragile things. Software manuals always tell you to store your original floppy disks "in a safe place," but they never say just what that is.

A safe place for floppies is somewhere where they won't be subjected to excessive heat or cold, are away from sources of electrical bursts, and won't get dusty. The boxes that the disks originally come in are fine for storing them.

Remember, information is saved magnetically on floppy disks, so anything that creates a magnetic field is dangerous. Things you wouldn't think of, like a ringing phone or an electric pencil sharpener too close to a disk, could scramble the data stored on it. Don't leave your disks lying on top of the computer because it, too, creates magnetic fields.

In the next chapter, you'll learn about backing up—making sure that if something does happen to data on your floppies or on your hard disk, you'll have an extra copy handy.

Backing Up

In PC-speak, "backing up" doesn't mean going back to where you started. It means taking steps so that you never have to.

Keeping your work in electronic form has the advantage of keeping your work compactly stored, in a form that's easy to work with. The disadvantage is that electronic components are subject to all sorts of dangers. The magnetic data on a floppy disk can be scrambled if you leave the disk near a television set, lying on top of your computer, or in other places near magnetic fields. Hard disks are subject to their own perils. It may never happen to you, but I know lots of people (including yours truly) who have, at least once, turned on their PC only to discover that their hard disk was corrupted. If that happens to you, you had better have a backup copy of your files or, well, you're in trouble.

When you're talking about electronic files, just remember: One copy is never enough.

Backing Up Your Hard Disk

If, like most people, you keep all your working files on your hard disk, you'll need to make extra copies of all those files. And you can't rest after you've backed everything up once. Since those files are added to and changed all the time, you'll need to back up your new work periodically.

The best rule to follow is: Back up whenever you'd be distraught if you lost the work you've done since the last backup.

How often you need to back up depends on how much work you do each day. Businesses that store many workers' files on a central hard disk back it up at least once a day. If you're working intensely on a single document, you'll probably want to back up that document every evening. If your work is less intensive, you can get away with backing up every week or so.

The simplest way to back up your daily work is to just keep a backup disk in your computer's floppy drive and save a copy to the floppy when you close a file.

It's also a good idea, however, to make regular backups of everything on your hard disk, or at least everything you've changed since the last big backup. You can automate the process with backup software. DOS 6.0 has a good backup program; instructions for using it are included in the DOS Cookbook at the end of this book. (Earlier versions of DOS also had a backup program, but it was very hard to use.) You can also get commercial programs, including **Norton Backup** (from Symantec, for DOS or Windows), **Central Point Backup** (from Central Point Software), or **Fastback** (from Fifth Generation Systems). Having a high-capacity backup device, such as a tape drive, can make the process easier, but you can also back up to floppies. (See "When a Floppy Isn't Big Enough" in Chapter 13 for more on tape drives.)

Resources

Central Point Backup
Central Point Software,
800-964-6896, 503-690-8090.

Fastback
Fifth Generation Systems,
800-873-4384, 504-291-7221.

Norton Backup
Symantec, 800-441-7234,
408-253-9600.

Backing Up Floppies

If you have any files that you keep only on floppy disk, it's wise to have extra copies of them, too. It's especially important to back up floppies in these cases:

- When you buy a new piece of software, you should make a copy of your original program disks to back up your software.
- After a while, your hard disk may become so full that you'll need to take some of your old work off and archive it on floppies. When you archive old files, be sure to make two copies of each disk, in case one gets damaged.

The Cookbook section at the end of this book tells you how to make copies of floppy disks.

Creating an Extra System Disk

You should always have a floppy **system disk** on hand—a floppy disk that has the boot files DOS uses to start up. I'm not trying to be a doomsayer here, but if your hard disk crashes (it could happen), you won't even be able to start up your computer unless you have your system files on a floppy.

The system files can't just be copied to a floppy; you can only create a system disk by telling DOS you want to make a disk a system disk as you format it. (See Chapter 29 for more on formatting disks, and see the cookbooks at the end of this book for instructions how.)

Once you've created a system disk, label it "System Disk" and put it in a convenient place. Then, if you ever have trouble booting from the hard disk, you can boot from the floppy.

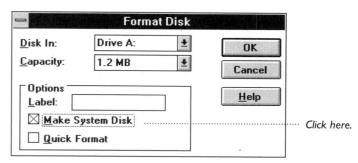

Click here.

In Windows, you create a system disk by clicking a check box in the Format dialog box.

Storing Backups

Of course, you should clearly label your backup disks and store them as you would store any floppies—away from extremes in temperature and electrical fields. (For more on storing floppies, see Chapter 29.)

If you want to be really safe, you need to keep a set of backup disks off your premises. I hope it will never happen, but if there is a fire or other catastrophe, having a set of backup disks in the same room as your computer won't do you any good.

If You Get Stuck

31 *Sometimes, especially when you're just getting the hang of the computer, you'll run into a situation that completely baffles you but is actually quite easy to fix. This chapter will run through a few of the most common such hang-ups.*

1. You're working with an application program and the computer just beeps at you whenever you press a key.

You're working on a program and you get stuck somewhere. The program is working OK, but you just can't figure out how to get back to the main menu or even quit the program. The first thing to try is press the Esc (short for Escape) key one or more times. As good as its name, the Esc key usually backs you out of whatever situation you're in, one step at a time.

2. You've messed up a file you're working on.

If you're working in Windows, your program should have an Undo command that lets you undo the last thing you did (look in the Edit menu). With this command, you can remove the last sentence you typed, reinstate the text you just deleted—undo any simple command.

Unfortunately, in some cases, the Undo command won't work. If the command was very complicated, Undo might not be available. And if you've done anything else since the command you want to retract, you're out of luck. Generally, Undo only works on the action you've just finished, although some programs have a multiple undo feature that can step backward through several actions.

If the problem is past fixing with Undo, you can always go back to the last version you saved to disk (the state the file was in when you last gave a Save command). To do that, just close the file without saving your changes. When you open it again, it will be the earlier version. (Some software has an automatic save feature that saves your file at regular intervals. If you're using software that does that, it will be hard to tell just what state the file was in when it was last saved, but this method is still worth a try.)

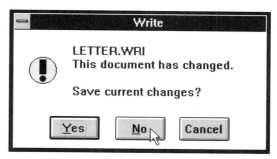

If you click No, the program will discard all the changes you made since you last saved the file.

3. Your computer freezes up.

Sometimes you'll press the keys on your keyboard, or move your mouse, and nothing happens. There's often no apparent reason. Programs sometimes just "lock up." It could be a **bug** or some combination of actions that you just can't figure out.

If this happens, first give the computer about a minute to try to work things out itself. Sometimes the software just needs time to catch up.

If you test it again a bit later and, still, nothing is happening, you'll need to **reboot** the computer. You do that by holding down the Ctrl, Alt, and Del keys all at the same time. If you're in Windows you might luck out and the program will quit, but Windows and other programs you have open won't. (That's the way it's supposed to happen.) Otherwise, the computer will go through its startup procedure again, leaving you back at the DOS or Windows opening screen.

When you use Ctrl-Alt-Del, all the work you've done since you last saved will be lost. Well, it happens.

Once in awhile, even Ctrl-Alt-Del won't work. The next maneuver is to push your PC's "reset" switch, if it has one. If that doesn't work (or if you can't find the switch), turn off the power for a few seconds (until it sounds like it's really stopped), and turn the computer back on again. Unless there is a serious problem, the machine should restart as it normally does. If it doesn't start properly, try inserting a floppy system disk in Drive A:. (That's the disk with the DOS system on it that you formatted earlier, as described in the last chapter.) If that doesn't work, you're going to need help from an expert.

4. Nothing appears on your monitor.
Fiddle wih the darkness and contrast controls. Nine times out of ten, this is the problem.

5. The computer makes a loud, rapid beeping sound when you turn it on.
Check to see whether the keyboard is plugged in or whether something is holding down a key.

6. You turn on your computer and nothing happens.
Start with the obvious. Is the machine plugged into the wall and is everything plugged into the computer? Check the monitor, the keyboard, the mouse, and the printer cables. Also check the brightness control on the monitor, in case it's turned way down.

OK—that was too easy. If the obvious didn't work, there is a good chance the problem is with your hard disk. Before you do anything, turn off the PC for about 15 minutes so it cools down, and try again. Sometimes components fail because of heat, especially on hot days.

If that doesn't work, try starting your computer with a floppy system disk in the A: drive. (For more on creating a floppy system disk, see Chapter 30.) If you have Norton Utilities or PC Tools, you should run the Disk Doctor (in Norton Utilities) or Disk Fix (in PC Tools) program, which can sometimes take care of drive troubles in a single step. (For more on those utilities, see Chapter 42.)

If your problem isn't listed here, and you just can't figure out what to do, remember to check your on-line help and the Troubleshooting section in the user's guide for more tips. Also, remember that the computer community is there to help you out. On-line tech support, user groups, your local computer guru, and if it comes to it, professional computer repair technicians can all help you figure out how to get unstuck. (Chapter 6 has a rundown of all those resources.)

Shutting Down

When you're done working at your computer for the **32**
day and you're ready to turn it off, don't just flip the
switch. It's important that you close all your files and
applications before you shut down.

This is not just a safeguard to make sure that your work is saved,
though it does serve that purpose. And if you don't do it, you won't
actually harm your computer. It's just better housekeeping. It enables
DOS to close all its files and empty its memory in an orderly way. This
is especially important if you use Windows, because Windows creates
all sorts of temporary files that it deletes when you exit properly. Again,
it's not the end of the world if your system crashes or you turn off your
PC while you're running Windows, but it is a good idea to exit properly.

Some people will tell you that you should never turn off your computer. The conventional wisdom used to be that a computer would last longer if you left it on all the time and just turned off the monitor to prevent the image from being burned into the screen. That reasoning was based on the idea that the internal components of the computer, and especially the hard disk, could be worn out by repeated starts and stops. These days, however, the life of your hard disk, the part most prone to failure, isn't likely to be diminished by being turned off and on. Most hard disks are rated to last an average of 10,000 starts and stops, which means that you could expect to turn the computer off and on every day for 27 years before you would wear it out. On the other hand, if you simply keep the computer on all the time, a typical hard disk will wear out, on average, after 150,000 hours, or 17 years.

Of course, your current computer will be obsolete long before either 17 or 27 years have passed, so the bottom line is, it doesn't matter whether you leave your computer running or turn it off when it's not in use. I recommend turning it off, at least at night, simply to minimize energy consumption, fire danger, and noise.

Congratulations. You've mastered the basic concepts. That, and knowing where to go if you get stuck, should get you through any computer task that comes your way.

Now it's time to get down to work. If you've got Windows, or if you got a good deal from your computer dealer, you've already got a few applications installed on your hard disk. If you don't, you need software— and pronto. Software lets you do the jobs you bought the computer for: writing letters and reports, balancing budgets, playing games.

In Part 4, I'll provide an overview of the basic kinds of software, along with advice about what to look for in each category.

Stocking Up on Software

How Much Software Do You Need?

33 *There are thousands of programs for IBM-compatible PCs. There's no doubt you'll be able to find programs to take care of everything you want to use your PC for. And that's just the beginning. Once you get used to working with a few basic pieces of software and start hunting through the magazines and catalogs, you'll find all sorts of games, utilities, and accessory software you won't want to do without.*

Although there is an enormous number of programs to choose from, you'll find that most of them fall into a few categories, which take care of most of the work you'll do on the computer (see the box below).

Of course, not all software falls into those categories. DOS—operating system software—is another type. Still other programs handle specialized tasks like accounting, type design, or music composition. Another group helps professionals from video store owners to landscape gardeners run their businesses. But the categories named in the box are the types for general use.

Software Categories

Category	What it's For
Word processing and desktop publishing	Writing and formatting documents
Spreadsheet	Working with numbers
Database management	Organizing information
Graphics	Working with pictures
Utilities	Managing the computer itself
Games	Stuff to do in all your spare time
Children's software	Having fun and teaching skills

In the following chapters, I'll tell you what to look for in each of the major categories and give recommendations for specific products. I've also thrown in a chapter on financial management software, which is a category I've found especially helpful and think you should know about. In most cases, I'll suggest one piece of software for people who don't use it professionally, and another for those who need an industrial-strength product. For example, if you only need a database to keep track of your personal address book and household inventories, you'll want a less expensive and easier-to-learn product than if you're planning on using it to automate your business's inventory system.

Software You Already Have, If You Have Windows

If you have Microsoft Windows, you already own several application programs. To find them, double-click on the Accessories Group icon in the Program Manager.

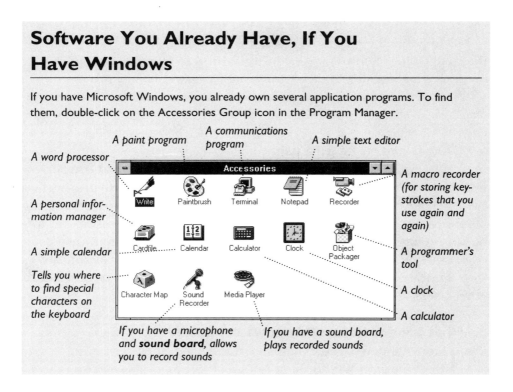

A word processor

A paint program

A communications program

A simple text editor

A macro recorder (for storing keystrokes that you use again and again)

A personal information manager

A simple calendar

Tells you where to find special characters on the keyboard

A programmer's tool

A clock

A calculator

If you have a microphone and **sound board**, allows you to record sounds

If you have a sound board, plays recorded sounds

How to Choose Software

34 *The fact that there are thousands of software programs to choose from has one drawback: With so many choices, how do you know which one is for you? Matching the list of features on the back of the box to your wish list is just one way.*

Programs differ in how easy they are to use, whether or not the company that makes them will give you technical support if you need it, how reliable the program is (will it crash a lot? does it have bugs that make it work in unexpected ways?), and in many other important areas. It's a good idea to do research on a product before you buy it.

Here are some things to consider before you choose a software package.

1. What is everyone else using?
In almost every software category, there are one or (at most) two runaway best-sellers. The best-selling program isn't necessarily the best on the market, or the best for your own needs, but it's an important signpost if you need a place to start looking. Sometimes best-sellers get to be best-sellers because they were the first on the market and they got a head start on the others. However, usually programs gain popularity through word of mouth—people who have tried the program praise it to other users who go out and buy it themselves.

2. What programs are Windows compatible?
If you have Windows, you'll almost certainly want to get programs that are compatible with Windows. Although DOS programs will run under Windows, they won't give you the advantages you bought Windows for. And if you don't have Windows, you'll need to make sure the program you want is available for DOS-only machines.

3. What do your friends like?

If you know some other people who have a PC, ask them what they use and how they like it. People who have used a program for a while can give you insights into how a program works that you wouldn't have thought to ask about. A program might have a lot of important features, but it might also have a really annoying way of making you give commands. Or it could have other interface problems that might make it a bad choice. Ask everyone you know what they would recommend. You'll probably quickly find one or two top choices.

4. What do the dealers suggest?

People who sell software may or may not know a lot about the products they sell, but asking them is worth a shot. After all, they have day-to-day contact with users of all sorts of software, and they know if a lot of customers are happy or unhappy with certain products. Many computer dealers, including mail-order companies, are happy to advise you on your purchases. After all, they want satisfied customers. Having said that, though, don't forget that Latin phrase, caveat emptor—let the buyer beware. Look hard enough and you're bound to find some software dealers who don't know what they're talking about.

5. What programs offer free support?

Make sure any program you buy offers free telephone support, and it's even better if it offers a toll-free number to call. Believe me, it's something you'll use. In fact, before you buy a product—especially a fairly complex one—you might try calling the technical support line to see how long it takes you to get through.

6. What do reviewers say?

Every computer magazine puts new products through rigorous tests and publishes the results. By all means, take advantage of this resource. If the program isn't covered in a current issue, check the back issues in a library. (See Chapter 6 for a rundown of the leading computer magazines and what they cover.)

7. What will your computer run?

Not all software runs on all computers. The hardware requirements are listed on the back of every box of software; if you can't find it there, ask the dealer or the manufacturer. The first thing to check, of course, is whether the program requires Windows. Another common limitation is RAM: Many of today's top programs, especially Windows programs, require 1 or 2 MB of RAM to run properly. Others require several megabytes of hard disk space, or a graphics adapter, or other add-ons. Of course, you may want to buy the extra equipment in order to run the program, but it's best to be forewarned.

Where to Get Software

You can get software from all sorts of sources, some
of them surprising. The software marketplace ranges
from specialty software stores that you can find in any
business district, to bulletin boards on on-line services,
to thriving mail-order businesses. You can also buy
software directly from the publisher.

35

Depending on where you buy, you can save hundreds of dollars on one piece of software, get money-back guarantees, and even get free upgrades. It pays to shop around.

The Software Publisher

Usually, when software is reviewed or mentioned in a magazine, the publication also provides the phone number of the software publisher, as if that were where you should buy the product. (I do it in this book, too.) Well, sometimes you can buy from the software publisher, but I wouldn't recommend it. The publisher usually won't give you a discount. That number can be useful, however, if you want to find out information about the software, including where it's sold in your area.

Specialty Stores

If you shop around, you can find good deals and good service at software specialty stores such as **Egghead Software** and **Computer City**. The best have knowledgeable staffs, good prices, and enlightened return policies. The worst, of course, have none of those things. Some, including Egghead, also sell by mail order.

Resources

Computer City
817-390-3000.

Egghead Software
800-EGGHEAD.

Mail Order

It's relatively easy to buy software via mail order. Actually, mail order is probably the wrong term, because you usually order it by phone, using a toll-free 800 number. Then the company sends it to you, often by overnight air. Mail-order houses are typically a lot less expensive than stores, they generally offer money-back guarantees, and they usually have well-informed salespeople who can offer you advice on what to buy. The best way to find a mail-order house is to look in practically any computer magazine. You can't miss their ads. Leading mail-order houses include **PC Connection** and **PC Zone**. You can call them for a catalog.

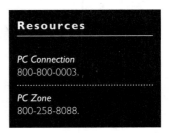

Resources

PC Connection
800-800-0003.

PC Zone
800-258-8088.

Shareware and Public Domain Software

Ever stand in line to buy a movie ticket and wonder whether you're really going to enjoy the film? Wouldn't it be nice if you could pay on the way out—after you've determined whether it's worth the price? That's the way shareware works, a category of computer software that is distributed on the honor system. You can get a copy for little or no money, but you're expected to pay for it if you find it useful.

There are thousands of shareware programs, in just about every category of software. In many cases, they are as good as commercial programs. You can get shareware in a number of ways. You can download programs from on-line information services, pick them up from a computer user group, or obtain them directly from the author. (See Chapter 19 for more on on-line services and Chapter 6 for more on user groups.) There are even mail-order companies that "sell" shareware for the cost of the disk plus a modest service charge.

Where to Get Shareware and Public Domain Software

Call these companies for a list of shareware and public domain software.

PC-SIG	800-245-6717
Public Brand Software	800-426-3475
Public Software Library	800-242-4775

Remember, shareware isn't really free. If you use a shareware program after a reasonable evaluation period, you are expected (even honor-bound) to send a check to the author for a specified, modest amount. The registration fee for most shareware programs ranges from as little as $5 to over $150, with the median being about $50—in most cases, far less than the cost of similar commercial programs.

Rules for Buying Software

Don't pay the retail price.
Software publishers generally establish a "suggested retail price" that has relatively little to do with what you actually pay for programs in the real world. Prices of popular programs are often heavily discounted, sometimes by as much as 50 percent or more off retail. Check the ads in the computer magazines to see what the street price really is.

Be sure you're getting the right version.
Every piece of software goes through several versions as its manufacturer adds features and fixes bugs. The version number follows the product name, as in Windows 3.1 or WordPerfect 5.2. I sometimes see ads for software at extremely attractive prices, but when I call or visit the dealer, I discover that the software is out of date. Make sure you know the latest version number before you order software. (You can find out with a quick call to the software company.) There's nothing wrong with using an older version of software, if you don't need the new features; just make sure you know what you're getting. If you're not getting the latest version, you should be getting a very substantial discount as well as an opportunity to upgrade to the new version at a reduced price.

Get a money-back guarantee.
I wouldn't consider buying a software program unless I knew that I could return it for a full refund if it turned out I didn't like it. Many stores refuse to accept returns because they think people are buying programs, making copies, and then returning the original as a way of "stealing" the software. Fortunately, some dealers have a more enlightened policy. Egghead Software, which has retail stores throughout the country as well as a mail-order service, will give you back your money within 30 days if you're not happy with the product. Most mail-order companies offer the same deal.

Buy with a credit card.
Even if the company you buy from has a good return policy, it's always best to buy computer products with a credit card. Most bank cards offer a dispute clause that allows you to get a refund on a product you're unhappy with, and some now double the warranty for products purchased with their card. It also makes refunds easy if a return is necessary.

In most cases, once you register, you'll be immediately rewarded by getting a printed manual (most shareware comes with a text file that you can read with any word processing program), and you'll be put on a mailing list to get information on new versions. You might also get a new set of disks. In some cases, shareware programs are slightly disabled, as an incentive for you to get the full-featured version. A shareware database program, for example, may limit you to a hundred or so listings, whereas the full-featured version has no such limit. Other shareware programs have all the features but burden you with notices requesting your money. When you pay the registration fee, you get a version that doesn't nag.

Another category of software, similar to shareware, is called public domain software or freeware. Unlike shareware, these programs are really free. No one even asks you to pay for them.

The Five-Finger Discount

You've paid all this money for your computer and now you find out that you have to buy your software, too. If you're not careful, you can spend more for the software than you did for the computer. Is it really necessary? After all, the guy next door offered to give you a copy of one of the leading word processing programs that's worth about $400. It would be as simple as copying the disks. You don't get the manuals, but for about $20, you can buy a book that will teach you the program.

Should you accept the gift? Legally, you shouldn't. Commercial software is copyrighted, which means it's illegal to distribute copies to people who don't pay for it. (The same issues apply to making copies of music and movies.) Copyrights protect the people who own the rights to the software, book, or other property, and they also protect the rights of the creative people who make it. Creating a piece of software is an expensive business, and the practice of illegally copying software deprives companies of the revenue they feel they have earned.

Copying software illegally is dubbed **piracy**, and many software companies vigorously defend their copyrights. According to the legal department of the Software Publishers Association, the SPA tends to go after businesses that buy a single copy of a program and distribute it throughout the organization. It also investigates claims that people are illegally reselling their programs. If you have "borrowed" your neighbor's disks, chances are you won't be wakened from a sound sleep one night by the FBI pounding on your door.

Even if you're not worried about the legal consequences, however, there are good reasons to buy your own copies of software. What happens if you run into a serious problem and can't get help from the software company? What if there's a bug in the program that you'll never learn about because you're not on the list of registered owners? I wouldn't dream of trusting my tax records or business information to a program that I didn't legally own. Moral and legal issues aside, it might just be worth it to buy a legitimate copy.

Word Processing: Writing Made Easy

36   *Basically, a word processing program turns a PC into a very advanced electronic typewriter. It not only provides tools that make it easier to write and edit your words, but it also makes it easy to dress them up.*

In a word processor, you can format your text with a variety of typefaces, add graphics, and set your work in sophisticated formats, such as newspaperlike columns. With a word processor, you type, edit, and design your work on screen, rather than on paper. When you're done, you print it. And with a high-quality ink jet or laser printer, your final document can look as if it were professionally printed.

Best of all, a word processing system lets you make changes to your work with amazing ease. Word processors let you delete, insert, copy, and move text whenever you get a new idea, and this will change the way you write. It takes some of the anxiety out of committing something to paper because you know that you can keep what you like and easily change what you don't.

Most word processing programs can also check your spelling, and some can help you find the right word with a built-in thesaurus. The best word processors make it easy to automatically create parts of documents, like tables of contents and indexes, that could otherwise take days to create, check, and recheck. And an electronic index or table of contents generated by the word processing program can be automatically updated when you change the text.

Scorecard: Word Processors

	DOS	Windows
Most Popular	WordPerfect for Windows	Microsoft Word
Shareware Alternative	PC Write (early versions)	—
Recommendation		
Everyday strength	Microsoft Works	Microsoft Works for Windows
		Word for Windows
Industrial strength	WordPerfect	Word for Windows
		Ami Pro

Windows Write: The Word Processor You May Already Own

Basically, everyone who owns a PC should have a word processor, and if you have Windows, you already have one, called **Windows Write** (you'll find it in the Accessories group in the Program Manager). Write has everything you'll need to be able to write letters, memos, or reports. You can change fonts (character sizes and type styles), insert graphics

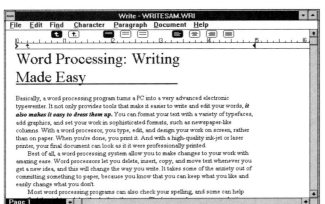

Working in a word processor is like working with a typewriter that has a lot of whiz-bang features. You type on screen instead of on paper.

from other Windows programs, and print very attractive documents. The only really important feature missing is a spell checker, which is something I can't do without any more. Write is a good program to start with, and even if you decide you need something else later on, practicing with Write will give you an opportunity to get used to word processing. Most other Windows word processors can import Write documents, so sharing files with other programs is no problem.

When you're ready for something more sophisticated, or if you don't have Windows, there are dozens of PC word processors to choose from.

What to Look for in a Word Processor

• **automatic footnotes** Automatically numbers footnotes and places them at the bottom of the proper page, or at the end of the document if that's what you prefer.

• **automatic index generator** Lets you tag certain words in your document for inclusion in the index, then creates the index, with page numbers, from those words. If the page breaks change while you edit, the page numbers in the index are automatically updated.

• **automatic table of contents** Looks for all the headings in your document and puts them together as a table of contents, complete with page numbers.

• **equation formatting** Some word processors are better than others at creating good-looking equations (the kinds that have all sorts of fractions within fractions). If you create technical documents, make sure your word processor handles equations well.

file management from within the application If you're working in DOS, it's helpful to have a word processor that includes commands for deleting, renaming, and moving files. If you're working in Windows, it's less important, since you'll always have access to the File Manager.

graphics support Some word processors let you incorporate graphics in your document and wrap text around the picture. Virtually all Windows word processing programs let you copy a picture from a graphics program to your word processing document.

• **macros** A macro is a keyboard shortcut. Using a macro feature, you could distill commonly used text into a single keystroke. For example, I've set up the key combination Ctrl-L to type *Sincerely, Lawrence J. Magid* at the bottom of my letters. You can also use macros to set into motion an entire sequence of commands by issuing a single keystroke. (You can also get separate utility programs that create macros.)

• **mail merge** The most common use for mail merge is merging a form letter with a list of names and addresses to personalize a business mailing. You've seen this at work in junk mail

The Best for Windows

If you want something that's inexpensive, easy to use, and reasonably powerful, I recommend **Microsoft Works for Windows**. You'll hear a lot about Microsoft Works in this part of the book because, for all but the most demanding users, it's my favorite word processing program, spreadsheet program, and database program all wrapped into one, plus it has a calendar for keeping track of appointments. (I'll have more on this and other **integrated programs** in Chapter 41.) The Works word processor is very easy to use, has a spell checker, a thesaurus, and

• indicates a feature found in industrial-strength programs

that addresses you by name, you know, "Congratulations, Mr. Marion Smith, you may already have won a valuable prize."

multicolumn formatting Some word processors enable you to set up multiple columns per page, as in a newspaper.

outlining Gives you an overview of your document by letting you collapse it down so that you see just the headings or just the first lines of each paragraph.

saving in different formats If you're sharing your documents with another person—a secretary, an editor, a boss, a graphics department—you'll have to make sure you can give them the document in a file format they can read with their own programs. (See Chapter 24 for more on formats commonly used to share word processing files.)

spell checking Checks every word in your document against an electronic dictionary. If a word isn't in the dictionary, it will ask you if you want to change it or add the word to your dictionary. It may also offer other possible spellings for the word.

• ***style sheets*** This feature allows you to change the format (the appearance) of all or part of a document by selecting a menu item or issuing one or two keystrokes. A style is a preset format that, once created, can be used over again.

thesaurus If you want to vary the words you use in your writing (always a good idea), you can look up alternative words in an on-line thesaurus. You can just highlight the word, activate the thesaurus, and the word processor will give you a list of other words that mean the same thing.

WYSIWYG formatting WYSIWYG is computer talk for "what you see is what you get," meaning that the program displays your document on screen just as it will look when you print it—type, indents, boldface, and all. It comes for free with Windows, but in DOS, it's a feature you'll have to check for.

most of the other bells and whistles most people will need. The whole package, including the word processor, has a suggested retail price of about $150, which means that you can probably get it for less than $100 if you shop around.

If you want a word processor with every feature you can imagine, try **Microsoft Word for Windows** (the program I used to write this book).

What's All This About Desktop Publishing?

With a good word processor and a laser printer, you can easily create documents that, just a few years ago, would have only been possible using professional typesetting and printing. In fact, personal computer software for creating documents has gotten so good that it has pretty much put professional typesetters out of business. More and more, professional graphic designers do all their work on PCs and Macintoshes.

To support these professionals, a new kind of software, called "page-layout software," has sprung up. Programs like **PageMaker** from Aldus and **QuarkXPress** offer all the tools for typographic refinements and four-color printing that designers need for the most sophisticated color publications. Other programs, such as **FrameMaker** and **Ventura Publisher**, specialize in helping publishers of books, technical manuals, and other long documents in which regular formats, complicated tables, and indexes are the most challenging tasks.

Although professional publishers will turn to these page-layout programs, most people will find that high-end word processing programs such as Microsoft Word and WordPerfect offer all the design flourishes they're likely to use. In fact, the top-of-the-line word processors offer a lot of the same capabilities, including multicolumn (newspaper-like) layouts and the ability to import color graphics and wrap text around them. Although these programs aren't as good at the kind of free-form layouts that page-layout programs specialize in, they can easily handle most day-to-day documents, and even pretty fancy newsletters.

If you find you're pushing the boundaries of your word processing program and want to try something a bit fancier, you might look into one of a group of page-layout programs designed for nonprofessionals. Programs like **Microsoft Publisher** offer many of the features of the professional-level packages, at a much lower price. They're also easier to master than the professional programs.

Resources

FrameMaker
Frame Technologies,
800-843-7263.

....

Microsoft Publisher
Microsoft, 800-426-9400,
206-882-8080.

....

PageMaker
Aldus, 800-945-4480.

....

QuarkXPress
Quark, 800-788-7835.

....

Ventura Publisher
Ventura, 800-822-8221,
619-673-0172.

This one has more features than a Boeing 747. It can automatically create tables of contents and indexes, and it has good features for formatting tables for data. It lets you zoom in close to see the small print, or zoom out to see a whole page. It also has a nice little macro feature, and you can even create your own menu items. A grammar checker completes the package. You name it, Word for Windows has it.

The two other leading Windows word processing programs are **Ami Pro for Windows** from Lotus and **WordPerfect for Windows**. They're both quite good, and Ami Pro is especially good for people who plan to integrate a lot of drawings into their documents. WordPerfect for Windows is a good choice for people who use WordPerfect for DOS at the office. (Lots of people use WordPerfect at lots of offices.)

Resources

Ami Pro for Windows
Lotus Development,
800-343-5414, 617-577-8500.

Microsoft Word for Windows
Microsoft, 800-426-9400,
206-882-8080.

Microsoft Works for Windows
Microsoft, 800-426-9400,
206-882-8080.

WordPerfect for Windows
WordPerfect, 800-321-4566,
801-225-5000.

The Best for DOS

If you don't have Windows, you still have a word processor of sorts. It's called EDIT, and it's a very basic **text editor** that comes with DOS. (You launch it by typing `EDIT` and then pressing Enter at the DOS prompt.) EDIT won't let you work with fonts or add any kind of formatting in documents, and it has no extra features like a spell checker. But it's handy for doing simple tasks like editing your AUTOEXEC.BAT file.

For more sophisticated tasks, I recommend the MS-DOS version of **Microsoft Works**, the same excellent integrated program I just described for Windows. The DOS version even adds a communications module. The MS-DOS version has pull-down menus (just like Windows programs), and you can use a mouse to issue commands and select data. Works lets you work on more than one document at a time, and it even lets you simultaneously process words and work with numbers—rare features in DOS.

The DOS version uses less than 640 K of memory, making it an excellent choice for laptops and other computers that have small hard disks, limited memory, or slower processors. Unlike most word processing programs, it doesn't even require a hard disk, although a hard disk makes it easier to use. And you don't need to worry about data compatibility: Works word processing files can be imported into most other word processing programs.

For the industrial-strength user, I recommend **WordPerfect**, the best-selling word processor on the market. Like a Windows program, it lets you use a mouse, has pull-down menus, allows you to edit two documents at a time, and integrates graphics into your text. It has every feature in the book, including an outliner, mail merge, table of contents and index generators, great file management, macros, and context-sensitive help.

Resources

Microsoft Works for DOS
Microsoft, 800-426-9400, 206-882-8080.

WordPerfect
WordPerfect, 800-321-4566, 801-225-5000.

Spreadsheets: Working With Numbers

37

If you work with numbers at all, you're probably a candidate for a spreadsheet program. Spreadsheet programs let you enter numbers into a grid of rows and columns and then perform calculations on them.

A spreadsheet is like a giant piece of electronic ledger paper. When you revise a figure or modify a formula, all the numbers affected by the change are revised as well. Most spreadsheets can also turn your numbers into a bar chart or a pie chart for a quick visual summary of what it all means. Spreadsheets can include text as well as numbers, and most offer basic text-formatting capabilities so you can also create good-looking reports from a spreadsheet.

Scorecard: Spreadsheets

	DOS	Windows
Most Popular	Lotus 1-2-3	Microsoft Excel
Shareware Alternative	AsEasyAs	—
Recommendation		
Everyday strength	Microsoft Works	Microsoft Works for Windows
	1-2-3 for Home	
Industrial strength	1-2-3	Microsoft Excel
	Quattro Pro	

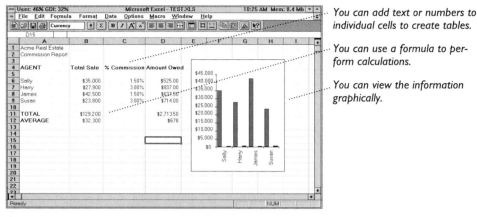

You can add text or numbers to individual cells to create tables.

You can use a formula to perform calculations.

You can view the information graphically.

A spreadsheet document is modeled on a piece of ledger paper, with rows and columns that make it easy to create tables. In each "cell" (the box that results from an intersection of a row and a column), you can enter numbers, text, or a formula that performs a calculation on other cells. (Microsoft Excel is shown here.)

Spreadsheets are amazingly versatile programs. They're used by the accounting departments of multinational corporations to do budgets and sales forecasts, but they're also useful for simpler tasks, like quickly adding up a set of personal expenses. Even a beginner can quickly master the few commands necessary for simple tasks.

As with word processors, there are lots of spreadsheets to choose from but just a couple leaders in the field. Also like word processors, you can get a quite adequate spreadsheet in an integrated program like Microsoft Works.

The Best for Windows

For Windows, my favorite full-featured spreadsheet program is *Microsoft Excel*. Excel is easy to use, and it offers all the features anyone could ever need. Like any Windows program, it puts all the commands in pull-down menus that are always available. Many of the most popular formulas can be implemented by using the mouse to press an on-screen button that writes the formula for you. To add up a row

Resources

Microsoft Excel
Microsoft, 800-426-9400,
206-882-8080.

Microsoft Works for Windows
Microsoft , 800-426-9400,
206-882-8080.

of numbers, for example, you simply place your **insertion point** at the bottom of the column you want to add and click on the Sum button.

The drawback to Excel is that it's expensive and it takes up a lot of hard disk space. That's why, for most users, I go back to the same advice I gave for word processing. If you have Windows, just get **Microsoft Works for Windows**, which includes a very good basic spreadsheet. It's what I use, and it has everything I need.

What to Look for in a Spreadsheet

• indicates a feature found in industrial-strength programs

• **the ability to link spreadsheets** This feature lets you pull data from multiple spreadsheets for your calculations. For example, you could create one spreadsheet documenting sales for each month of the year, and then create a summary spreadsheet that pulls the data from the monthly spreadsheets to calculate yearly totals.

automatic formula writing Formulas tell a spreadsheet what cells you want added, multiplied, or otherwise operated on. Once you get the hang of them, they're not too hard to put together, but the syntax can be somewhat complicated. Some programs, such as Excel for Windows, let you select just the cells you want to work on; you click a button and the program writes the formula for you.

graphics Most spreadsheets include the ability to generate business graphics such as pie charts and bar graphs from your spreadsheet data.

import and export other formats Most spreadsheets can read and save to ASCII and Lotus 1-2-3 formats. The ability to save to leading formats is important not only for sharing data, but in case you want to change to another program later and want to take all your old models with you. It would be a shame to lose all your work if you should change spreadsheet programs.

• **lots of useful functions** Functions are little programs built into the spreadsheet that automatically calculate the numbers. Any spreadsheets will have basic ones, like SUM (which adds a row of numbers), but from there they can get pretty wild. If you're interested in really putting your spreadsheet program to work, automating accounts payable and such, check out what it offers in the way of advanced functions.

• **macros** A macro capability lets you create your own programs within the spreadsheet, to automate updates and reports, for instance. Again, macros are for people who want to do sophisticated jobs with their spreadsheet program.

text formatting In order to use a spreadsheet for presentations, you'll need some control over how the text looks, especially the ability to italicize and boldface words and to pick appropriate typefaces.

The Best for DOS

For DOS users who aren't in corporate accounting departments and don't need to share files with corporate accounting departments, my advice is the same as for Windows users: Get an integrated program that includes a spreadsheet, such as **Microsoft Works for MS-DOS** or **LotusWorks for DOS**. (I talk more about those and other integrated programs in Chapter 41.)

If you're into high-level financial wizardry, you have a few choices.

The most popular spreadsheet program in the world is **Lotus 1-2-3** for DOS. That alone might be reason enough for you to get it. Chances are, it's the standard at your company.

But before you spring for the industrial-strength version of 1-2-3, check out **1-2-3 for Home**. The home version costs about a third of the price of the regular version and does many of the same things. The main difference between the two is the size of the spreadsheet. The regular version of 1-2-3 offers 256 rows by a whopping 8,192 columns; the home version is limited to 256 columns by 512 rows. For most users, that's more than enough.

Unlike the professional version, the home version of 1-2-3 comes with 50 useful spreadsheet templates—ready-made spreadsheets set up to handle many home and small-business problems, including an expense budget, college costs, a net worth statement, invoices, tax planning, accounts receivable, an auto expense record, and more.

The other king of DOS spreadsheets is **Quattro Pro**, from Borland International. Despite 1-2-3's position as an industry standard, Quattro Pro is giving it a run for its money and comes out on top in many reviews. The program has enough features to fill up this and several other books, and it's fully compatible with 1-2-3, so you and co-workers who use either program can freely share files.

Resources

Lotus 1-2-3
Lotus Development,
800-343-5414, 617-577-8500.

Lotus 1-2-3 for Home
Lotus Development,
800-343-5414, 617-577-8500.

Quattro Pro
Borland International,
800-331-0877, 408-438-8400.

Database Management: Organizing Information

38

Even if you've never touched a computer, you've already used a database, which is simply any collection of information. Your phone book—a list of names, addresses, and phone numbers for a city—is the most obvious example. Database software is more accurately called a database management program—a way to manage a bunch of information that you store in the computer.

    PC database programs are used for all kinds of tasks. Customer mailing lists are one common use. So are personnel records, inventories, and people's CD collections. Database software enables you to keep track of lots of information and easily pull out just the pieces of information you need in the form of database "reports." It also lets you "sort" the information in different ways. For example, let's say you have put your personal address book into a database. You can tell the database program to arrange the names in the address book in alphabetical order and print out the list. Alternatively, you can tell the database to arrange them in zip code order and print the list that way.

Although database software is one of the most common and useful types of PC software, the fact is, most people don't actually need it. If they do, they can usually get away with a very simple database program like (you guessed it) the one built into Microsoft Works. The Works database handles up to 32,000 items—plenty to account for my circle of friends, and probably more than adequate for keeping track of your CD collection, insurance records, or just about any other personal data. In many cases, people are best served by a category of database software called **personal information managers**, which are specially designed to keep track of personal phone lists and other common information. (I'll say more about them later.)

The more powerful database programs, like dBase IV, Paradox, Microsoft Access, and FoxBase are called **relational databases** because they can connect the information from more than one file at a time. Simpler ones are called **flat-file databases**. The more powerful database programs also include their own programming languages, which allow you to create a customized program that includes data entry forms for a specific purpose, such as entering sales for an inventory database or entering customer queries for a product database.

Do you need a powerful database program? That's like asking if you need a big truck. Big trucks are more expen-

Scorecard: Database Management Programs

	DOS	Windows
Most Popular	dBase IV	Paradox for Windows
Shareware Alternative	PC-File	Win/db
Recommendation		
Everyday strength	Q&A	Ace*File
	Microsoft Works	Microsoft Works
	PC-File	
Industrial Strength	Paradox	Approach
		Paradox for Windows

```
┌─────────────────────────────────────────┐
│ ▭           PRODUCTS.WDB                 │
├─────────────────────────────────────────┤
│ Name: _____        │
│ Address: _____       │
│ City: _____       │
│ State: __    Zip Code: _____           │
│ Product: _____       │
│ Price: _____                            │
│ ▐Purchase Date:▌ _____        │
│                                          │
│                                          │
│                                          │
│                                          │
└─────────────────────────────────────────┘
```

There are usually two types of screens in a database program: data entry forms (like the one shown here) and reports. Once the information is entered, you can organize it any way you like, calling up reports that list just the people who live in Oregon, or who bought a product that cost over $100.

sive, more powerful, and more macho than little cars, but if all you're doing is commuting to work, you don't need one. You do need one if you have lots of stuff to haul. Well, you'll need an industrial-strength database program if you have tons and tons of data. While the Works database has more than enough features for my needs, that wouldn't be the case if I ran the subscription department of a large magazine or handled the inventory for a chain of stores.

Creating a Database

Working with a database program requires a certain amount of organization. It's not rocket science, but it doesn't exactly come naturally, either.

Setting up a database usually requires that you identify the **fields** you'll be using. Fields are the categories used by a particular database. In a mailing list, for example, you would have one field for name, another for street address, another for phone number, and so on. (A collection of fields that makes up one entry is called a "record" in database language.) So, you have to think about the kind of information you'll enter later. Fortunately, you don't have to anticipate every field you might possibly need down the road because virtually all database programs allow you to add new fields (or get rid of fields you don't want) at any time.

Industrial-Strength Databases

As I indicated earlier, I don't recommend industrial-strength databases for anyone who doesn't absolutely need one. If you do need one, then I suggest you read reviews in *PC Magazine, DataBase Adviser,* and other publications that put these industrial-strength programs through industrial-strength review processes.

Paradox (DOS and Windows) is not only popular but quite well regarded by database wizards. It has a lot of power and is (relatively) easy to use. The program lets you enter and view your data in table and form views and is very good at letting you get data from a variety of files at the same time. I'm not a big-time database user, but with just a little help, I was able to set up a relational database in Paradox for Windows in about half an hour. Paradox has a powerful programming language, which I stay away from. But it's great for professionals who

What to Look for in a Database Program

• indicates a feature found in industrial-strength programs

• *the ability to link files* This feature, which usually defines a relational database, allows you to draw reports from a number of different database files.

easy addition, modification, and deletion of fields Make sure your database program lets you add, modify, and delete fields in already-created databases.

easy data entry Entering data should be a piece of cake. All commands should be obvious to anyone looking at the screen.

easy report creation The best database programs let you create forms by using a mouse to select possible fields from a field palette. It goes downhill from there to programs that make you write a program to create even the simplest form.

• *a programming language* If you want to create a database program tailored to your own business, you'll need a programming language.

saving in different formats Most full-strength databases will save in dBase or ASCII format. (dBase is the best-selling database program.) Other formats to look for are standard spread-sheet formats such as Lotus 1-2-3's .WKS format.

simple setup If you want to get right to work with a database program, you'll need one that's easy to set up. Most have some kind of point-and-click setup routine, but even some of those can be daunting. Personal information managers are essentially databases set up with predesigned forms for address books and schedules.

want to create customized applications for corporations.

Approach for Windows, from Lotus Development, is easy to use and still has more features than most people need. It doesn't have a programming language but uses commands that you issue with the mouse to easily create and change reports.

When most people think of database programs, they think of **dBase**, the granddaddy of them all. dBase was the first really powerful database on the market, and it's still the most popular database around. It's good, but only one of several database programs you should consider—it's probably a lot more than you need.

Resources

Approach for Windows
Lotus Development,
800-277-7622, 617-577-8500.

dBase IV
Borland International,
800-331-0877, 408-438-8400.

Paradox and Paradox for Windows
Borland International,
800-331-0877, 408-438-8400.

Everyday Database Programs

Ace*File from Ace Software is an easy-to-use flat-file database program for Windows. It includes dBase file compatibility and offers built-in forms. **Q&A**, from Symantec, is a respectable database for DOS. **PC-File**, a shareware program, is also an excellent choice for DOS users who don't need industrial strength. It has all the features you'll need in a flat-file database program. And, of course, there's also the database program that comes with **Microsoft Works**. Like all the other components of Microsoft Works, it's up to most jobs you'll want to throw at it.

Resources

Ace•File
Ace Software, 800-345-3223,
408-451-0100.

Microsoft Works
Microsoft, 800-426-9400,
206-882-8080.

PC-File
ButtonWare, 800-528-8866,
206-454-0479.

Q&A
Symantec, 800-441-7234,
408-253-9600.

Personal Information Managers

Not everyone needs to computerize their personal data, but storing all your phone numbers and addresses on your computer disk can alleviate the problem of shuffling through piles of papers to find notes or hunting for your address book to find a phone number. What's more, you'll have a convenient place to enter information that you know you'll need later.

Personal information managers (PIMs) are a special type of database program designed to keep track of names, addresses, phone numbers, and other "personal" information. They're relatively inexpensive, typically costing around $100. Most PIMs can also be

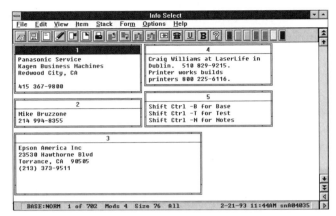

Personal information managers, like Info Select, shown here, are database programs specialized to take care of contact and schedule information.

used to keep track of your schedule, and others let you record notes and other information. Many will even dial your phone for you if you have a modem. You can't turn around and create an inventory management system with one, but if a database of business contacts is your main database need, a PIM is for you.

What to Look for in a Personal Information Manager

address book Most PIMs have a convenient place to keep addresses and phone numbers. You should be able to search on a field (first name, last name, etc.) or look at the entire list.

calendar and appointment book Most good PIMs have some type of calendar and appointment book. If there is a calendar, it should offer month-at-a-glance and week-at-a-glance features.

moving and copying data You should be able to easily move or copy data between parts of the program.

telephone dialing Dialing the phone isn't exactly my idea of an onerous chore, but if the program can do it for you (via a modem), why not? Most PIMs will do this.

universal search You should be able to search for any data across all modules. Enter someone's name, and you should find his or her address, phone number, and any appointments you have scheduled with that person.

Most PIMs have predefined fields for basic information—name, phone number, and so on—although many allow you to change and add fields as well. That type of PIM is ideal for anyone who wants a lot of control over how the information is displayed and printed. Data kept in a structured PIM can easily be sorted or formatted for mailing labels, printed phone directories, and other purposes. There are lots to choose from. Leaders in the field are **Lotus Organizer for Windows**, **Okna Desktop Set** (for Windows), and Borland's **SideKick II** (for MS-DOS).

For DOS, I like SideKick II from Borland. It offers a notepad, a calendar, an address book, a simple communications program, an appointment scheduler, a calculator, and a Rolodex with an auto dialer. What's more, you can get access to all those accessories while you're running any other program. (In Windows, such "multitasking" is a given, but in DOS it's an extra feature.)

There are a lot of good PIMs for Windows. I especially like **Info Select** from Micro Logic Software (there's also an MS-DOS version). This free-form database permits you to enter information in whatever order you choose, without the constraints of designated fields. You don't even have to decide what kind of information you want to store. The same file that stores your addresses and phone numbers can also store information about your credit cards, prescription drugs, personal possessions, telephone messages, or any other type of data.

In this category I can also heartily recommend a shareware program, **Time & Chaos**, from iSBiSTER. It's a Windows PIM with three very useful features: a calendar, a to-do list, and a telephone book. Personally, I like it better than most commercial PIMs because it's easy to use and it presents your information in a clear, easy-to-understand form. You can get it from the normal shareware sources (see Chapter 35) or you can call the number listed in the Resources box at right. When I last checked, it was $30 for a registered copy.

Resources

Info Select
Micro Logic Software,
800-342-5930, 201-342-6518.

Lotus Organizer for Windows
Lotus Development,
800-343-5414, 617-577-8500.

Okna Desktop Set
Okna, 201-460-0677.

SideKick II
Borland International,
800-331-0877, 408-438-8400.

Time & Chaos
iSBiSTER International,
214-495-6724.

Graphics: Working With Pictures

39

For some people, the notion of computer graphics implies crude drawings that immediately betray their origin. For other people, computer graphics are associated with the slick special-effects animation used in TV advertisements and science-fiction movies. The reality is that computer graphics touch both extremes, with a lot of different effects possible in between.

Having a computer graphics program won't make you an artist if you can't draw, any more than having a word processor will turn you into a professional writer. In fact, even professional artists have to learn new skills to use computer graphics programs. What a graphics program can do, though, is give people who work with graphics the ability to try out different versions of their work more easily, more quickly, and much more inexpensively than they could with traditional methods. Professional graphics programs will draw perfect circles for you, let you experiment with different color schemes, and even let you see how a photograph would look if it were a painting by Van Gogh.

The split between novice-level and professional-level programs is a wide one in the graphics area. Computers have revolutionized the way professional artists work, and graphics programs that are specialized for professional-level requirements have sprung up to meet their needs. In a lot of the categories I'll describe here, the professional-level program is the category's best-seller, but those programs come with a lot of tools you don't need if you're working more casually with graphics. They also have price tags that can be justified in a professional setting but are harder to reconcile if you're just experimenting. I'm assuming that most of you reading this book are in the latter group. If you're a professional graphic artist, you'll need to do more research into what program you'll need than I can supply here. Therefore, in this chapter, I'll talk briefly about the professional-level applications, but I'll mostly be recommending the more affordable, less ambitious ones.

Most graphics programs for the PC are now created for Windows. That's probably because software publishers assume that if you're going to be using a lot of graphics, you'll probably want to be working in Windows, which offers an icon-based interface that makes working with graphics much easier. Windows also builds in the ability to move graphics between applications, which is important if you want

Scorecard: Graphics Programs

	DOS	Windows
Most Popular		
Painting programs	PC Paintbrush V	Windows Paintbrush (everyday strength; comes with Windows)
Drawing programs	—	CorelDraw (industrial strength)
		Windows Draw (everyday strength)
Recommendation		
Painting program	PC Paintbrush V	Windows Paintbrush (for beginners)
Drawing program	AutoSketch	Visio

to move your works of art into a word processing document, for example.

There are lots of different types of graphics programs, from programs specialized for business slide presentations, to professional drawing and painting tools, to programs that help architects and industrial designers visualize their projects. I'll run through each category, with quick suggestions for what to try in each category.

Drawing Programs

Drawing programs provide the user with a set of tools that simulate pencil strokes, paintbrush lines, and other natural drawing effects. Pictures created with a drawing program, called **object-based graphics**, are easy to edit because the program organizes the information that makes up a picture as a set of objects (curves, rectangles, irregular polygons, and other shapes) that can be moved, colored, and edited separately. These days, a lot of drawing programs also offer 3-D effects.

The most popular drawing program for Windows is *CorelDraw*. Although one version of CorelDraw is available for $199 suggested retail, which makes it very affordable (version 4.0 was going for $399

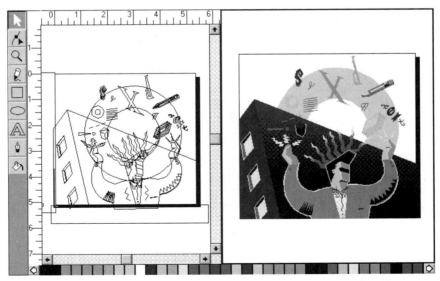

Drawing programs, such as CorelDraw (shown here) compile collections of shapes, or objects, into complex graphics. You can edit each object separately.

when I wrote this), this is one of those programs I recommend for those who are really serious about creating professional-level drawings. It's big and complicated. Adobe Illustrator and Aldus Freehand, two programs that have gained all-star status in their Macintosh versions are now also available for Windows. Like CorelDraw, these are professional-level drawing programs that offer every graphics trick in the book, at a price suitable for the design offices they serve rather than for nonprofessional artists.

What to Look for in a Drawing Program

• indicates a feature available in industrial-strength programs

• **Bezier curves** The more advanced drawing packages work with Bezier curves, which allow you to shape forms with mathematical precision.

clip art Most packages come with a large selection of clip art to use in your own work.

a good set of drawing tools Drawing programs come with a set of basic shapes to draw with, including rectangles, circles, lines, and polygons. The more the merrier.

fills Most drawing programs allow you to fill shapes with a variety of patterns and colors.

• **flip and rotate** These tools allow you to change your drawing's orientation on the page.

font manipulation tools Creating special effects with type is one of the most popular uses of drawing packages. CorelDraw is particularly good at this, and it comes bundled with a lot of fonts.

good color handling Your drawing program should support the number of colors available on your monitor, plus it should allow you to work in shades of gray. The more advanced programs support color standards, such as Pantone and Trumatch, used by graphics professionals.

rulers and grids These tools make your drawings conform to measurements you choose.

support for a variety of file formats Historically, every PC drawing program has had its own file format. The most well-defined and reliable formats are TIFF and EPS. Use those formats if at all possible.

text effects In some programs, you can play with text as with any other graphic form, reshaping it and wrapping it around curves.

• **3-D effects** Some drawing programs enable you to extrude shapes into three-dimensional forms. More advanced packages offer very sophisticated 3-D effects, including the ability to realistically wrap text and other patterns around 3-D objects.

Windows Draw from Micrografx, at about $120 last time I checked, is a much easier-to-use, more affordable, but still solid program for the masses. Another Windows program, *Arts & Letters Apprentice* (a cut-down version of the company's industrial-strength Arts & Letters) also has strong features and comes with 3,000 **clip art** images and lots of typefaces at a similarly reasonable price.

Visio for Windows, from Shapeware, is a more specialized package. Billed as an "intelligent drawing package for nonartists," it provides a collection of 15 stencils and shapes designed to make it easier to create organizational charts, office layouts, flowcharts, and drawings. Visio has a unique interface that lets you to work with drawings even if you can't draw a straight line. When I wrote this, it had a suggested retail price of $299.

For MS-DOS users searching for an easy-to-use program, I recommend *AutoSketch* from Autodesk. It lets you work with lines, arcs, circles, boxes, and other shapes. You can place text anywhere on your drawing and move, copy, stretch, mirror, scale, and rotate shapes.

Resources

Arts & Letters Apprentice
Computer Support,
214-661-8960.

AutoSketch
Autodesk, 800-228-3601,
206-487-2233.

CorelDraw
Corel, 800-836-3729,
613-728-8200.

Visio
Shapeware, 800-446-3335,
206-467-6723.

Windows Draw
Micrografx, 800-733-3729,
214-234-1769.

Painting Programs

Painting programs not only let you create graphics with tools supplied in the program itself, but they also let you use a device called a scanner to turn photographs, line drawings, and other artwork created outside the computer into computer files that you can edit yourself. Paint-style graphics are called **bit-mapped graphics**. Unlike the object graphics used by drawing programs, bit-mapped graphics are built up from a collection of different-colored dots. (They're called bit-mapped graphics because in black-and-white graphics, each dot is stored as a digital bit, an on/off signal stored by the computer). This means you have to edit the files in a different way. The format makes it more difficult to isolate different objects in a picture (a person, a tree, or other subject), but it creates a more naturalistic, softer look than you generally get from drawing programs.

Clip Art

Clip art is a collection of precooked graphics that you can use in your own publications. It's for people who don't want to (or can't) draw but want to spice up their publications with appropriate art. You can get clip art collections of people in business or sports, of company logos, of wildlife, of textures to use as backgrounds—of just about anything you need. Clip art comes in different formats that can be imported into most graphic programs and printed at any size. Here's just a sampling of the many companies that produce clip art and the many subjects and styles you can experiment with. Clip art is also available from on-line services (see Chapter 19).

Product: Click Art
Company: T/Maker,
  415-962-0195
Package: Animals &
  Nature
Format: EPS

Product: Click Art
Company: T/Maker,
  415-962-0195
Package: Newsletter
  Cartoons
Format: PCX

Product: Cliptures
Company: Dream Maker
  303-762-1001
Package: World Flags
Format: EPS

Product: ProArt
Company: MultiAd Services
  800-447-1950, 800-322-3941
Package: Borders & Headings
Format: EPS

Product: Electronic Art
Company: Metro Image Base,
  800-525-1552, 818-881-4557
Package: Business Graphics
  (left), People (right)
Format: TIFF, PCX, IMG

Product: DigitArt
Company: Image Club
  403-262-8008
Package: Business Cartoons
  (left), Fabulous Fifites (right)
Format: EPS

Paint programs, such as Windows Paintbrush, shown here, and image-retouching programs work with bit-mapped graphics, which are made up of a collection of individual dots, producing pictures with subtle, photographic variations of tone and line.

If you have Windows you already have a simple painting program called **Windows Paintbrush**. (It's in the Accessories group in the Program Manager window.) Windows Paintbrush isn't very sophisticated by computer graphics standards, but it's actually quite a handy program. You can use it to paint freehand or draw circles, squares, rectangles, and lines. It works in color or black and white, and you can easily integrate Paintbrush graphics into most other Windows documents, including those created with any Windows-based word processor.

If your needs are more sophisticated, you might consider **PhotoFinish** from Z-Soft. PhotoFinish is a sophisticated program for Windows that lets you convert images between black and white, shades of gray, and different levels of color. It's sold as an image-editing program, but it has good paint tools as well. It exports files in PCX, TIFF, GIF, BMP, TGA, MSP, and EPS formats and offers numerous special effects.

Resources

PC PaintBrush V+
Z-Soft, 800-227-5609.

PhotoFinish
Z-Soft, 800-227-5609.

For those of you who are not using Windows, consider the $149 **PC PaintBrush V+**, also from Z-Soft. In addition to providing regular painting features, it can be used to scan, crop, modify, and retouch photographic images. All this, and it's easy to use, too.

Image-Manipulation Software

Image-manipulation programs, like paint programs, work with bit-mapped images. Image-manipulation programs, however, are specially designed to work with scanned photographs and other images. These turn your computer into an electronic darkroom, where you can apply

What to Look for in a Paint or Image-Manipulation Program

• indicates a feature available in industrial-strength programs

• *color separation* If you will be printing your images professionally, your paint program should offer automatic color separation of its files.

filters Most image programs give you a set of "filters" that let you sharpen, blur, and add special effects to your image.

• *gamma correction* Professional-level programs have a gamma-correction tool, which allows you to change the overall brightness and contrast in your image.

good color support Your program should work with at least 16 colors (256 for professional work or photographic slides) or in gray scale.

• *good font support* If you have Windows, this comes for free. As with drawing programs, some paint programs include extra fonts in addition to the ability to handle type creatively.

a good set of tools Particularly look for a rubber-stamp tool, which lets you copy a part of your image and duplicate it in another part of the picture, and an eye dropper or sampling tool, which lets you pick up colors from one part of the picture to use in another.

photo retouching tools for scanned images Paint programs should be able to work with scanned photographs. Some even let you scan from within the program, and all should offer common photo-retouching tools like airbrushes.

support for TIFF and PCX TIFF is the standard format for bit-mapped files; PCX is a standard Windows format.

undo When you're working with bit-mapped images, where changes are made dot by dot, a good undo feature is important.

sophisticated or far-out effects to photographs. Adobe's **Photoshop** for Windows is now used by a lot of professional magazine and newspaper publishers to retouch their published photos. Another popular industrial-strength program is **PhotoStyler** from Aldus.

PhotoFinish, from Z-Soft, is one of the best low-cost (under $200) image-editing programs on the market. The program works directly with leading scanners, allowing you to scan and edit images with one program. It supports a wide variety of file formats and has "floating toolbars" that give you quick access to many of its features. PhotoFinish has some excellent retouching tools, plus special effects filters that give you the ability to make drastic or subtle changes to your images.

Desktop Presentation Software

Want to make a splash and impress your friends and colleagues? Your computer can help. Desktop presentation software is designed to help you create visual aids for business presentations. These programs can help you create sophisticated slides, overhead transparencies, or colorful screens that you can display on a computer while you talk. (Sales and marketing professionals often bring along notebook computers on which they can display their presentation when they visit clients.) Some packages even let you create "multimedia" presentations that include animation, video, and sound.

The leading presentation programs include **Persuasion** from Aldus, **Freelance Graphics for Windows** from Lotus Development, **Harvard Graphics** from Software Publishing, and **Microsoft PowerPoint**. All these programs are excellent choices. Freelance Graphics for Windows or Microsoft Powerpoint are probably the best options for novice users because they're so easy to use.

What to Look for in a Presentation Program

• indicates a feature available in industrial-strength programs

• *ability to create graphics from spreadsheet data* For business presentations, a program's ability to create pie charts or other graphs from raw data is important. The graphics program should be able to import data from your spreadsheet program so you don't have to reenter the information. And in this day and age, two-dimensional charts won't do; you'll want to present your information in three dimensions.

• *ability to define your own bullets* Bulletted lists are used a lot in business presentations. The ability to use interesting bullets—from arrows to your company logo to smiling faces—is an important factor in creating interesting slides.

ability to import common graphics formats Likewise, you should be able to import the graphics you've created in another program. This is useful for things like company logos and other business graphics that you want to include in your slides.

• *animation* Animation effects can range from blinking or moving arrows to zooms to the on-screen assembly of pieces of a technical drawing.

ease of use Most people who use presentation programs do so on an occasional basis. As a result, it's important to find one that's easy to learn and easy to use.

• *outliner* Many new programs allow you to view your presentation as an outline. You can then "expand" the outline to see what topics are covered in each slide and move headings to rearrange the presentation. Outlines are a good way to see how your presentation is developing as a whole.

• *run-time player* A run-time player is a limited version of the presentation software, which you can put on a disk and distribute to clients along with your presentation so that they can run the presentation on their own computers.

templates Templates, or preformatted slides and screens, can make it easy to create a professional-looking presentation. The type, borders, and colors are already chosen. You just add your own text.

• *varied transitions* You can add life to an on-screen presentation by varying the way one slide is replaced by the next on screen. Many programs offer dissolves, wipes, explosions, and other dynamic transitions.

Computer Aided Design Software

Computer aided design (CAD) software is used by industrial-design professionals to plan products, buildings, printed circuit boards, and other objects. The professional-level offerings are incredibly sophisticated and incredibly expensive. The most popular CAD program for personal computers, **AutoCAD**, from Autodesk, costs several thousand dollars. It enables industrial designers to envision their creations in 3-D, from any angle, and in lifelike settings. If you're about to invest millions of dollars in product development, it's worth it.

The good news is that more modest versions of CAD software are available for nonprofessional users. Autodesk also makes a product called **Generic Cadd**, which is suitable for the drafting needs of home-based architects and industrial artists.

The same kind of visualization aids are also available for more specialized uses. Autodesk's **Office Layout** helps office designers with their jobs. The **Design Your Own Home** series from Abracadata includes programs that handle architectural, landscape, and interior design. Each package comes with a library of architectural shapes, structural details, plants, and furniture.

Resources

AutoCAD, Generic Cadd, Office Layout
Autodesk, 800-964-6432, 415-332-2344.

Design Your Own Home series
Abracadata, 800-451-4871, 503-342-3030.

Communications Software: Talking to Other Computers

40

Modems—the devices that link your computer to a telephone line and then to on-line services and other information sources—can do wonders, but they can't operate by themselves. You need communications software to run them. Communications software will take care of dialing the phone, determining what communications standards to use, and making the connection. (See Chapter 19 for more on modems, communications standards, and the rest.)

You may not actually have to buy communications software yourself. If you have Microsoft Windows, you have a simple communications program called **Terminal**. (It's in the Accessories group in the Program Manager.)

Scorecard: Communications Software

	DOS	Windows
Most Popular	Procomm	CrossTalk for Windows
	BitCom	
	SmartCom	
Shareware Alternative	Qmodem	—
Recommendation	Qmodem	Microphone II

Many modems are packaged with communications software, and most on-line services, such as CompuServe, Prodigy, and America Online, come with their own software that's designed to interact with the features available on that particular service. If you're using one of those services, you don't need any other software for communications. If the service you use doesn't have its own software, though, or if you want to access any other on-line bulletin boards, you'll need to get your own communications software.

In many cases, you won't need to buy communications software at all: Often, it comes free when you buy a modem or sign up for an on-line service.

Like almost every other type of software I've talked about here, communications software ranges from the fairly simple to what I've called industrial strength, with every bell and whistle in the book. Programs like **BitCom Deluxe**, **SmartCom III**, and **ProComm Plus**, which are the three programs generally packaged with modems, will give you everything you could possibly use, and more. They all include scripting languages, with which you can write simple programs that can make fairly complex on-line actions as easy as giving a single command. The most advanced programs, like **CrossTalk Mk4**, not only have their own programming language, but also can handle communica-

Resources

BitCom Deluxe
Bit Software, 510-490-2928.

CrossTalk Mk4
DCA, 800-348-3221.

Procomm Plus
DataStorm Technologies, 314-443-3282.

SmartCom III
Hayes Microcomputer Products, 404-840-9200.

tions for an entire **network**, running several sessions at one time. Unless you're setting up your company's communications, though, the simpler scripting available in everyday-strength programs like the ones I recommend below should take care of all your needs, for a much more reasonable price.

Communicating With Windows

Terminal, the communications program that comes with Microsoft Windows, is a very basic communications program, but it could be quite adequate for users who don't spend a lot of time on line. Terminal will let you connect your PC to any other modem-equipped PC to exchange messages or files. Terminal is about the easiest communications program to use, because it has all the familiar Windows pull-down menus. It supports both the XMODEM and Kermit error-correction standards (they are the protocols supported by most other communications programs), which make sure that the data you send is exactly what the other person receives. Terminal also has a dialing directory you can set up with frequently called numbers so that it can automatically dial your phone, and it enables you to set up your function keys to perform frequently issued commands, such as entering your password when signing on to an on-line service.

What to Look for in a Communications Program

• indicates features available in industrial-strength programs

auto-dialing directories Lets you set up directories of frequently called numbers and then dial those numbers automatically.

macros Lets you set up the function keys to carry out frequently used commands.

popular error-correction standards When a communications program sets up a session betweeen two modems, one thing that must be agreed on is the **error-checking protocol** to be used. Popular standards, which should be included in any communications software, are XMODEM, YMODEM, ZMODEM, and Kermit.

• *scripting language* Gives you the ability to create little programs that automate your connections. For example, you can set up a script to dial your on-line service, retrieve your mail, then log off again, and do it all at a time when rates are lowest.

If you want to get a little fancier, I recommend **Microphone II** from Software Ventures. It has a very powerful yet easy to use scripting language that allows you to automate all your on-line sessions. At a retail price of $129 (at presstime), it's still relatively inexpensive. Software Ventures also publishes Microphone Pro, which includes all sorts of features that no one, including advanced users like me, really cares about.

Resources

Microphone II
Software Ventures,
510-644-3232.

If You Have MS-DOS

MS-DOS doesn't come with a communications program, so if you don't get software with your modem or from your on-line service, you'll have to do some shopping. And you guessed it, **Microsoft Works**, which I've recommended as a good all-purpose word processor, spreadsheet, and database program, also has a built-in communications program that should be adequate for most users.

Another good option is **Qmodem**, from Mustang Software. Qmodem is a shareware program that you can obtain from all the usual shareware sources (described in Chapter 35), or straight from the publisher (see Resources at right). Qmodem, like Terminal, has all the features most people will need, and it's relatively easy to use and quite powerful.

Resources

Qmodem
Mustang Software,
800-999-9619, 805-395-0223.

Microsoft Works
Microsoft, 800-426-9400,
206-882-8080.

Integrated Software: All in One

41

SO YOU FIGURE THAT RUNNING "WORKS" ON FOUR COMPUTERS MAKES YOU JUST AS PRODUCTIVE AS 16 "NORMAL" PEOPLE.

Most PC programs are designed to perform a single task, such as processing words, creating spreadsheets, or managing lists. But some programs can do more than one task. These are known as "integrated programs" because they integrate several tasks into a single program.

The biggest advantage of integrated software is that you don't have to buy or use a lot of different programs. Surprisingly, integrated software tends to be less expensive than programs designed to perform a single task. Most are priced under $200, and Better Working Eight in One, from Spinnaker Software, is even cheaper, going for $60, when I wrote this. People who buy integrated software are a little like the folks who buy integrated stereo systems. They are not looking for the most

In an integrated program, you can work in different modules that provide the features of several different kinds of applications. Microsoft Works (shown here) supplies word processing, spreadsheet, database management, and drawing modules.

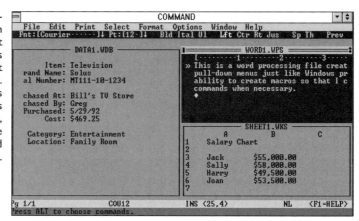

```
┌─────────────────────────────────────────────────────────────┐
│ ═                        COMMAND                        ▼ ▲│
│   File  Edit  Print  Select  Format  Options  Window  Help  │
│ Fnt:[Courier·····]↓ Pt:[12·]↓   Bld Ital Ul   Lft Ctr Rt Jus   Sp Th   Prev │
│ ┌───────DATA1.WDB──────┐ ┌────────WORD1.WPS════════┐│
│ │                       │ │[······1·····2·····3····│
│ │      Item: Television │ │» This is a word processing file creat││
│ │ rand Name: Solus      │ │  pull-down menus just like Windows pr││
│ │ al Number: MT111-10-1234│ │  ability to create macros so that I c││
│ │                       │ │  commands when necessary.           ││
│ │ chased At: Bill's TV Store│ │◆                                  ││
│ │ chased By: Greg       │ └─────────────────────────┘│
│ │  Purchased: 5/29/92   │ ┌────────SHEET1.WKS───────┐│
│ │      Cost: $469.25    │ │           A       B       C ││
│ │                       │ │1   Salary Chart            ││
│ │  Category: Entertainment│ │2                          ││
│ │  Location: Family Room│ │3   Jack    $55,000.00      ││
│ │                       │ │4   Sally   $58,000.00      ││
│ │                       │ │5   Harry   $49,500.00      ││
│ │                       │ │6   Joan    $53,500.00      ││
│ │                       │ │7                          ││
│ └───────────────────────┘ └─────────────────────────┘│
│ Pg 1/1          COU12       INS (25,4)      NL   <F1=HELP> │
│ Press ALT to choose commands.                               │
└─────────────────────────────────────────────────────────────┘
```

powerful product on the market, they just want something that is economical, practical, and easy to use.

Integrated programs aren't necessarily easy to use, but all the different modules—word processing, spreadsheet, database, and so on—work similarly, so once you've learned the basics, you are able to use all the modules pretty easily.

The most popular integrated programs offer word processing, communications, database, and spreadsheet modules. Others offer additional features such as drawing, and scheduling modules.

As you've probably guessed by now, the program that's the favorite with most people—**Microsoft Works**—is my favorite as well, for both Windows and DOS. It has a word processor, a spreadsheet, a database manager, and either a communications program (with the DOS version) or a drawing program (with the Windows version), all rolled into one.

There are two versions of Works, one for DOS and one for Windows. I use the DOS version on my laptop computer, and I would recommend the program highly to anyone whose computer is not powerful enough to run Windows. That's because Works does fine on just about any type of PC, regardless of how fast it is and whether or not it has a hard disk.

You can use more than one of the Works modules at a time, making it possible to search for an address in your

Scorecard: Integrated Software

	DOS	Windows
Most Popular	Microsoft Works	Microsoft Works
Recommendation	Microsoft Works	Microsoft Works

mailing list, calculate your budget in the spreadsheet, and communicate with another computer via a phone line, all without ever having to exit a program.

Ease of use is one of Works' strong points, and it's one of my main reasons for liking the program. Even the DOS version uses pull-down menus so that you can easily use all the program's commands. Both Works for DOS and Works for Windows let you have more than one document open at a time.

Microsoft Works is not the only good integrated package on the market. For DOS, you might also look at **Lotus Works**, from Lotus Development, and **WordPerfect Works**, from WordPerfect Corp. Spinnaker Software's two offerings—**PFS: First Choice** and **Better Working Eight in One**, both well under $100—are especially affordable. All of them have the basic categories—word processing, spreadsheet, database, and communications modules, plus assorted extras. Better Working Eight in One, for example, has a word processor, spell-checker/thesaurus, outliner, database, graphics, spreadsheet, and communications, plus an extensive set of desktop utilities, including an individual label-maker. WordPerfect Works includes the LetterPerfect word processor, which is a scaled-down version of WordPerfect. For Windows, **Claris Works** is excellent. You might find that one of those integrated packages suits you best.

Resources

Claris Works
Claris, 800-544-8554,
408-987-7000.

Better Working Eight in One
Spinnaker Software,
800-323-8088.

Lotus Works
Lotus Development,
800-343-5414, 617-577-8500.

Microsoft Works
Microsoft, 800-426-9400,
206-882-8080.

PFS: First Choice
Spinnaker Software,
800-323-8088.

WordPerfect Works
WordPerfect, 800-321-4566,
801-225-5000.

Utility Software: Computer Housekeeping

42

Utilities is a rather general category, but in general it has come to mean software that helps your computer operate more efficiently or more safely.

There are all sorts of utility programs. In this chapter, I'll run through the ones I consider the most important, which fall into three categories:

- General utilities, which help protect your data from possible corruption and rescue you in case your data has been damaged.
- Virus-protection software, which checks for the harmful **virus** programs that are becoming more and more prevalent.
- Compression software, which helps you effectively double your hard disk space by compressing your files.

With each version of DOS, more and more of these basic utility functions have become part of the operating system. DOS 6.0 includes backup, virus-protection, and compression programs that could provide all the help you need with these functions. (Instructions for using them are included in the Cookbook at the end of this book.) That said, there is still a reason to check out the offerings of commercial utilities. They stay in business by keeping one step ahead of the abilities of DOS, and they are especially useful in the disk-fixing category covered by Norton Utilities and PC Tools. In the following descriptions, I'll cover both the features of DOS 6.0 and those of commercial software in each category.

Scorecard: Utility Software

	DOS	Windows
Most Popular		
General Utilities	Norton Utilities	Norton Utilities
	PC Tools	
Antivirus	Norton Anti-Virus	Norton Anti-Virus
	McAfee Virus Scan	
Compression	Stacker	—
Recommended		
General Utilities	Norton Utilities	—
	DOS 6.0	
Antivirus	Norton Anti-Virus	Norton Anti-Virus
	McAfee Virus Scan	
Compression	Stacker	—
	DOS 6.0	

Norton Utilities and PC Tools: General Housekeeping

My favorite general utility program is called **Norton Utilities** (there are versions for both DOS and Windows). It has lots of different utilities that let you manage files. Most important, though, it has a Disk Doctor program that can almost magically fix whatever goes wrong with your hard disk. It has saved my data on several occasions. If you have DOS 6.0, be sure you get Norton Utilities version 7.0 or higher. It is optimized to work with DOS 6.0's optional compressed drives. (See the DOS Cookbook for more on compressing files with DOS 6.0.)

Resources

Norton Utilities
Symantec, 800-441-7234,
408-253-9600.

PC Tools
Central Point Software,
800-964-6896, 503-690-8090.

Equally popular is **PC Tools** from Central Point Software, which is pretty much the same as Norton Utilities except it comes with several other programs, including virus protection, a text editor, and a communications program.

Antivirus Software: An Ounce of Prevention

Antivirus software helps safeguard your computer against destructive programs—"viruses"—that are sometimes planted on floppy disks and networks. If you get a virus, your computer could undergo damage that ranges from the annoying to the disastrous (see the box "How Bad Can a Computer Virus Be?")

A virus-protection program scans your hard disk and memory for known viruses and, if it finds one, removes it. These programs can also load software into memory to protect you by continually checking for possible infections.

How Bad Can a Computer Virus Be?

You've probably heard about viruses attacking computer systems. Viruses are bugs that have been deliberately planted by vandals who are out to destroy other people's property. A virus gets into your computer by infecting a program or floppy disk. Most viruses attach themselves to programs and are activated as soon as the infected program is run. Some viruses aren't carried by programs but are spread by floppy disks. All it takes to be infected with such a virus is for you to turn on your computer while an infected disk is in the floppy drive. The virus copies itself to your computer's memory and infects any other disks in the computer, including your hard disk.

Before I go on, let me give you a word of assurance. Although viruses are a real threat, they're not nearly as common as some people claim. I use an enormous number of programs and I download software from on-line services and bulletin boards. I've been using a computer almost every day for more than a decade. Yet I've only once caught a virus, and I was able to detect it and get rid of it before it did any damage. There is a good chance you'll never encounter a virus. Nevertheless, it's worth taking precautions, just in case. If a virus enters your system, you could lose everything on your hard disk, or you could find that your computer just starts doing crazy things.

New viruses are always being introduced, and it's important to make sure that your virus-protection program can detect all the newest strains. Companies that make virus-protection utilities make new versions of their virus data files available regularly. You can get them by calling the company or contacting your local user group, or you can download them from on-line services.

DOS 6.0 comes with an antivirus program that should be adequate for most users. There are also a number of other programs that offer greater degrees of protection or may be easier to use or more regularly updated. Leading antivirus programs include **Norton Anti-Virus** from Symantec, **Untouchable** from Fifth Generation Systems, and **Central Point Anti-Virus**. McAfee Associates distributes its antivirus software, **Viruscan**, **Clean-Up**, and **VShield**, as shareware. When it comes to protection, McAfee's shareware is as good as any of the commercial programs, although it isn't quite as easy to use.

See the DOS and Windows cookbooks at the end of this book for more on how to run DOS's virus-protection program.

File Compression: Doubling the Size of Your Hard Disk

As I predicted in Chapter 12, you'll be amazed at how quickly your hard disk fills up. Before you go out and get another one, however, you should look into compression software. Compression software is a way of shrinking your files so that you can fit much more—even twice as much—on the hard disk you already have.

Compression programs accomplish this seemingly miraculous trick by removing redundant information from your files. It's like squeezing the air out of your data, and it's perfectly safe. Although compressing and decompressing files takes a little bit of time and can result in your files opening more slowly, most compression programs are set up to get in your way as little as possible, automatically taking advantage of idle time on your computer to recompress files.

DOS 6.0 has a built-in compression program, called DoubleSpace, that you can use to either compress everything on your hard disk or just create double the free space you had before compression. (The Cookbook in the last part of this book tells how to use DoubleSpace.) The most popular stand-alone hard disk compression program is called **Stacker**, a program from Stac Electronics.

Another kind of compression software is designed to compress specific files or directories. By far the most widely used is **PKZIP**, a shareware compression program that will compress one or more files into a single file that is typically one-tenth to one-half the size of the original. Unlike with Stacker and DoubleSpace, files that are "zipped" must be manually decompressed before you can use them. This is done via a companion shareware program called **PKUNZIP**.

There are three primary uses for PKZIP and PKUNZIP:

- Most shareware programs that you get on bulletin boards and on-line services are compressed as ZIP files so they take less time to transmit. You'll need PKUNZIP before you can use those files.

- Sometimes a floppy isn't big enough to hold all the files you want to put on it, or even big enough to hold a single file you want to transfer. You can compress the files to make them fit.

- If you don't use DOS or Stacker to compress your entire hard disk, you can use PKZIP to compress programs or data files that you use on rare occasions. You can then "unzip" them when you need them.

Resources

PKZIP, PKUNZIP
PKWARE, 414-354-8699.
....
Stacker
Stac Electronics, 800-522-7822,
619-431-7474.

Financial Software: Running Your Home Like a Business

43

Your computer can't make you wealthy, but it can help you better manage the money you already have. After all, computation—what most of us haven't done since grade school, and what computers do best—is what finances are all about. Financial management packages are relatively inexpensive, and I have found that they save me lots of trouble. Since you have a computer, you should take a look at some of the features available in these packages and consider whether they would help you.

Organize Your Finances

Quicken, from Intuit, is the best-selling program of all time for the PC. It's an inexpensive, all-around personal finance program that helps you pay your bills and keep track of various accounts, including stocks and mutual funds, and see how you're doing at managing your money for retirement and other financial goals. You can categorize each expense and track your income sources so that you can print out detailed reports. Another great program that offers the same features is **Managing Your Money**, from MECA. Both come in DOS and Windows versions.

In the DOS versions, both programs enable users with a modem to pay their bills via CheckFree, an electronic bill-paying service. (This is also a feature in Quicken for Windows.) You enter the information in the program, and instead of printing the check, the software dials CheckFree's processing center and transmits the check order. CheckFree pays the bills on your behalf and deducts the funds from your checking account. Mortgage, car payments, deposits to an investment account can all happen automatically via the "recurring payment" option. There is a nominal fee for using the service. I've been using CheckFree for years and am very happy with it.

Managing Your Money includes several extra utilities, including a reminder pad where you can maintain your schedule; keep track of anniversaries; and have the program remind you to pay bills, transfer funds, or make time-sensitive investments. There is also a word processing module, called MYM-Write, that lets you write documents without having to leave the program. It can also be used to edit the financial reports that Managing Your Money generates.

Scorecard: Financial Software

	DOS	Windows
Most Popular		
Financial management	Quicken	Quicken for Windows
Tax preparation	TurboTax	TurboTax
Recommendation		
Financial management	Managing Your Money	Quicken for Windows
	Quicken	
Tax preparation	Tax Cut	Tax Cut
	TurboTax	TurboTax

The DOS version of Managing Your Money also comes with QuoteLink, a feature that lets you automatically dial in to CompuServe to update the value of each of your securities. QuoteLink is available as a $19.95 option in Quicken for Windows.

Personally, I prefer the DOS version of Managing Your Money and the Windows version of Quicken. That's because Managing Your Money's DOS version has a Windows-like feel to it and includes better planning modules and on-line help than the DOS version of Quicken. Quicken for Windows version 2.0 has more features than Managing Your Money for Windows version 1.0 (Managing Your Money for Windows doesn't have CheckFree or an automatic stock update feature), but both companies will continue to improve their products, so check to see their current status before deciding.

Resources

Quicken
Intuit, 800-624-8742,
415-322-0573.

Managing Your Money
MECA Software,
800-288-MECA.

Tax Preparation Software: Making Tax Time Less Taxing

There are lots of advantages to using a computer to do your taxes. First of all, the software does all the arithmetic for you, eliminating a lot of human error. Tax preparation programs can automatically sort and add all of those receipts you're keeping in shoe boxes. Once they're entered in the program, the program keeps them all straight.

More important, all the forms that most taxpayers need are included with the programs. You don't have to order forms or even search around your desk. You just bring them up on the screen, fill them out, and then print them out and send them in. The programs automatically carry forward data from each form and schedule to the appropriate line of the 1040.

The leading tax preparation programs are **Personal Tax Edge** from Parsons Technology, **TurboTax** from ChipSoft, and **TaxCut** from MECA Software. If you use a personal finance program such as Quicken or Managing Your Money to keep track of your finances during the year, you can even import the data into

Resources

Personal Tax Edge
Parsons Technology,
800-223-6925, 319-395-9626.

TurboTax
ChipSoft, 619-587-3900

TaxCut
MECA Software,
800-288-MECA.

any of these programs. None of the programs gives you the kind of strategic advice you can get from a good tax professional, but they will help you better understand which deductions you're entitled to and how to enter them on the forms. I recommend TaxCut for people who are novices when it comes to preparing taxes. TurboTax is excellent for people who are savvy with IRS forms.

Just as I was finishing this book, ChipSoft, the company that makes TurboTax, announced that it had acquired MECA, the company that makes TaxCut (so much for healthy competition). However, both products are likely to remain available.

Entertainment Software: Just for Fun

44

Judging by the sales of games and "entertainment software," a lot of people love to use their computers to play games. Around $400 million was spent on game software in 1991, according to figures from the Software Publisher's Association, and that number just seems to keep rising.

Contrary to popular myth, the majority of game players are not teenagers. Most are adults who have been seduced by the ability of computer games to test their powers of deduction and quick thinking. In addition to old standbys like Solitaire and Scrabble, you can get the kinds of interactive games that are possible only on computers, which offer impressive animation and intelligent responses to your actions.

Most computer games offer levels of play from very easy to almost impossible, so as you get better, the game gets harder.

There are quite a few companies—such as Sierra On-Line, Broderbund, and Spectrum Holobyte—that specialize in computer games, but even companies you might think of as more serious-minded—including Microsoft—have their own game offerings.

If you're interested in learning about more games, pick up a copy of *Dvorak's Guide to PC Games* by John C. Dvorak and Peter Spear (Bantam Computer Books, 1991, $29.95).

Now that I've said all that, though, I've got to admit that I'm not that much of a game player—my idea of fun is testing out a new word processor. When I need to know what's going on in the world of computer games, I turn to my friend Peter Spear. Spear, a former TV producer, is now a full-time computer-game expert. He writes books for game players and helps entertainment software companies develop more challenging products.

For much of the material in this chapter, then, I've asked Spear to recommend the games he thinks are the ones most worth calling to your attention.

Simulation Games

Starting with Microsoft's Flight Simulator, which, when it was introduced in the early 1980s, became the first blockbuster game for the PC, simulation games featuring the excitement of flying a fighter jet or helicopter have been hot sellers. As you fly the plane, the computer throws you into battlelike situations to test your reflexes and strategy. The best of these games have truly impressive graphics that make you feel like you're actually fighting an enemy.

Game guru Peter Spear calls *JetFighter II* from Velocity Development "the ultimate flight simulator." You fight against an enemy over the skies of Southern California in a variety of aircraft. Careful. You may have to land on a carrier (not easy) somewhere off the coast of Los Angeles.

Resources

JetFighter II
Velocity Development,
415-776-8000.

Links
Access Software, 800-800-4880,
801-359-2900.

Microsoft Golf for Windows
Microsoft, 800-426-9400,
206-882-8080.

Stunt Island
Walt Disney Computer
Software, 800-688-1520,
818-973-4015.

JetFighter II, from Velocity Development, puts you in the pilot's seat of a variety of military jets. You fight your battles above Southern California.

Stunt Island from Disney Software is a flight simulator with a twist. Here you fly through a movie set for a movie that you produce as you go along. You start by flying over pylons and through barns and the action escalates as you help create some great aviation movies. When the movie is complete, you can edit it and play it back to your heart's content.

Links from Access Software is in a different, very popular, simulation category: sports. This one puts you on the golf course. The graphics and strategy are based on real courses that were taped and

Links, from Access Software, puts you on the fairways of some of the world's best golf courses.

digitized. Links gives you a chance to play some of the leading courses with 360-degree views of the greens. A Windows version, called **Microsoft Golf for Windows**, is available from Microsoft.

Fantasy and Role Playing

Fantasy adventure games put you in settings like an ogre's castle or a labyrinth, where you use your native wit and quick reflexes to find the right paths, choose the right weapons, and team up with the right allies to win your way to the treasure or rescue the princess. Some of the situations can get incredibly complicated. If you make the wrong choice, you can die a bloody death. But don't worry—you get a chance to learn from your mistakes: You can enter the game again, making different choices at crucial points.

The **King's Quest** games from Sierra On-Line have been on the market since 1984, and they're now considered classics. There are five in the series, which includes titles like "Quest for the Crown," "Romancing the Throne," "To Heir Is Human," and "The Perils of Rosella."

In the Kings Quest series, from Sierra On-Line, you become an adventurer in search of lost treasure and romance.

If your taste tends to be less romantic, you've got your choice of plenty of other roles to play. You can be a sleazy but lovable loser, a railroad tycoon, a supreme being, or almost any other role. As you make choices in the setup situation, the game responds to show you the results of your actions. The outcome can be daunting or hilarious.

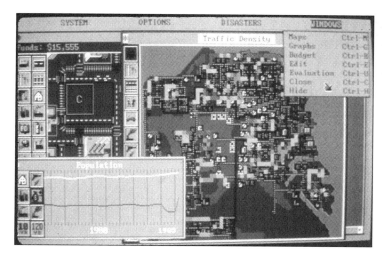

In SimCity, from Maxis Software, you test your creative powers by building cities from scratch.

Leisure Suit Larry, also from Sierra On-Line, features a character you might call a sexist pig, but that would be giving him too much credit. In this self-mocking series of games, Larry, the hero, is on a quest for true love—or at least a little companionship.

In **Railroad Tycoon**, from Microprose, the object is to create your own railroad empire. You not only have to lay tracks, but you also have to handle finances and worry about hostile takeovers.

SimCity and **SimEarth**, both from Maxis Software, launch you to an even more heady position. In these reality simulators, you get to play God. These are games for people who like to think and save the world at the same time. In SimCity, your job is to create the ideal city. In SimEarth, you create the ideal world. Screw up and, well, your screen might look as bad as the real world. Do a good job and you'll be the envy of your neighbors and the political establishment. I think playing these games should be required for politicians and ambassadors.

Resources

King's Quest
Sierra On-Line, 800-326-6654, 209-683-4468.

Leisure Suit Larry
Sierra On-Line, 209-683-4468.

Railroad Tycoon
Microprose, 800-879-7529, 410-771-1151.

SimCity, SImEarth
Maxis, 510-254-9700.

Arcade Games

Computer arcade games offer the kind of reflex-testing sport you'd find in a coin-operated video arcade.

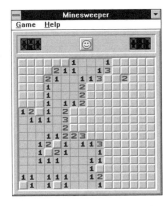

Spectrum Holobyte offers a series of very popular arcade games based on a very simple premise. In *Tetris*, *Welltris*, *Faces*, and *Wordtris*, objects fall from the sky. Your job is to move and rotate them so they fall in orderly rows. Sounds simple, but, of course, it's not. In Tetris and Welltris, the objects have a variety of shapes that you need to assess and realign to fit the grid before they hit the ground. With

Minesweeper, a simple arcade game, comes with Windows 3.1.

Faces, the blocks are replaced with facial parts (noses, eyes, etc.). In Wordtris, the blocks hold letters, with which you must form words. With all these "Tris" games, the objects drop at an ever-accelerating speed. Watch out below!

Windows comes with a simple arcade game called *Minesweeper*. Minesweeper offers a blank grid that has bombs hidden randomly beneath it. You click each square to discover either a bomb or a blank tile. If the tile lies next to a bomb, a number there tells you how many mines are around. You win by clearing the grid without landing on a mine. You can choose easy, medium, or hard levels of play, or specify a custom grid for which you choose the size of the grid and the number of bombs.

Resources

Tetris, Welltris, Faces, Wordtris
Spectrum Holobyte,
800-695-4263, 510-522-3584.

Crosswords, Anyone?

A lot of people have turned common games that you generally play with a deck of cards or a pencil and paper into computer programs. Solitaire, Cribbage, Poker, Blackjack, and Hangman are all available in computerized versions from SWFTE, Microsoft, Symantec, and others, in game packs that combine several simple programs starting at around $30. (Solitaire also comes free with Windows.)

One of the most popular is the **New York Times Crossword Puzzle** on disk from SWFTE. It's a Windows program with 250 crossword puzzles. The computerized edition lets you select your skill level. Novice and intermediate players can check their answers as they enter them.

Kid Stuff

Games for children are covered in the next chapter, but some of those kids' programs could just as well be for adults. Check out the Carmen Sandiego series from Broderbund. I listed it in the kids section, but adults love it, too.

Resources

New York Times Crossword Puzzle
SWFTE International,
800-237-9383.

Symantec Game Packs
Symantec, 800-441-7234,
408-253-9600.

Microsoft Game Packs
Microsoft, 800-426-9400,
206-882-8080.

Games Can Require Some Serious Hardware

Don't think that fun and games means you can get away with lightweight hardware. Some games will work on 640-K machines, but virtually all require some kind of graphic display. Many games, like any graphics-driven application, require VGA boards, 386 CPUs, and as much as 4 MB of memory. Games that run under Windows work best on a system with a 386 or 486 CPU and at least 4 MB of memory.

You also need a sound adapter board to fully enjoy many games. If you buy a sound board, make sure it's Sound Blaster–compatible. Sound Blaster boards, from Creative Labs (800-998-5227, 408-428-6600), are able to reproduce voice as well as music. Sound Blaster–compatible boards, which are available from a number of companies, have the same capabilities and work with the same software.

Children's Software: Learning and Playing

45

WATCH THIS, TOMMY: IN ONE KEYSTROKE, I TAKE CONTROL OF THE UNIVERSE AND GET A FIVE DOLLAR BUMP IN MY ALLOWANCE!

This book is for adults. That's because kids don't need a computer book; they take to computers naturally.

I have two kids. Katherine is nine years old and William is seven. Both have been playing with computers since before they could walk or talk. During the first year or two they were content to pound on the keyboard. In fact, William still has my old extra keyboard that I put in his room when he was a toddler. As they began to get older, they enjoyed watching the letters form on the screen. During her first few years, Katherine would get very excited about seeing her name on the screen. William still enjoys typing his own name.

As my kids reached prekindergarten, we began to experiment with children's software. They both enjoyed most of the Disney titles because the characters, Mickey, Donald, and the gang, were so familiar. The kids love games that have music, and they insist on color. In fact, they're now bugging me to get a color printer. For a while I had them convinced that the reason the printouts were in black and white was so they could color them in themselves.

My kids have definite favorites. Here are some comments on each of them as well as some others I think you and your kids might enjoy.

Kid Desk: A Desktop for Kids

Your kids mean well, but accidents do happen. The fact that the kids are enjoying themselves is small consolation if they accidentally wipe out your financial files or that important report you took home from the office. It's not likely, but it can happen. The best way to protect your data from the kids is to make it so they can't get to the key parts of your system. This probably isn't necessary with older kids, but it's a good precaution with the younger set.

An easy and fun way to accomplish this is with **Kid Desk** from Edmark. This program, which works under both DOS and Windows, lets you to keep your kids away from your files and programs while it makes it easier for them to get to their own. It also provides some fun and useful utilities, including a clock that tells the time aloud, a calculator, and a calendar that can be marked with important dates. You can create a separate "desk" for each member of your family. If you have a sound board, you can record a greeting for your children, and they can record their own messages.

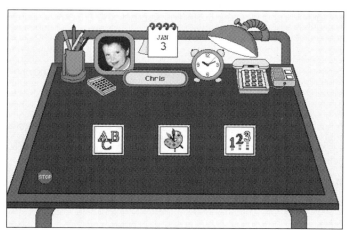

Kid Desk, from Edmark, provides an easy-to-work-with interface for kids. Clicking on an object on the desk brings up different games and tools. And not incidentally, the new interface hides access to the grown-ups' files.

Once in Kid Desk, the children can run the programs set up for them by clicking on a colorful icon. By pressing a secret sequence of keys, you put the program into "adult mode," where you can add or delete icons, access MS-DOS, and make any other changes.

Resources

Kid Desk
Edmark, 800-426-0856, 206-556-8400.

KidPix: Kid-Style Graphics

KidPix, from Broderbund Software, lets children create their own artwork. It is a lot easier to use than painting programs designed for adults, and it offers lots of extra goodies, including sounds, predrawn images, and plenty of special effects. You can actually hear the paint gurgle as it's poured from the can. The pencil makes a faint scratching sound as you drag it about the screen. When you select a letter or number, the program reads it aloud in either English or Spanish.

Resources

KidPix
Broderbund Software,
800-521-6263, 415-382-4400.

Playroom and Treehouse: Electronic Playgrounds

Another fun children's game, also from Broderbund, is called *Playroom*. In this educational game, children use the mouse to enter various doors, which take them on a variety of adventures, including one that allows them to create a weird-looking monster and another that lets them build their own outdoor environment. There are lots of things to explore using the mouse to navigate through Pepper Mouse's magical world. William loved Playroom when he was in preschool.

Treehouse, another offering from Broderbund, is a similar game, although it is aimed at a somewhat older audience—kids from six to ten. Treehouse contains a number of games that require and sharpen reading skills, including musical games, a money game, and a road

Pepper Mouse is your guide in Broderbund's Playroom.

rally, among others. William and I had a great time playing the Treehouse Theater, where we got to stage our own show. The child chooses from a cast of characters, scenes, and kinds of action.

Resources

Playroom, Treehouse
Broderbund Software,
800-521-6263, 415-382-4400.

Kid Works: A Talking Picture Book

Kid Works, from Davidson & Associates, enables children to write, illustrate, print, and hear their own stories. It's aimed at the four- to ten-year-old set: Little kids can create stories by manipulating icons or pre-drawn pictures; older kids can add words that they type themselves. Click on the lips icon and the program reads the story aloud, albeit in a computerlike voice.

Kid Works is based around a painting module reminiscent of the one used in KidPix. Children can start with a blank slate or load in 1 of 12 predrawn backgrounds, including a farm, outer space, a forest, and an underwater scene. There are also about 60 "stamps" that the child can use to add illustrations to the drawing.

Resources

Kid Works
Davidson & Associates,
800-556-6141.

Reader Rabbit: Serious Fun

Both my children like the Reader Rabbit series from the Learning Company, a firm that is serious about education and fun. All its games are developed in consultation with teachers and are play-tested at schools, and the company publishes educational guidelines for teachers. Parents really don't need any guidelines—a little trial and error and a few minutes with the manual should be fine. The newest version, *Reader Rabbit 2*, comes with four games. For each game, a parent or teacher can set the individual "challenge" level for each child. The parent can set a different difficulty level for each game for each child, so if a child is good at rhymes but not so good at vowels, the parent can adjust the levels accordingly.

Resources

Reader Rabbit 2
The Learning Company,
800-852-2255.

Broderbund's Where is Carmen Sandiego? is the most popular game series for older kids. The games test your ingenuity and your knowledge of geography. In one recent edition, Carmen's adventures extend into outer space.

Where Is Carmen Sandiego?

Broderbund's *Where Is Carmen Sandiego?* series is by far the most popular educational software in the age range from ten to young adult. In each of the games, kids search for the elusive Ms. Carmen Sandiego and her cohorts by using clues to solve a variety of mysteries. In some games, like "Where in the World" and "Where in the U.S.A.," you find Carmen by demonstrating your understanding of geography as well as your deductive skills. In others, you focus on time, culture, or even politics.

In each game, you, the player, are an agent with the San Francisco–based Acme Detective Agency. You're assigned a case and sent on a high-tech, high-flying adventure to find Carmen and her companions. Each game comes with a book of facts and clues. These aren't just game manuals. "Where in the World" comes with the *World Almanac* and the *Book of Facts.* "Where in the U.S.A." comes with *Fodor's U.S.A.* travel guide, and so on.

Resources

Where Is Carmen Sandiego?
Broderbund Software,
800-521-6263, 415-382-4400.

Mickey's Jigsaw Puzzle: Fun With Familiar Friends

When buying children's software, don't overlook the company that has been entertaining children since before I was a boy. Disney Software has a number of entertaining programs that feature Mickey, Donald, and other classic characters.

Katherine and William both enjoy **Mickey's Jigsaw Puzzle**. It provides for various levels of difficulty, making it appropriate for a range of age groups. Come to think of it, it's challenging for me, too.

The game starts out with a child-friendly screen from which the child picks the puzzle he or she wants to complete. Mickey then says, "Let's choose how many pieces we want in our puzzle," and the child gets to choose 4, 9, 16, 25, 36, 49, or 64 pieces. When you're finished putting all the pieces in the correct place, you can click on the movie camera to get a short animated cartoon, complete with sound. You can also click on individual characters to animate them.

Resources

Mickey's Jigsaw Puzzle
Disney Computer Software,
800-688-1520, 818-973-4015.

Headline Harry and the Great Paper Race

Do you have any would-be Pulitzer Prize winners in your family? If so, put them to the test with **Headline Harry and the Great Paper Race** from Davidson & Associates. This game, in the spirit of Broderbund's Carmen Sandiego series, sends the user on a rash of cross-country treks in search of news stories. You, a reporter, work for Headline Harry, editor of the *U.S. Daily Star*. Your goal is to beat the reporter from the *Diabolical Daily*, a smut-sheet edited by Marvin Muckracker.

The neat thing about Headline Harry and the Great Paper Race is that all the news is real, based on major events that took place between 1950 and 1990. You do the research to get the facts on the story and record it in your notebook. When you've filled in all the blanks, select "File the Story" and the computer writes it out for you. Harry is happy, you're happy, and you've learned some skills and a bit of history.

The program is aimed at ages ten to adult, and it's fun and challenging even to this adult journalist. The program requires a hard disk and a graphics monitor.

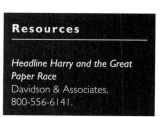

Resources

Headline Harry and the Great Paper Race
Davidson & Associates,
800-556-6141.

Millie's MathHouse: The Most Basic Math

This delightful game teaches very young children (ages two to six) to recognize sizes, shapes, patterns, and numbers. A mere list of activities—building houses for mice; putting jelly beans on cookies; bouncing an object over ducks, pigs, and Millie herself—doesn't do the program justice. It's the combination of sounds, music, animation, characters, humor, and ease of play that makes this one an instant classic.

Resources

Millie's MathHouse
Edmark, 800-426-0856,
206-556-8400.

The Treasure Series: Hunting for Skills

A tremendous winter storm has wreaked havoc on treasure mountain, scattering the treasures and freezing the magic crown. *Treasure MathStorm!* is an educational game aimed at five- to nine-year-olds. Only your child can stop the mischief, but he or she must use math and thinking skills. You get clues by catching elves and answering their questions. But there's more. If you run out of nets or other resources, you have to stop to earn money and shop at the store. There is a lot of learning hidden beneath a fun game that builds hand-eye coordination and critical thinking. One part of the game requires the child to translate between a digital and an analog clock. Both Katherine and William love it.

In Treasure MathStorm! from the Learning Company, elves help young children with math skills.

Treasure Mountain uses similarly playful techniques to work on reading, thinking, and math skills. *Treasure Cove* focuses on reading, science, thinking, and math.

Resources

The Treasure Series
The Learning Company,
800-852-2255.

Operation Neptune: Learning Math as If Your Life Depended on It

The space capsule *Galaxy* has crashed into the South Pacific, where it has released dangerous levels of toxic chemicals. As captain and crew of the rescue diving pod *Neptune*, it is your task to recover *Galaxy* and protect the undersea ecology from further danger. Aimed at 8- to 12-year-olds, **Operation Neptune** hones math skills by requiring numerous calculations regarding the diving pod's fuel, depth, and other critical indicators. The action is convincing, and kids get a chance to test their arcade-style maneuvering skills.

Resources

Operation Neptune
The Learning Company,
800-852-2255.

Installing Software

46   *Now that you've chosen the software you need, have bought it from the appropriate source, and gotten it home, how do you get it working on your computer?*

Software generally comes on floppy disks. In most cases, however, you don't run the programs from the original floppy disks—you copy them first to the hard drive. Sometimes, that requires copying the files from the floppy into a new directory on your hard disk. More often, however, the process involves using an installation program, which creates new directories and copies the application files for you.

Caution: Before installing the program disks, make sure the floppies are locked (see Chapter 29) so you can't accidentally erase them while you're copying them.

"Install" is an ominous-sounding term. It evokes images of a service person with a truck, a set of tools, and specialized skills. In most cases, though, installing software is pretty simple. The installation program makes it easy, prompting you for the information it needs to configure the software so that it works with your hardware.

The next step is to look for the section in your manual called "Installation" or "Getting Started" or something like that. You don't

The READ.ME File

More often than not, the software disk will include a file called READ.ME, in ASCII (plain text) format. You can open it with any software that reads ASCII. First try opening it with your word processor. (If you don't have a word processor yet, try the EDIT program that comes with DOS; that's a very basic word processing program.)

This file includes information that the programmers found out about too late to include in the manual. Here you'll find any late-breaking news about additional features, features that work differently from the way the manual describes them, and any known bugs or incompatibilities with other software or hardware.

You might not understand most of the information in the **READ.ME file** (no one does), but it's a good idea to scan through it anyway, just in case there's something that's important for you to know.

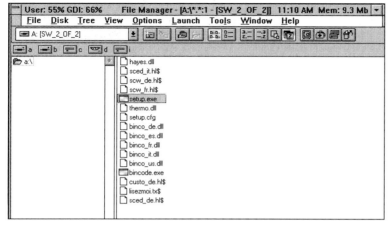

In the Windows File Manager, look for a file with a name like INSTALL.EXE or STARTUP.EXE on the first software disk and double-click on it. That will launch the installation program.

have to read the manual cover to cover. Usually that section will be near the beginning or in a separate pamphlet. The installation program itself will lead you through the installation procedure, so there may be no need to actually read that section unless you have a problem, but have it handy anyway.

The manual will tell you right away whether there is an installation program and what it is called. If there is one, you use it by placing the first disk in the floppy drive and running the program called Install. (Sometimes the installation programs will have a different name, like Setup, Start, Hello, or Go.) Then you just follow any instructions displayed on screen.

The program will either figure out what it needs to know on its own or will ask you questions about your hardware. Many of these programs are smart enough to know what type of display you have, whether or not you have a mouse, and whether you have enough room on your hard disk. They will almost always ask you

The Three Steps of Software Installation

1. Look for the section called "Installing" in your user's guide, or just put disk 1 into your A: drive and run the installation program.

2. Put your original packaging and original disks in a safe place, and send in the registration card.

3. Make backup copies of your original disks.

(The Cookbook section at the end of this book has instructions on formatting and copying disks and for running programs in DOS and Windows.)

While you're installing a new pro-gram, the installation program may inform you that it will be changing your AUTOEXEC.BAT and CONFIG.SYS files. If the pro-gram asks your permission to change those files, tell it to go ahead.

what type of printer you have. And it will tell you when you need to insert other disks and when installation is complete.

If you're working with Windows, you will probably need to be running Windows before you run the installation program. Select the File menu in the Program Manager, and choose the Run command.

Now type `A: INSTALL` and press Enter.

As an alternative, you can use the File Manager to display all the files on the A: drive and double-click on the one called INSTALL.EXE or SETUP.EXE.

If the program you're installing doesn't have an installation proce-dure, installation should still be fairly easy. In that case, though, you'll really need to read the installation section of the manual and follow its instructions.

And last but not least, register your software. Registering makes you eligible for benefits like technical support and free bug fixes. It's worth the trouble.

Registering Software

When you open a box of software, most likely a registration card will fall out. It's usually a postcard that asks you to fill in your name and address, along with some other information that will be useful to the software company's marketing department, and return it to the company. They're like the warranty cards you get with many consumer items. I don't know if it makes any sense to register your new toaster, but it is a good idea to register your software.

Registering software makes you eligible for benefits that you can't get any other way. To begin with, registering makes you eligible for a free upgrade if serious bugs are found in the program. Second, registered users receive information on program updates and generally get a steep discount on new releases. Some companies require you to be registered in order to use their telephone support lines.

All you have to do to register is fill out the form. If you don't want to fill in the marketing information, just leave it blank. Your name and address will still make it into the database.

Congratulations. You're not a computer novice anymore. In record time, you've learned everything you need to know to work confidently with your PC.

Now that you've got a solid grounding in all the basics, it's time to get practical. The last parts of this book, the DOS and Windows Cookbooks, provide you with recipes for carrying out common tasks you'll need to do in DOS and Windows. A glossary at the back of the book provides a quick reference for any jargon you may need to brush up on.

Have fun.

The DOS Cookbook

cookbooks

The DOS Cookbook

Disk Housekeeping 224

Setting Up Your System 249

Using DOS

You use DOS, instead of an application program, to do housekeeping on your system. This cookbook will take you, step by step, through the DOS commands you'll need to use for those tasks.

This cookbook won't cover every available DOS command. The full set is documented in the DOS manual that came with your system, in the help system you can use by typing HELP in DOS, or in books on DOS like Peachpit's *The Little DOS 6 Book*. The commands I tell you about here are the ones you will find most useful for the file, disk, and system management and housekeeping tasks that you'll need to do regularly.

Most—but not all—of the functions available in DOS are also available through Windows. If you have Windows, you might want to go straight to the Windows Cookbook, where you'll learn how to do many of the same tasks from within Windows' more friendly interface. Even if you have Windows, though, you may want to use DOS for some tasks.

Using DOS Commands

To use a DOS command, you type it on the DOS command line, at the DOS prompt:

```
c:\>
```

After you've typed it, you press the Enter (or Return) key, and DOS will execute the command.

It's rarely dangerous to make a mistake in a DOS command. Usually, if you type something wrong, DOS will simply give you the message

`Bad command or filename`

or some variation on that, and display the DOS prompt so you can try again. If you're not careful, though, you can get into trouble using commands that delete lots of files at one time. In this cookbook, I'll try to give you some warning about when to be careful.

Parameters and Options

Some DOS commands have extra parts to them, called "parameters" and "options."

Parameters tell DOS what disk drive or file you want the command to act on. They are preceded by spaces on the DOS command line.

Options, also known as "switches," tell DOS that you want the command to act in a special way. They are preceded by a space and a slash character (/).

Here's an example of a command that uses both parameters and options:

```
C:\>dir a: /w
```

DIR is the command that tells DOS to display a directory (list) of files. The parameter A: tells DOS that you want the DIR command to act on the disk in drive A: (that is, display a list of the files in drive A:). The option /w tells DOS to display the directory in a wide format so that more file names fit on the screen. (For more on the DIR command, see the recipe "To See a List of Files in the Current Directory.")

Many DOS commands have options, and some DOS commands have several of them, but only a few options are really important to know. I tell you all about the options that you'll use a lot. You can find out about others with DOS's HELP command. (See the recipe "To Get an Explanation of a DOS Command" for more details.)

Using Paths in DOS Commands

DOS always assumes that you want to apply your command to the current directory, unless you specify otherwise. If you want to apply a command to a file or files in a different directory, you have two choices:

1. You can move to the directory where the files you want to act on are stored, as described in the "To Change the Current Drive" and "To Change the Current Directory" recipes.

2. Alternatively, you can stay right where you are and provide a path in the command's parameter, either as the parameter itself or as an addition to a file name used as a parameter.

For example, let's say you're working in the root directory of drive C: and you want to delete some files in the business directory. You can either move there and then delete the files, like this:

```
C:\>cd \business

C:\BUSINESS>del toharry*.*
```

Or you can do it with a single command, like this:

```
C:\>del \business\toharry*.*
```

Moving to the directory you'll be working on can reduce the possibility of error when you're typing DOS commands. Those paths can be long!

There is one other situation in which you might need to use a path in a DOS command, but it happens only rarely. Some DOS commands rely on files that are stored in the DOS directory. If you use a DOS command and get an error message that says "Bad command or filename," first make sure you've typed the command correctly. If you have, try adding a path to the \DOS directory in the command, like this:

```
C:\>\dos\format a:
```

On most systems this is unnecessary because the AUTOEXEC.BAT file includes a PATH command that tells DOS to look in the \DOS directory for any command file it needs. If your system isn't set up that way, you can add the command yourself, using the recipe "To Add a PATH Command to Your AUTOEXEC.BAT File."

Some Notes About Using This Cookbook

- In the examples I show in these recipes, everything you type on the DOS command line is shown in lowercase. That's because that's probably the easiest way to type them; but in practice, you can type commands in uppercase, lowercase, or any combination of uppercase and lowercase.

- These recipes assume that you have DOS 6.0. Most of the commands will also work for earlier versions of DOS, but some won't, and some will work, but slightly differently. In cases where the command is available only in DOS 6.0, but you can perform the same task in a different way with DOS 5.0, I describe the alternate method in the notes to the recipe. If you have a version of DOS earlier than 5.0, I can't promise that these recipes will cover you.

- The instructions in these recipes assume that the files you want to act on are in the current directory. In the examples, the current directory is shown in the DOS prompt, as it probably is on your own system. If you want the command to act on files that are in a different directory, you will need to either move to that directory or use a path in the parameter of the command. (See the box "Using Paths in DOS Commands.")

Using Wildcards in DOS Commands

DOS provides special symbols called wildcard characters that let you work on several commands at the same time.

- The asterisk character (*) can stand for any number of characters in a file name.

- The characters *.* (an asterisk, the period that separates the file name and the file extension, and another asterisk) stands for "any file in the directory."

- The question mark (?) can stand for any one character.

You can use these wildcard characters to operate on more than one file at once.

For example, you can copy every file in the current directory to the NEW directory by giving the command:

```
C:\>copy *.* \new
```

You can display only files with the .DOC extension by typing:

```
C:\>dir *.doc
```

You can display only files beginning with the word "old" by typing:

```
C:\>dir old*.*
```

Try these characters in the parameters of any DOS command where you think they might be useful. A few DOS commands don't allow wildcards, but you won't hurt anything by trying them—unless, of course, you use DEL (Delete) *.* or ERASE *.* on the wrong directory.

To Get an Explanation of a DOS Command

Why Anytime you need information about a DOS command, you can get help from DOS itself. Both DOS 6.0 and DOS 5.0 have a help feature, but the help feature in 6.0 is a lot more complete. That's the one I'll describe here.

How 1. If you don't know which DOS command you need to use for your task, type **HELP** at the DOS command line and press Enter:

```
C:\>help
```

You will see a screen listing all of the available DOS commands:

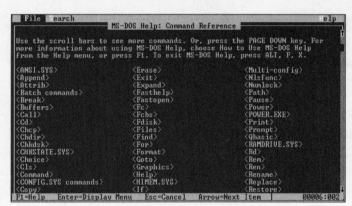

2. Using the mouse and scroll bars (or the PgUp, PgDn, and Tab keys), you can "browse" the list to find the command you want information about. Click on the command you want with the mouse, or, when the command you want is highlighted, press Enter.

DOS Cookbook

3. Once you've chosen a command, a help screen showing information about that command will be displayed. For example, the help screen for the DIR command looks like this:

Words in brackets at the top of the help screen indicate that there are additional pages of information. Clicking on the topic with the mouse or highlighting it and pressing Enter moves you to that page.

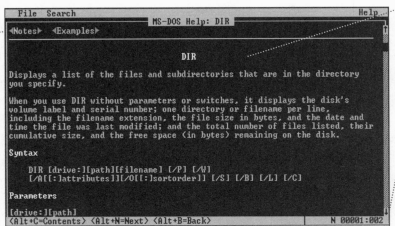

Each help screen describes what the command is used for, the syntax of the command (how you type it), and the parameters and options you can use with it.

You can click on the scroll arrows (if you have a mouse) to move through the help information.

4. Use the PgUp and PgDn keys to move through the help screen, or use the scroll arrows (if you have a mouse).

5. To look for all the help screens that include a particular word or phrase, you can press Alt-S (or click with the mouse) to open the Search menu. Choose Find from the menu. A text box will appear. Type in the word or phrase that describes the topic you are interested in. For example, if you want to learn about different techniques for copying files, try typing copy files. By repeatedly selecting Repeat Last Find from the Search menu, you can browse through the help screens for all commands that involve copying files.

6. To print the text from a help screen, open the File menu and choose the Print command.

7. To exit the on-line help system, open the File menu and choose Exit.

Notes • If you know which DOS command you want to read about, type **HELP** followed by the name of the command. For example:

```
C:\>help dir
```

You will go directly to the main help screen for the DIR command.

• DOS 5.0 includes a much more abbreviated help system. Type **HELP** followed by a command name to get a brief summary of the parameters and options you can use with the command. Type **HELP** by itself to get a list of commands.

To Start a Program

Why To work with any file, you run its application program first. For example, to make changes in a text document, you will need to run your word processing or text editing program.

How Type the name of the program and press Enter. For example, to run WordPerfect, you type:

```
C:\>wp
```

After you press Enter, the DOS screen will disappear and be replaced by the screen for the program you just launched.

Notes • The user's manual that comes with the program will tell you what command to type so you can start the program.

• If after you type the command you get the message "Bad command or filename" and a DOS prompt, check your spelling to make sure you've typed the command properly. If your spelling is OK, you need to either change to the directory the program is in before running the program (see the "To Change the Current Directory" recipe) or add a path to the command name. (You can also make sure this doesn't happen again by adding the program's directory name to the PATH command in your AUTOEXEC.BAT file.)

To Change the Current Directory

Why When you first start your computer, the current directory will probably be the root directory. If you're working with a number of files in one directory, you can move to that directory so you don't have to type paths for each file.

How Type CD followed by the path for the directory to which you want to change, and press Enter. For example, to change to the BUSINESS directory, type:

`C:\>cd \business`

On most systems, the DOS prompt will change to reflect the new current directory:

`C:\BUSINESS>`

Notes • If the directory you name with the CD command is on another drive, the effect of the command will be to change the current directory on that drive, but it will not have an effect on the current directory on the current drive. For example, say your current directory is the root directory on drive C:. (Your DOS prompt reads "C:\>.") Then you type "CD A:." On drive A:, the current directory will be changed to the root directory, but your DOS prompt will still say "C:\>"; the current directory will be unchanged. To change the current directory to a directory on a new drive, see the next recipe.

To Change the Current Drive

Why   Changing the current drive is like changing the current directory —it lets you work on files at the new destination without putting a disk drive designation in front of the file names.

How   Type the letter for the drive to which you wish to change, followed by a colon, and press Enter. For example, to change from the hard drive C: to floppy drive A:, type:

```
C:\>a:
```

The prompt will change to show the new current drive:

```
A:\>
```

Notes   • When changing to a floppy drive, you will have to put a disk in the drive first, or you will get a "Not ready" error message. If you get this error message, put a disk in the drive and press r, for "retry."

• Changing the current drive has no effect on the current directory on that drive. To change the current directory, see the previous recipe.

To Change the Name of a File

Why There are lots of reasons you'll want to rename files. Let's say, for example, you decide that renaming the file LETTER23.TXT to MARY.LET would make it much more likely that you will remember what's in that file. Or you have a graphics program that names the pictures you save as PICT1.PIC, PICT2.PIC, and so on, and you want to give the files more descriptive names.

How Type **REN** (rename), followed by the name of the file to be renamed and the file's new name, and press Enter. For example:

```
C:\CORRES>ren letter23.txt mary.let
```

The file LETTER23.TXT in the CORRES directory will now be called MARY.LET. The file hasn't been moved or changed in any way; it merely has been given a different name.

Notes • If the file to be renamed isn't in the current directory, just add a path to the old name and leave it off the new name:

```
C:\DOS>ren \corres\letter23.txt mary.let
```

Adding it to the new name too will get you an error message.

• You can also have a file's name change when it is copied or moved to another directory. (See the "To Copy a File" and "To Move a File" recipes for details.)

• If you try to rename a file with the name of a file that already exists in the destination directory, you will get the message "Duplicate filename or file not found." Try again with another name.

To Copy a File

Why   You will copy files for lots of reasons—to back up files to a floppy disk, to share a file with a colleague, or to create a second version of a file without changing the original.

How   Type `COPY`, the name of the file to be copied, and the name for the new copy, and then press Enter. For example, to make a copy of PLAN93.WKS and call it 1993RPT.WKS, type:

```
C:\BUSINESS>copy plan93.wks 1993rpt.wks
```

Notes • The COPY command uses paths in a number of different ways, but if you think about them, they all follow common sense.

The above command copies a file to a new file in the same directory. If the file you're copying isn't in the current directory, you need to add a path to the file name of the original file—but not to the copy. For example, the command

```
C:\>copy \business\plan93.wks 1993rpt.wks
```

does the same thing as the first example, but it does it from the root directory.

If you want to copy a file to a different disk or directory, you must add the path to the second file name. For example:

```
C:\BUSINESS>copy plan93.wks a:1993rpt.wks
```

This command copies the PLAN93.WKS file in the current directory (BUSINESS) to a file called 1993RPT.WKS in the root directory on drive A:.

If you are copying from a different (not current) directory to a different (not current) directory, you have to use paths for both file names.

• If you are copying a file to a different disk or directory, and you want to keep the same file name for the new file, you don't need to give a second file name; just supply the path for the new directory as the second parameter:

```
C:\BUSINESS>copy plan93.wks \outbasket
```

To Create a New Directory

Why Creating a new directory is like starting a file folder for a project. Whenever you start a new project, install a new program, or, in general, start a new activity on your computer, creating a new directory lets you keep the files in a single place where you can always find them.

How Type **MD** (Make Directory), followed by the name of the new directory, and press Enter. For example, to create a directory called BUSINESS, type:

```
C:\>md \business
```

Notes • DOS does not automatically make the new directory the current directory. After you create the directory, you can move to it using the CD command (described in the "To Change the Current Directory" recipe).

To Delete a Directory

Why When you've finished a project and have archived the files, or if you just decide you want to organize your disk differently, you'll want to delete directories you've made. With DOS 6.0, you can delete a directory, all of its files, and all of its subdirectories in one shot. If you are using earlier versions of DOS, you will need to empty the directory first. In either case, you will want to make sure you have taken care of all the files appropriately, by copying them elsewhere or archiving them, if necessary, before you delete the directory.

Caution The DELTREE command can get you into serious trouble because, unlike DEL and ERASE, it can erase hidden, system, and read-only files. Some of those files are necessary for DOS itself or for running a program. Be very sure you know what you're doing before using DELTREE to delete an entire directory.

How **1.** First type `DIR`, the name of the directory in question, the /s option, and press Enter. For example:

```
C:\>dir \business /s
```

This will get you a listing of all the files and subdirectories in the BUSINESS directory. Make sure you really want to delete everything, and that you've copied or moved any files that you want to keep.

2. Now type `DELTREE`, followed by the name of the directory to be deleted, and press Enter. For example, to delete the BUSINESS directory and all of its files and subdirectories, type:

```
C:\>deltree business
```

DOS will ask if you're sure you really want to delete everything:

```
Delete directory "temp2" and all its subdirectories? [y/n]
```

3. Type **Y** if you're sure you want to delete everything; type **N** if you want to reconsider the situation.

Notes • With DOS versions earlier than 6.0, you'll need to remove any files that are in the directory before you delete it. After you've made sure you don't need any of the files in the directory, use the DEL *.* command to delete all the files. Watch out, though: Make sure that you're in the correct directory before you type that command! Then move to another directory and type **RD** (Remove Directory), followed by the directory name:

```
C:>rd \business
```

If the directory you want to delete has subdirectories, you have to perform these steps for each subdirectory and then for the main directory.

• If, when trying to delete what you think is an empty directory, you see the message

```
Invalid path, not directory,
or directory not empty
```

there's a chance that you have "hidden files" in that directory. To erase the files, you must first "unhide" them. To do that, type this at the DOS prompt:

```
attrib *.* -h
```

At this point, you can erase the files in the normal way.

Caution Only "unhide" files in directories you're sure you want to erase. Generally, files that are hidden should remain hidden.

To Delete a File

Why You may need to delete files to avoid running low on disk space.

How Type DEL, followed by the name of the file to be deleted. For example, to delete the file TO-BOB.DOC, type:

```
C:\>del to-bob.doc
```

Notes • Be careful when using wildcards with this command. DEL *.* will delete everything in the current directory.

• If you delete a file by mistake, don't panic. Turn to the "To Restore a File You've Deleted" recipe.

• If you want to delete both the directory and its files, see the "To Delete a Directory" recipe.

To Find a File on Your Hard Disk

Why You won't always remember which of your dozens of directories contains a file you need.

How **1.** Make sure you are in the root directory of the disk you are searching. This is usually indicated by a DOS prompt of C:\>. (To find out how to change directories, see the "To Change the Current Directory" recipe.)

2. Type `DIR`, followed by the file name and the /s switch, and press Enter. For example, if you were looking for the file QUERY.LET, you would type this:

```
C:\>dir query.let /s
```

DOS will search every directory on the disk, and it will display a directory listing for each place it finds the file name you specify. For example, the following display shows that the QUERY.LET file was found in three places: the \CORRES and \JOBHUNT directories and the CORRES subdirectory of the \PERSONAL directory:

```
 Volume in drive C is DBL_DISK
 Volume Serial Number is 11E5-3D3E
Directory of C:\CORRES
QUERY LET   356 05-01-93 12:40a
   1 file(s)   356 bytes
Directory of C:\JOBHUNT
QUERY LET   356 05-01-93 12:40a
   1 file(s)   356 bytes
Directory of C:\PERSONAL\CORRES
QUERY LET   356 05-02-93 11:01a
   1 file(s)   356 bytes
Total files listed:
   3 file(s)   1068 bytes
      131858432 bytes free
```

Notes • If more than one copy of the file is found, you can compare the dates and times in the directory listings to see which version of the file is the most recent. (In this case, the one in \PERSONAL\CORRES is the latest version.)

• If there are a lot of files that meet your criteria, the file names and locations may scroll off your screen. To prevent that, add the /p option to the command:

```
dir *.bat /s /p
```

After the first screenful of information, DOS will display the message "Press any key to continue..." Then you can press any key to see the next screenful.

To Find Out Whether a Certain File Is in a Directory

Why To find out whether a file you want is in a certain directory, you can always type DIR followed by the directory name to list all the files in the directory (see the recipe "To See a List of Files in the Current Directory"). Searching through a long directory listing can be dificult, however, so if you just want to know whether a certain file is there, it's often easier to ask for the specific file name you want.

How Type DIR followed by the name of the file you want to find, and press Enter. For example, to find out if the file BUSPLAN.DOC is in the BUSINESS directory, type:

```
C:\BUSINESS>dir busplan.doc
```

If DOS finds the file there, it will list it, along with information about the \BUSINESS directory:

```
 Volume in drive C is DBL_DISK
 Volume Serial Number is 11E5-3D3E
 Directory of C:\BUSINESS
 .     <DIR>   05-24-93 1:06a
 ..    <DIR>   05-24-93 1:06a
BUSPLAN DOC   9349 03-10-93 6:00a
   3 file(s)   9349 bytes
        132251648 bytes free
```

If the file isn't found, DOS will tell you so:

```
 Volume in drive C is DBL_DISK
 Volume Serial Number is 11E5-3D3E
 Directory of C:\BUSINESS

File not found
```

To Move a File

Why You're likely to want to reorganize your directories and files as your needs change. For example, let's say you have a directory called \TEMP that you use as a kind of catchall to store all the files that you receive from your friends and colleagues. Pretty soon it will get pretty cluttered in there. To make things more orderly, you might want to start keeping files from each person in a separate directory.

How Type MOVE, followed by the name of the file, a space, and the name of the directory to which you're moving the file, and press Enter. For example:

```
C:\TEMP>move george1.txt \george
```

This command moves the GEORGE1.TXT file from the \TEMP directory to the \GEORGE directory.

When DOS has made the move, it gives you the complete paths of the original and moved files, followed by "[ok]" if the operation was successful. It would look like this:

```
C:\temp\george1.txt => c:\george\george1.txt [ok]
```

Notes • Watch out: If you move a file to a directory that already has a file with the same name, the copy at the destination will be replaced without warning. You might want to ask for a list of the files in the destination directory before you make the move if you think that file name may have already be used there.

• If you have DOS 5.0 or earlier, you can't move a file from one place to another in a single step. Instead, you will need to copy the file to the new directory and then delete the original. See the "To Copy a File" recipe and the "To Delete a File" recipe for instructions on those operations.

To See a List of Files in the Current Directory

Why You want to check what files are in a directory.

How Type DIR and press Enter. For example, to see what files are in the BUSINESS directory, type:

```
C:\BUSINESS>dir
```

DOS displays the list of files in the directory, along with a bunch of other information, in this format:

```
 Volume in drive C is DBL_DISK
 Volume Serial Number is 11E5-3D3E
 Directory of C:\BUSINESS
.    <DIR>   05-24-93 11:19a
..   <DIR>   05-24-93 11:19a
INVENTRY RPT   20906 12-07-89 9:00a
JULY   LET   4226 05-23-93 11:19a
REPORT1    4000 05-23-93 11:19a
TODO   LST   5489 12-21-89 8:42p
   6 file(s)   34621 bytes
       131768320 bytes free
```

The columns in the directory listing, from left to right, give the file name, extension, size, date last changed, and time last changed.

Notes • You can list the files in another directory by adding the path of that directory as a parameter. For example,

```
C:\>dir \business
```

gets the same result.

• You can get a directory listing that includes all of the subdirectories (and their files) in addition to the listing of the main
directory. Just add the /s option to your DIR command. (This
option is available starting with DOS 5.0.)

• DOS's DIR display keeps scrolling until all the files in the
directory are listed on the screen. That means that, usually, the
top names in the directory will scroll off the screen before you
can see them. To avoid that, you can use a couple of options.

The /w (wide) option tells DOS to display the information in two
columns (leaving out some of the information) so that more files
fit on the screen.

The /p (pause) option tells DOS to display a screenful of information at a time. After each screenful, DOS displays the line
"Press any key to continue . . ." and waits for the user to press a
key before it displays the next screenful.

To See the Directory Structure of Your Hard Disk

Why Sometimes you can't remember how your disk is organized or just what you've named a certain directory. At those times, you need an overview of your directory structure.

How Type TREE, a space, and the path of the directory you want to see, and then press Enter:

```
C:\>tree \home
```

You will see the directory structure of your current directory, in a form like this:

```
Directory PATH listing
Volume Serial Number is 1AB9-5397
C:\HOME
|___BUDGET
|___LETTERS

C:\
```

Notes • The TREE command, with no parameter, displays the directory structure of the current directory. If you want to see the directory structure of the whole disk, make sure you're in the root directory, or use the disk name as a parameter for the command, like so:

```
C:\>tree c:
```

• If you want the report to include not only the directories but all of the files as well, add the /f (files) option to your TREE command:

```
C:\>tree /f
```

• Often, especially if you have asked to see the directory structure of the entire disk, the TREE display will be too large to fit on the screen and will scroll right off it before you get a chance to see it. See the box "Controlling the Output of DOS Commands," below, for tips on how to capture the output so that you can see it at your own pace.

Controlling the Output of DOS Commands

Sometimes DOS commands display a lot of information—so much, in fact that it will scroll off the screen before you get a chance to read it. DOS has a couple of options that you can use to control the output of any command.

• The first option involves the MORE command. To use it, you type the command followed by the | symbol (a vertical bar), and then the MORE command. For example, the command

```
C:\>tree | more
```

will display the directory structure of your hard disk, one screen at a time. After the information fills the screen, the display will stop and wait for you to press a key before it continues displaying the report. (The | character is usually Shift-\.)

• Another command, the greater-than symbol (>), sends the command's output to a file. To use it, type the command, followed by the > symbol, and then the name of a file in which the report will be stored. For example,

```
C:\>dir *.* /s > mydirs
```

gets a directory listing of the whole disk and stores it in the file MYDIRS, where you can read or print it later.

To Back Up Your Hard Disk

Why It's a good idea (as you know) to keep current backup copies of all your work. If you work mostly on just one or two files, you can easily keep a backup version of them using the COPY command (see the "To Copy a File" recipe for details). If, however, you work with a variety of files, or with programs that use a variety of files that are constantly updated, you can't count on remembering which files you have created or changed each day. You need a more systematic backup strategy. DOS 6.0 provides a command called MSBACKUP that helps you back up your hard disk to floppies.

How **1.** Decide what you need to back up. If you think about it, many files seldom, if ever, change. If you organize your hard disk so that each application has a directory for its program files, and data files (documents) are in their own directories, you don't need to back up those tens of megabytes of program files. If something goes wrong, you can always reinstall the program from its installation disks, which you should have backup copies of.

2. Run the MSBACKUP program by typing `MSBACKUP` at the DOS prompt and pressing Enter:

```
C:\>msbackup
```

The first time you run MSBACKUP, the program will check out your hardware (disk drives, processor, etc.) and test it to determine its most efficient use. Just follow the prompts and make selections with the mouse, or by using the Tab key and pressing Enter. (You can press F1 at any time to get help.) MSBACKUP will make a small test backup and then compare the backed up files with the originals on your hard disk to ensure that it is making accurate backups.

3. Once MSBACKUP has configured itself for your system, you will see the program's main screen.

Choose the Backup button; you will see the Backup options screen, which looks like this:

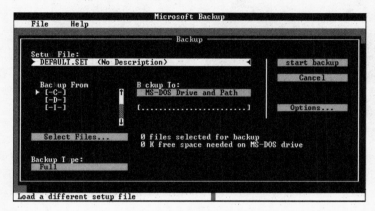

4. Make sure that you specify what drive you are backing up from and what drive you are backing up to. Normally, the defaults, which specify backing up from drive C: to drive A:, will be fine, though you might want to back up to drive B: instead if that is your 3.5-inch drive (3.5-inch disks hold a little more data than 5.25-inch disks, and they're easier to store). If you need to change any of the options shown on this screen, just click on the highlighted area (or use the Tab key and press Enter), and a menu of possible choices will pop up.

5. Now specify which files you are going to back up. If you want to back up everything on the hard drive, click on the drive letter in the Backup From box with the *right* mouse button, or move there with the Tab key and press the space bar.

6. If you just want to back up certain files, click on or select the Select Files button. You will see a screen that looks like this:

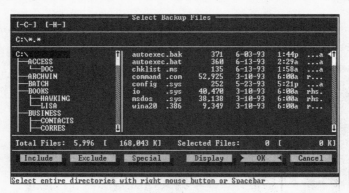

If you have worked with either the DOS Shell or the Windows File Manager, the format of this screen will look familiar. The window on the left shows your directory tree structure, with subdirectories indented under their parent directories. The window on the right has a list of files in the currently selected directory. To select a directory (and all of its files), click on the directory with the *right* mouse button, or use the arrow keys and space bar. To select just certain files in a directory, select the directory with the *left* mouse button or arrow keys and then use the mouse or arrow and spacebar keys in the file list window to select the files that you want to back up. Select the OK button at the bottom of the screen when you are through selecting files.

7. Another way to select files is to choose the Include button from the main Backup screen. You will see a dialog box that looks like this:

This box lets you select all files that match a particular file name pattern, without your having to select them "by hand." First, fill in the PATH specification with the directory from which you want to back up files. (If you do not want to include subdirectories of this directory, click on or select the Include All Subdirectories box to uncheck it.)

8. Now type in a file specification using wildcards. For example, if you want all .DOC files in the specified directory (and subdirectories, if checked) to be backed up, type *.DOC in the File specification. Click on or select the OK button to return to the Select files screen. You can make more than one file inclusion specification if you want, by repeatedly selecting the Include button. MSBACKUP keeps a list of all your inclusions and exclusions; you can review and edit them by selecting the Edit Include/Exclude List button from the Include or Exclude box.

9. You can do any combination of manual or automatic file selections that you want. You can also use the Exclude box, which works just like the Include box, except that it specifies a pattern for files that won't be backed up. A typical example would use the file pattern *.EXE to exclude all program files from the backup.

10. Once you've specified the files you want to back up, return to the main Backup screen by selecting the OK button. Note the message that tells you how many floppies you will need and approximately how long the backup process will take. If you have the time and enough disks, select Start Backup to begin the backup process. MSBACKUP will prompt you to insert disks, which need not be formatted, though they must all be of the same capacity.

Caution Be sure to label your backup disks in order! Include the "backup catalog number" that MSBACKUP assigns you. You will need this if you have to restore files later.

Notes • It can take some time to specify all your backup settings, including the drives to be used, directories to be backed up, and files to be included. Fortunately, MSBACKUP lets you save the current settings to a "setup file." To save the current settings, select Save Setup from the File menu on the main MSBACKUP screen.

Next time you back up, you can choose Open Setup to load a saved setup file. You can have several setup files for different backup needs, such as a full disk backup, a backup of document files only, or a backup of just a few key directories.

• For later backups, you may want to select the Backup Type button and change the kind of backup from full backup (the default) to "incremental" backup. An incremental backup backs up just those files that have been created or changed since the last full or incremental backup. If you use this method, you end up with a large set of floppies from the full backup plus separate sets that reflect the changes made since the last backup.

A "differential" backup is similar, except that each time it backs up everything that's been changed since the last full backup. With this method, you end up with your original full backup disk set and one new set that gradually grows larger as more files are changed.

• While running MSBACKUP, you can press F1 at any time to get help. Use these help screens and the DOS 6.0 *User's Guide* to learn about other options and features of the MSBACKUP program.

• DOS versions before 6.0 don't have MSBACKUP, but they do have a BACKUP command that can back up files and directories. To peform a backup, type BACKUP at the DOS prompt, followed by the drive and directory that you want to back up, and the drive to be backed up to. For example, type

```
C:\>backup c:\*.* a: /s
```

to back up all files on drive C: to a set of floppies in drive A:. The *.* specifies that all files are to be backed up, and the /s specifies that all subdirectories are to be included.

To back up all files that have a certain extension, type a command like this:

```
C:\>backup c:\*.doc a: /s
```

This specifies that all files on drive C: with the *.DOC extension will be backed up. The command

```
C:\>backup c:\writing\*.* b:
```

would back up all files in the C:\WRITING directory (but not any subdirectories) to drive B:.

To Check How Much Space Is Left on Your Hard Disk

Why Every once in a while, you should check to see how much space is left on your hard disk, in case it's getting too full. (You should always leave some empty space, since programs often create temporary files while they are running.) You might also want to check to make sure you have enough room to install a new program. (The program's installation guide should tell you how much disk space it needs.)

How Type CHKDSK and press Enter. (If you want to check a disk other than the current drive, add the drive letter and a colon.)

```
C:\>chkdsk
```

The resulting display will look like this:

```
Volume Serial Number is 1AB9-5397

199852032 bytes total disk space
  4210688 bytes in 7 hidden files
   622529 bytes in 135 directories
164212736 bytes in 4894 user files
 28147712 bytes available on disk
```
.... *This line tells you how much space is left on your disk.*

```
     4096 bytes in each allocation unit
    48792 total allocation units on disk
     6872 available allocation units on disk

   655360 total bytes memory
   578544 bytes free

C:\>
```

As you can see, this gives you a lot more information than just the remaining disk space; it also tells you how the space on your disk is being used and how much RAM you have available.

Notes • If you just want to find out how much room is on your hard disk, there is another way. Whenever you use the DIR command (see the recipe "To See a List of Files in the Current Directory"), the last line of the listing will tell you how much space is on the hard disk. The method I describe here, though, gives you a lot more information about the state of your system.

• Sometimes the CHKDSK report will tell you that there are errors on your hard disk. If it does, see the recipe "To Recover a Damaged File."

• If you are running CHKDSK from a DOS prompt in Windows, you will often get an error message, even when nothing is wrong. It is best to exit Windows completely before running CHKDSK.

To Check for Viruses

Why Just about everyone has read about how computer viruses can stealthily enter a system and destroy precious data. While the risk of viruses has been somewhat exaggerated, it's a good idea to check your system regularly to find and remove any viral "infections" before they threaten your data and programs. DOS 6.0 has a built-in virus protection utility that will help you.

How **1.** Type **MSAV** at the DOS prompt and press Enter:

```
C:\>msav
```

You will see a screen like this:

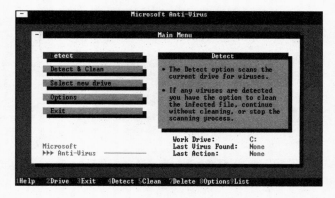

2. To scan for viruses on the current disk drive (probably C:), press Enter to choose the Detect option. If you want MSAV to automatically detect and remove any viruses it finds without prompting you, you can choose Detect & Clean instead of Detect.

The MSAV program will first check memory (RAM) for viruses, and then it will check the files on the disk. This may take several minutes, depending on the size of your hard disk. When the scanning is completed, and if you've chosen Detect rather than Detect & Clean, you will see a report like this:

3. If a virus is found during the scanning process, you will see a dialog box that tells you what type of virus was found and where. The dialog box will include buttons you can use to tell MSAV how to proceed. Press Enter to choose the Clean button and remove the virus from the UTIL.EXE program. If this operation is successful, the virus will be gone.

Notes • MSAV has some additional options I won't talk about here. After running MSAV, you can press F1 at any time to get information about them.

• Sometimes a virus will have already damaged a program, rendering it unusable even after the virus has been removed. In that case, you'll need to reinstall the software.

• DOS 6.0 also includes a program called VSAFE that checks for viruses on an ongoing basis. You can read about it in your DOS 6.0 *User's Guide.*

• MSAV and VSAFE use a file called MSAVIRUS.LST to get information on what various viruses act like. The folks who make computer viruses are always at work, so it's a good idea to keep this file up to date. See Appendix D of the DOS 6.0 *User's Guide* for information on how to obtain updated versions of this file.

• If you have a version of DOS earlier than 6.0, you will need to get a virus-protection program from another source. See Chapter 42 for more on virus protection.

To Copy a Floppy Disk

Why You will probably need to make copies of disks fairly often. Before you install a new software product, for example, it's a good idea to make a backup copy of each of the installation disks. You can copy all the files on a floppy by using the COPY command (see the "To Copy a File" recipe). The method I'll describe here makes an exact copy of the floppy, including any hidden files on it. Generally, you'll use this method to copy software installation disks and boot disks, and you'll use COPY or XCOPY to copy sets of files from floppy disks to your hard disk (and vice versa).

How **1.** Write-protect the disk you want to copy. This will ensure that, if you do get your disks mixed up in the following procedure, no harm will be done. Now put the disk in your floppy drive. (See Chapter 29 for more on write-protecting disks.)

2. Type `DISKCOPY`, followed by the letter of the drive containing the disk to be copied (the "source disk") and the letter of the drive that will contain the copy (the "destination disk"). For example:

```
C:\>diskcopy a: a:
```

The above command assumes that you have just one floppy disk drive of a single size. If you have two floppy drives of the same size, you can use this command:

```
C:\>diskcopy a: b:
```

If you are using the same drive for source and destination, DOS will prompt you to exchange disks in the drive as necessary.

After you press Enter, DOS will tell you to

```
Insert SOURCE diskette in drive A:
Press any key to continue . . .
```

3. Make sure the disk you want to copy is in drive A:, and then press any key on the keyboard. DOS will begin to copy the disk, displaying a message about disk tracks and sectors, which you can ignore.

When DOS has read its first batch of information, it will display the message:

```
Insert TARGET diskette in drive A:
Press any key to continue . . .
```

When you see that message, remove the first disk, insert the disk you want the first disk copied to into drive A:, and then press any key on the keyboard. DOS will copy the information it read from the source disk to the target disk.

If you're using a single disk drive, you will probably need to switch disks several times. DOS will tell you when.

Notes
• DISKCOPY formats the target disk and erases all data on that disk, so be sure to use a disk that is either blank or that has information that you no longer need.

• Since DISKCOPY makes an identical physical copy of the disk, you can't use DISKCOPY to copy a disk from a 5.25-inch drive to a 3.5-inch drive, or vice versa.

To Create More Disk Space

Why Remember when I said that you'd use up your hard disk space faster than you ever imagined? You should review your directories and files periodically and delete unneeded files. You can also create more disk space by using CHKDSK to recover and delete any "lost" disk sectors. But once you've done all that and still need more space, it's time for a disk compression program.

DOS 6.0 has a compression utiltiy, called DoubleSpace, built in. It allows you to "compress" files so that you can store about twice as much data on your hard disk as you were able to before. (For example, a hard disk with 20 MB of free capacity could have as much as 40 MB after compression.)

How **1.** Exit any programs you are running (including Windows, if you're running it).

2. Although the chance of something going wrong during the compression process is very small, you should back up the files on your hard disk before running DoubleSpace. (See the "To Back Up Your Hard Disk" recipe to find out how to use the MSBACKUP command.)

3. Type `DBLSPACE` at the DOS prompt, and press Enter:

```
C:\>dblspace
```

4. Read the welcome screen that DBLSPACE displays, and then press Enter. Assuming that you want to compress drive C:, press Enter again to choose Express Setup. DBLSPACE will take it from there. It will compress all the files on drive C:, except for certain system files used by DOS and Windows. The process may take as long as several hours, depending on how fast your PC is and how much data is on the disk. (You might want to let it run overnight or before a very long lunch.)

When DBLSPACE is finished, you will find that drive C: now has about twice as much space as it had before.

You will also find that DOS has created another drive, usually called drive H: (in some cases, DOS uses another letter), that contains system files that DBLSPACE is unable to compress.

The compressed drive C: works in exactly the same way as the old, uncompressed one did. You simply continue to use your programs and DOS commands as before. (There are a few games and utility programs that may not run properly from a compressed drive, but you can copy them over to the new, uncompressed drive H:.)

Caution DOS creates a hidden file called DBLSPACE.000 on the new drive H. You won't see it when you display the directory of drive H:. Whatever you do, don't mess with that file. It contains information DOS needs so it can find all the data on your hard disk; changing or deleting that file will erase all the data from your hard disk.

Notes • You can compress a disk other than drive C: by choosing Custom Setup rather than Express Setup. Floppy disks as well as hard disks can be compressed.

• You can get on-line help while running DoubleSpace. Press F1 for helpful explanations of other features of the DoubleSpace utility.

• If your AUTOEXEC.BAT or CONFIG.SYS file has a command that includes the SMARTDRV.EXE disk cache, you may get an error message the first time you start your system after using DoubleSpace. You can solve the problem by changing SmartDrive's default drive to the new drive H: rather than to C:. (Ask an expert for advice if you have this problem.)

To Format a Floppy Disk

Why Before you use any floppy disk, you must "format" it with DOS so that it will accept information. (A few brands of disks are available preformatted for convenience.)

Reformatting disks you've already used erases them and gets them ready to be used again.

How **1.** Put the disk to be formatted in a floppy drive. Type FORMAT, followed by the letter of the drive containing the disk. For example, to format the disk in drive A:, type:

```
C:\>format a:
```

Because this command destroys any information on the target disk, DOS is pretty careful about executing it. Before it goes ahead and formats the disk in the specified drive, it gives you a chance to make sure you have the right disk in there, displaying the command:

```
Insert new diskette for drive A:
and press ENTER when ready . . .
```

After you insert the disk you want to format and press Enter, DOS displays messages showing its progress through the formatting procedure.

When it's done, DOS displays the message:

```
Format complete
Volume label (11 characters, ENTER for none)?
```

2. If you want to give the disk an electronic label, type in the name you want to use for the label and press Enter; otherwise, just press Enter.

DOS will display information about the amount of disk space available and show you the serial number it has assigned to the disk. DOS will then ask:

```
Format another (Y/N)?
```

3. Press **Y** to repeat the process with another disk, or **N** to return to the DOS prompt.

Notes • To make a disk that you can use to start the system (a "boot disk"), add the /s option to the FORMAT command:

```
C:\>format a: /s
```

It's a good idea to have a couple of boot disks so that you can start your system if something goes wrong with the hard disk.

• If you have a disk that is already formatted and contains information, and you just want to wipe it clean to use for another project, add the /q option to your FORMAT command. This does a "quick format."

• By default, FORMAT uses the full capacity of the floppy drive. For nearly all machines sold today, that means that FORMAT will make high-density disks (1.4-MB 3.5-inch disks or 1.2-MB 5.25-inch disks). Make sure that you use disks that say "high density" on their label. A "double density" disk formatted as high density will be unreliable. If you need to format double-density rather than high-density disks, use the command

```
C:\>format /f:720
```

for 3.5-inch (720-K) disks, or use

```
C:\>format /f:360
```

for 5.25-inch (360-K) disks.

To Recover a Damaged File

Why You sit down to work on your report. You try to open REPORT.DOC. Instead of your immortal words, you see an error message. If you have a current backup of your important files, this is not a disaster. But if you don't, you may still be able to recover most, if not all, of your data.

How **1.** Exit your application program (and Microsoft Windows or the DOS Task Swapper, if they are running). If you try to "fix" a file that is in use by some other program, the file may be permanently damaged.

2. Now give your hard disk a quick checkup. At the DOS prompt, type `CHKDSK` and press Enter:

```
C:\>chkdsk
```

CHKDSK will print a report that gives information about your hard disk and available memory. If one or more files have had their cluster lists damaged, you will see a report like this:

```
Volume DBL_DISK created 05-10-1993 2:11p
Volume Serial Number is 11E5-3D3E

Errors found, F parameter not specified
Corrections will not be written to disk

  649 lost allocation units found in 19 chains.
  2658304 bytes disk space would be freed

199852032 bytes total disk space
  4210688 bytes in 7 hidden files
   622529 bytes in 135 directories
164212736 bytes in 4894 user files
 28147712 bytes available on disk
```

```
 4096 bytes in each allocation unit
48792 total allocation units on disk
 6872 available allocation units on disk

655360 total bytes memory
578544 bytes free
```

```
C:\>
```

In another case, the second block of text might read something like this:

```
PROPOSAL.TXT is cross linked on allocation unit 18
ADDRESS.DAT is cross linked on allocation unit 18
```

You don't need to understand what this means, but pay attention to which message it shows.

3. If it says a file is "cross linked," try copying the file to another location on the disk (see the "To Copy a File" recipe). Then try opening the file with your application program (assuming it is a text file). Most of the file should be intact, though some data might be missing.

4. If it says "lost clusters," run the CHKDSK command again, but this time add the /f switch:

```
C:\>chkdsk /f
```

As it displays its report, CHKDSK will ask you whether you want to "convert lost chains to files?" Press y, and DOS will save the recovered information in a file called FILE0000.CHK in the root directory of the current disk. (If there is more than one set of lost clusters, DOS will create FILE0001.CHK, FILE0002.CHK, and so on, with one file for each set of lost clusters.)

5. You can now use your word processor or a text editor (such as the EDIT program that comes with DOS) to examine the recovered files to see if they contain useful data. This may enable you to recover part of a text document or database file.

6. If you decide that the data in a .CHK file is useful, use the REN command to give the file a more meaningful name (see the "To Change the Name of a File" recipe). If the data turns out to be useless, use the DEL command to delete the .CHK file and free up the disk space (see the "To Delete a File" recipe).

Notes • You cannot recover a program file. Instead, you'll need to put a fresh copy of the program file on your disk.

• CHKDSK cannot recover data if the disk is unreadable because of a hardware problem. However, some third-party utilities may be able to recover at least part of such data. (Utilities are covered in Chapter 42.)

To Restore a Disk You've Formatted

Why You discover that you have formatted a disk that had the only copy of some important files on it. Sometimes DOS will be able to get your files back—and sometimes it won't. It's worth a try.

How **1.** Type **UNFORMAT**, followed by the letter of the drive you will use for the floppy disk, and press Enter. For example:

```
C:\>unformat a:
```

DOS will display the message:

```
Insert disk to rebuild in drive A
and press ENTER when ready . . .
```

2. Put the disk in the drive and press Enter. DOS will display a screen of warnings, telling you that you should use this command only on a disk that you've used the FORMAT command on. At the end of the message will be the line:

```
Are you sure you want to update the system area of
your drive A (Y/N)?
```

3. It sounds a bit scary, but press **Y**. DOS will rebuild the disk. Then it will display

```
The system area of drive A has been rebuilt.
You may need to restart the system.
```

and will show the DOS prompt again.

Notes • The UNFORMAT command is available starting with DOS 5.0. Users of earlier DOS versions can obtain this capability as part of popular utility packages such as Norton Utilities and PC Tools.

To Restore a File You've Deleted

Why You've goofed with the DEL command, and you've erased something you want back. If you act promptly, before you've saved anything else to the disk, you may be able to get it back.

How **1.** Type **UNDELETE**, followed by the name of the file to be undeleted. For example:

```
C:\>undelete \business\corres\order.doc
```

DOS will examine the situation and report what it finds:

```
Directory: C:\BUSINESS\CORRES
File Specifications: ORDER.DOC
   Delete Sentry control file not found.
    Delete-tracking file not found.
   MS-DOS directory contains 1 deleted files.
   Of these, 1 files may be recovered.
Using the MS-DOS directory method.
   ?RDER.DOC    371 5-27-93 10:24a ..A Undelete (Y/N)?
   Please type the first character for ?RDER.DOC:
```

2. When DOS deleted the file, it marked the file as deleted by erasing the first character of the file name. Now, DOS needs to know what that character was. Usually, you can figure it out from context. (Here, you would probably type *o*.) After you've supplied the letter, DOS will respond:

```
File successfully undeleted.
```

(If you used a wildcard, as in the command "UNDELETE *.TXT," DOS may have found more than one deleted file. If so, you'll be prompted to undelete each one in turn.)

Notes • Undelete is available starting with DOS 5.0. Similar functions are provided by many third-party general utility programs such as PC Tools and Norton Utilities.

• UNDELETE is most reliable when used immediately after you delete the file. If you continue to work after accidentally deleting a file, you decrease the chance that UNDELETE will recover your file.

• For extra security, DOS 6.0 provides two additonal kinds of protection against accidental file deletion. Delete Sentry stores "deleted" files in a special area on the disk from which they can be recovered if you change your mind about deleting them. Delete Tracker keeps track of information that makes it more likely that DOS will be able to restore deleted files. See your DOS *User's Guide* or type **HELP UNDELETE** at the DOS prompt for more information on setting up those features.

To Restore Files You've Backed Up With MSBACKUP

Why It finally happened. You try to use a file and you get a message telling you the file is damaged. Or perhaps you've deleted a file and you can't recover it with the procedures described in the "To Restore a File You've Deleted" recipe. Fortunately, you've made a backup...

How 1. Type MSBACKUP at the DOS prompt, and press Enter:

```
C:\>msbackup
```

2. In the main backup screen, choose the Restore button by clicking on it with the mouse or by using the Tab key and pressing Enter.

The Restore screen shown below will appear:

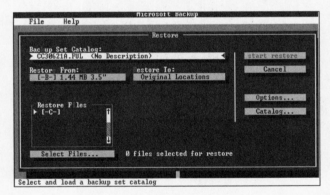

3. Click on (or select) the Backup Set Catalog button. From the list of catalogs that appears, find the catalog number that matches the one that you've put on the label of the disk set from which you'll be restoring files. (I hope you wrote it on your backup disks. I told you you would need it.) Click on the catalog name or highlight it with the arrow keys and press Enter.

4. In the same way, open the Restore From list box, and select the drive that contains the files that you want to restore.

5. If you want to restore all the files on the disks in your backup set, press the spacebar while the drive letter is highlighted (or click on the drive letter with the mouse).

6. If you want to restore only certain files, press Enter. The Select Restore Files screen will appear:

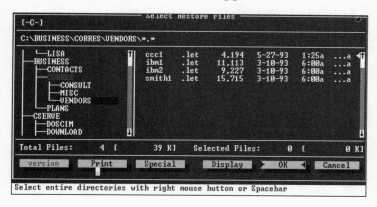

This screen works in much the same way as the one you used to select files to back up. (See the "To Back Up Your Hard Disk" recipe.) Choose a directory to which you want to restore files. If you want to restore only certain files in the directory, select the files to be restored from the file list window. Repeat until you have selected all directories and files to be restored.

7. By default, files will be restored to their original locations. If you want to restore the files to a different drive and/or directory, open the Restore To box and specify the location to which you wish to restore the files.

8. Choose the Start Restore button to begin restoring files. DOS will prompt you when it is time to insert a disk in the drive.

Notes • Be careful not to restore an older copy of a file over a newer one (unless that's what you want to do). To guard against this, you can open the Options box and check the Prompt Before Overwriting Existing Files box. DOS will then warn you when a restored file would overwrite an existing one, and you can decide whether to restore that file.

• Versions of DOS earlier than 6.0 don't have the MSBACKUP command. They use the BACKUP command to back up files and the RESTORE command to restore them. To use the RESTORE command, type **RESTORE** followed by the letter of the drive containing the first backup disk, and then type the path of the drive and/or directory to which the files are to be restored. For example,

```
C:\>restore a: c:\*.* /s
```

restores all files on the backup disks in drive A: to their locations on the hard drive C:. The /s option tells DOS to restore the files to their original subdirectories. In this example,

```
C:\>restore a: c:\corres\report.oct
```

restores just the REPORT.OCT file in the CORRES directory in drive C: from the backup disk in drive A:.

RESTORE will prompt you to insert disks as necessary. To have RESTORE prompt you before overwriting newer files with older ones, add the /p option to your RESTORE command.

To Add a PATH Command to Your AUTOEXEC.BAT File

Why You can run a program from any directory by supplying a path before the program command on the DOS command line, but it's easy to forget to do that. To make it easy on yourself, you can set up a special command in your AUTOEXEC.BAT file that lists directories you want DOS to look in when you type a command on the DOS command line. If the program or command you want to run is in any of the directories listed there, DOS will find it without your having to type the path each time.

Caution Before making any changes to your AUTOEXEC.BAT file or your CONFIG.SYS file, it's a good idea to be sure you have a floppy boot disk available just in case you do something that makes it hard to start your PC. For information on creating a bootable floppy disk, see the Notes section of the "To Format a Floppy Disk" recipe.

How 1. Before you start editing AUTOEXEC.BAT (or any other important file), make a backup copy of it. You can do this with the command:

```
C:\>copy autoexec.bat autoexec.bak
```

This makes a copy called AUTOEXEC.BAK in the same (root) directory. Now, if you make a mistake while you're editing the file, such as accidentally changing something you didn't mean to change, you can just restore the original file by reversing this command—copying AUTOEXEC.BAK to a new AUTOEXEC.BAT file.

2. Now open your AUTOEXEC.BAT file with a text editor, such as the EDIT command that comes with DOS:

```
C:\>edit autoexec.bat
```

3. Find the line in your AUTOEXEC.BAT file that begins with the word PATH. It will look something like this:

`PATH C:\DOS;C:\WINDOWS`

(The list of directories in the PATH statement will vary according to how your system was set up.)

4. Use the arrow keys to move the cursor to the end of the PATH statement (or just click there with the mouse). Add a semicolon followed by the directory for the application program that you want DOS to be able to find. For example, if you have a directory C:\WP that contains your word processor, add it to the PATH statement above so that it looks like this:

`PATH C:\DOS;C:\WINDOWS;C:\WP`

5. Save the revised file (in EDIT, click on the File menu with the mouse and then click on the Save command, or press the Alt key, then type **F**, then **S**). The new PATH setting will take effect the next time you start your PC. Now you can type the name of your word processing program and run it no matter where you are on the disk.

Notes • If your AUTOEXEC.BAT file doesn't have an existing PATH command, you'll need to start a new line for it. To do that, just move your cursor to the end of any line in the file and press Enter, then type **PATH**, a space, and the path to the directory you want to include. At the end of the line, press Enter again so that the PATH statement is on its own line.

• You can edit the AUTOEXEC.BAT file with any word processor that can save files in ASCII format. EDIT is the easiest to use, and everyone with a version of DOS later than 5.0 has it. If you use a different word processor, make sure you save the file in ASCII (plain-text) format.

To Run a Program Automatically

Why If you have a utility program or DOS command that you want to automatically run each time you use your PC, you can add that file to your AUTOEXEC.BAT file. For example, you may want to run your word processing program each time you start your PC.

Caution Before making any changes to your AUTOEXEC.BAT file or your CONFIG.SYS file, it's a good idea to be sure you have a floppy boot disk available just in case you do something that makes it hard to start your PC. For information on creating a bootable floppy disk, see the Notes section of the "To Format a Floppy Disk" recipe.

How **1.** Before you start editing AUTOEXEC.BAT (or any other important file), make a backup copy of it. You can do this with the command:

```
C:\>copy autoexec.bat autoexec.bak
```

This makes a copy called AUTOEXEC.BAK in the same (root) directory. Now, if you make a mistake while you're editing the file, you can just restore the original file by reversing this command—copying AUTOEXEC.BAK to a new AUTOEXEC.BAT file.

2. Now open your AUTOEXEC.BAT file with a text editor, such as the EDIT program that comes with DOS:

```
C:\>edit autoexec.bat
```

3. Use the arrow keys to move to the end of the file (or click on the end of the last line with the mouse). Then press Enter to start a new line.

4. Type in the command that you want to run. Follow the program name with any parameters and options that you usually use with the program. For example, to run WordPerfect, you would add this line:

`WP`

5. Save the revised file. (In EDIT, you do this by clicking on the File menu with the mouse and then clicking on the Save command, or by pressing the Alt key, then typing `F`, then `S`). The program will now run automatically each time you start your PC.

Notes • You can put any DOS command in your AUTOEXEC.BAT file and DOS will run it automatically on startup.

• You can edit the AUTOEXEC.BAT file with any word processor that can save files in ASCII format. EDIT is the easiest to use, and everyone with a version of DOS later than 5.0 has it. If you use a different word processor, make sure you save the file in ASCII (plain-text) format.

To Change Your CONFIG.SYS File

Why When you buy a new piece of add-on hardware (such as a mouse), you will often need to install a driver program for it in the CONFIG.SYS file. You may also need to change CONFIG.SYS to accommodate a piece of software that requires special FILES or BUFFERS settings. Often, installation software that comes with the hardware or software will make the changes automatically, or after prompting you for permission. If it doesn't, you will need to edit CONFIG.SYS, which is in your hard disk's root directory, to make the changes yourself.

Caution Before making any changes to your AUTOEXEC.BAT file or your CONFIG.SYS file, it's a good idea to be sure you have a floppy boot disk available just in case you do something that makes it hard to start your PC. For information on creating a bootable floppy disk, see the Notes section of the "To Format a Floppy Disk" recipe.

How **1.** First, make a backup copy of your CONFIG.SYS file by entering a command like this:

```
C:\>copy config.sys config.bak
```

This copies CONFIG.SYS to a new file called CONFIG.BAK in the root directory. Now, if something goes wrong while you're editing CONFIG.SYS, you can just reverse this command, copying CONFIG.BAK to CONFIG.SYS, and start over again.

2. Now open CONFIG.SYS with DOS's Edit program, using this command:

```
C:\>edit config.sys
```

3. Use the arrow keys (or click the mouse) to go to the place in the text where you want to make changes. (If you need to, you can press F1 to get help with EDIT's commands.)

4. Insert a new line (by pressing Enter) or change an existing line as necessary. The installation instructions in the user's manual for the hardware or software you are installing should tell you what to change.

5. When your changes are complete, save the file (in EDIT, click on the File menu with the mouse and then click on the Save command, or press the Alt key, then type **F**, then **S**).

6. Reboot your PC (by pressing Ctrl-Alt-Delete) so that your changes will take effect.

To Change Your System Date

Why Your PC contains a battery-powered clock that keeps track of the date and time even when the PC isn't running. If the battery runs down or is accidentally disconnected, you will need to reset the date for the PC's clock.

How 1. Type DATE and press Enter:

```
C:\>date
```

DOS will display a message like this:

```
Current date is Mon 05-10-1993
Enter new date (mm-dd-yy):
```

2. Type the correct numbers for the month, day, and year, separated by dashes. For example, to set the date to June 12, 1993, you would type 06-12-93. Press Enter, and DOS will set the clock to the new date.

Notes • If you don't want to see the current date before you set it, you can take a shortcut by typing DATE followed by the new date and then pressing Enter:

```
C:\>date 06-12-93
```

• If you don't want to set a new time, but just want to see what the current clock time is, just press Enter again without entering a new date.

To Change Your System Time

Why The PC doesn't know about Daylight Savings Time, so you'll probably have to change your system clock's time at least twice a year. Also, PC clocks are not 100 percent accurate so, over time, your clock may run a little fast or slow.

How **1.** Type **TIME** and press Enter:

```
C:\>time
```

DOS will display the current setting and ask for a new one:

```
Current time is 12:43:03.80p
Enter new time:
```

2. Type the correct numbers for the hours and minutes, separated by a colon (:). (The seconds are optional.) Follow the time with *p* for PM or *a* for AM. For example, to set the time to 1:43 PM, you would type **1:43p**. Press Enter, and DOS will set the clock to the new time.

Notes • If you don't need to see the current time, you can just type **TIME** followed by the new time, and then press Enter:

```
C:\>time 1:43p
```

To Create a Batch File

Why Say you frequently use a particular series of DOS commands or programs, and you'd like to be able to run them automatically without having to type them in each time. Or perhaps you have a command or program that uses a lot of options, and you don't want to have to remember (and type in) all the options each time you use the command. You can set up a batch file to give such commands automatically.

How **1.** Open DOS's Edit program by typing `EDIT` at the DOS prompt and pressing Enter:

```
C:\>edit
```

2. In the editor, type in the DOS command lines that you want the batch file to execute. Type one command per line and press Enter, just as you would when entering commands at the DOS prompt. For example:

```
@echo off
cls
dir /o:n /w
```

The first command, "@echo off," is a special batch file command that prevents the lines of the batch file from being "echoed" or displayed on the screen as the batch file runs.

The second command, "cls," clears the screen to make it easy to see the directory listing that is about to come.

The third command, "dir /o:n /w," uses two switches with the DIR command. The /o:n switch sorts the file names in the directory listing into alphabetical order. The second option, /w, displays a "wide" directory listing that fits as many file names as possible on the screen. (See the "To See a List of Files in the Current Directory" recipe.)

3. Save the file (in EDIT, click on the File menu with the mouse and then click on the Save command, or press the Alt key, then type **F**, then **S**). When asked for a file name, type in a name that describes what your batch file does, followed by the extension .BAT. (A batch file can have any legal file name, but it must have an extension of .BAT so DOS will recognize that it is a batch file.) Let's say you choose the name WDIR.BAT (for "Wide DIR").

4. Once you have your WDIR.BAT file, you can execute it by typing **WDIR** at the DOS prompt and pressing Enter. (You don't have to type the .BAT extension.) A batch file acts just like a regular DOS command or program.

Notes • As with a program, you must add a path to the batch file name if you're not in the directory that contains the batch file. Many people find it useful to create a directory called \BATCH that holds all their batch files and then add that directory to the PATH command in the AUTOEXEC.BAT file. (To learn how to change your PATH, see the "To Add a PATH Command to Your AUTOEXEC.BAT File" recips.)

• There are a number of special commands that you can use in batch files that let you add parameters to the batch file command, perform an action on each of a group of files, or ask the person running the batch file a question and make a decision based on the answer, among other things. For more information on batch files, see your MS-DOS manual or type **HELP BATCH** at the DOS prompt.

To Find Out What Version of DOS You're Running

DOS Cookbook

Why Some programs require a certain version of DOS to run, and sometimes, when you call a help line, the technician will want to know what version of DOS you're running. DOS includes a command that gives you that information.

How Type VER at the DOS prompt, and press Enter:

```
C:\>ver
```

You'll see a message like this:

```
MS-DOS Version 6.00
```

In this example, you're running DOS 6.0.

Notes • The part of the version number in front of the decimal point (6 in this case) is the most important piece of information. Versions with numbers like .1 or .01 after them represent only minor changes in features.

To Give Your Programs More Memory

Why You try to run a program, and you get an "insufficient memory" (or similar) message. You know you have 4 MB, 8 MB, or even more memory in your PC, so what gives? The problem is that DOS uses the first 640 K of memory for special purposes, and a program may not run well (or at all) if enough of that special memory isn't available—even if there is plenty of other memory. DOS 6.0 includes a program you can use to free up the "conventional" memory that other programs use.

How **1.** First, do a little housekeeping. Check your AUTOEXEC.BAT and CONFIG.SYS files to see if they run any programs that you don't need (for example, a driver for a piece of hardware that you no longer use). Delete those commands or put the word *REM* (it stands for "remark") in front of those lines to inactivate them. Then reboot your PC so that the revised AUTOEXEC.BAT and CONFIG.SYS files take effect. (If Windows or the DOS Shell starts running, exit it.)

2. Check how much memory your system has by typing MEM at the DOS prompt and pressing Enter:

```
C:\>mem
```

DOS will display a report that looks like this:

```
Memory Type  Total = Used + Free
-----------  -----  ----  ----
Conventional  640K   59K  581K
Upper         91K    91K  0K
Adapter RAM/ROM 384K  384K  0K

Extended (XMS)  7077K 6053K 1024K
-----------   -----  ----  ----
Total memory   8192K 6587K 1605K
Total under 1 MB 731K  150K  581K
```

```
Total Expanded (EMS)        1024K (1048576 bytes)
Free Expanded (EMS)         1024K (1048576 bytes)
Largest executable program size  581K (594560 bytes)
Largest free upper memory block  0K  (0 bytes)
MS-DOS is resident in the high memory area.
```

I know it looks intimidating, but don't worry. Right now, you're only concerned with the number that tells you how much free "conventional" memory you've got. In the example, 581 K out of 640 K of this memory is available.

3. Now type **MEMMAKER** at the DOS prompt, and press Enter:

```
C:\>memmaker
```

4. When you've seen enough of the welcome screen that appears, press Enter to continue. MEMMAKER will now ask you to choose between Express and Custom Setup.

5. Press Enter to choose Express.

MEMMAKER now asks if you have any programs that require "expanded memory." Unless you are sure you have such programs, press Enter to choose No. (Today's programs tend to use extended rather than expanded memory, or they can use both. Don't worry about the difference between the two.)

6. If you have Windows on your system, MEMMAKER may ask you for some more information. Follow the screen prompts and answer the questions (they're pretty simple).

7. MEMMAKER now says that it is ready to restart (reboot) your PC. (It has to do this in order to watch how your AUTOEXEC.BAT and CONFIG.SYS files load stuff into memory). Press Enter to give it permission. MEMMAKER will analyze your memory and make appropriate changes in your AUTOEXEC.BAT and CONFIG.SYS files.

8. When MEMMAKER is done, press Enter to start your PC with the new configuration. If the screen "freezes," or if programs being loaded from your AUTOEXEC.BAT or CONFIG.SYS files give error messages, try to make a note of the messages. If any problems occur, see the troubleshooting guides in Chapter 6 of the DOS 6.0 *User's Guide.* Otherwise, when your system has restarted, MEMMAKER will display a screen summarizing how much memory it has freed up for you. If the amount of memory available after MEMMAKER ran is less than the amount you started with, see the "Undoing the Changes MemMaker Made" section in Chapter 6 of the DOS 6.0 *User's Guide.*

Notes • For more information on the Custom Setup options for MEMMAKER, see Chapter 6 of the DOS 6.0 *User's Guide.*

The Windows Cookbook

cookbooks

The Windows Cookbook

Working With Documents 298

Managing Files and Directories 309

Housekeeping Tasks 328

Windows Cookbook

Using Windows

As I described in Chapter 5, Windows is more than just a friendly interface for DOS—it defines a whole way of working with your computer, based on using the mouse to select and manipulate text, graphics, and program controls on screen. Everything you do in Windows, and also in any program written to work with Windows, uses many of the same basic commands and the same ways of working with the mouse.

This Windows Cookbook isn't intended to teach you how to use Windows and Windows programs. Instead, it focuses on leading you through the basic tasks you will need to do with Windows itself as you work with your PC: managing programs, files, and directories. Many of these tasks, such as copying files, creating directories, and so on, are the same ones I described in the DOS Cookbook. (You can do them either in DOS or Windows.)

As you'll quickly find out, there are many ways of doing almost everything in Windows. In this cookbook, I don't explain them all. Instead, I usually just provide the way I think is easiest. Although it's possible to do every task from the keyboard, without using the mouse at all, I describe how the tasks are done with the mouse because, usually, that's the easiest way to do them. In a few cases, I'll provide alternative methods of doing the same thing because I think you will sometimes find it easier to do those things one way, sometimes another. In any case, I encourage you to use Windows' on-line help (described in the recipe "To Get Help With a Windows Program or Command") to find out about all the other things you can do in Windows and all the ways you can do them. The best way to learn the basics of Windows is to run the Windows Tutorial by choosing it from the Help menu in the Program Manager, which will familiarize you with basic mouse and keyboard techniques.

Now, before you go on, take a minute to become familiar with the illustrations on the next couple of pages. They introduce you to the basic parts of Windows and the on-screen controls you will be using in the recipes that follow.

The Program Manager

The first thing you will see when you start Windows is the Windows Program Manager. This is where you set up and launch programs—your main control panel.

The Program Manager, like any other program in Windows, has a menu bar across the top, from which you can choose commands.

This is the icon for the window control menu. You can click on it once to show its commands or click on it twice to close the Window.

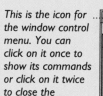

These icons show what programs are available in the program group. You can select an icon by clicking on it, or open it by double-clicking on it.

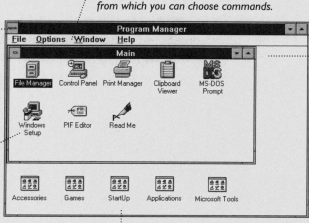

This is the Main program group, open on screen. This group contains some of the most important icons, including the File Manager and MS-DOS Prompt icons.

These are icons for program groups. You can open a program group by double-clicking on its icon.

The File Manager

The File Manager is where you open and organize directories and files in Windows. You open it by double-clicking on its icon in the Program Manager.

The title bar of the directory window shows the path of the current directory.

These disk icons show the drives on your computer. The current drive is boxed.

The left side of a File Manager window displays the directory structure of the current drive. Each folder stands for a directory. The open folder is the current directory.

The file list at the right side of the directory window shows the files in the current directory.

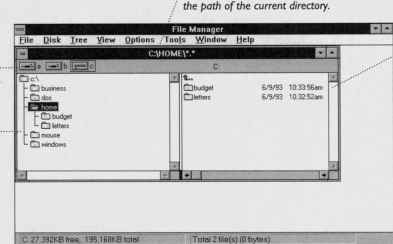

Dialog Boxes

The other kind of controls you'll see in Windows are in **dialog boxes**. Dialog boxes often appear on screen when you use a menu command. They supply a place where you can provide more information that will help Windows or the application program carry out the command. (When a menu command has three dots following its name, that means it has a dialog box associated with it.) For example, when you choose the Open command from the File menu in a Windows program, you will get a box that looks something like the one at right.

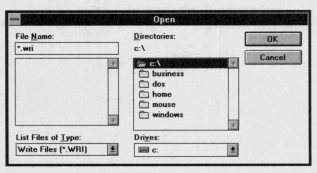

Dialog boxes have several different kinds of controls in them, which you will also find in application windows and other places throughout Windows and Windows programs. Here's a guide to how to use them.

Buttons are generally rectangular, tinted, and look sort of three-dimensional. To activate the command written on the button, you click on it.

Check boxes list options that you can either turn on or off. When the box has an X in it, the option is chosen. You can check a box (put an X in it), or uncheck it, if it is already chosen, by clicking on it.

When you can choose only one option of a set, the options are provided with **radio buttons**. Clicking on one button will select it and deselect the others in the set.

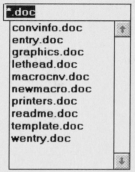

Text boxes provide a space where you can type your choice.

```
┌New──────────────────┐
│ ○ Program Group      │
│ ◉ Program Item       │
└─────────────────────┘
```

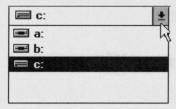

Sometimes a text box or other field will have a **drop-down list** associated with it. That means there are a limited number of choices you can make there. To see a list of possible choices, you click on the text box or on the down arrow at its right. Then you can select an entry in the list by clicking on it.

To Choose a Menu Command

Why In Windows and in Windows applications, almost all commands are available in menus, which are listed in a menu bar at the top of the screen. You can easily see the major commands in any program by browsing through its menus.

How 1. In the menu bar, click on the name of the menu you want to use, or press Alt and the letter that is underlined in the menu name. The menu will drop down.

2. Click on the name of the command you want to use, or type the letter that is underlined in the command name.

3. If a dialog box appears, choose the available options from each field in the dialog box. When you are finished, click on OK, or cancel the command by clicking on Cancel.

You can either click the menu name or press Alt and type the underlined letter in the menu name (in this case F) to drop down the menu.

You can either click the command name or type the underlined letter in the command name (in this case U) to activate the command.

If the command has a keyboard shortcut, it is listed next to the command name on the menu.

If the command name is followed by three dots, a dialog box will appear, in which you will need to supply extra information before the command is executed.

Notes • Many menu commands have keyboard shortcuts associated with them—keys you can press instead of using the menus. If a command has a keyboard shortcut, it is listed next to the command name in the menu.

• When you choose some more complicated commands, you will open a "submenu" that presents additional choices. Just click on the appropriate choice in the submenu, or type its underlined letter.

• If a menu command is grayed (appears in dim text), it means that the command is not currently available or isn't relevant to you at that point.

• If you open a menu and decide you don't want to choose a command from it after all, you can just click on the menu name again, and the menu will disappear.

To Get Help With a Windows Program or Command

Why Whenever you don't know how to do something in Windows or in a Windows application, the first place to turn to is the on-line help. Most Windows programs have a Help menu from which you can choose a topic, and many Windows dialog boxes include a help button, which brings up information directly related to the task at hand. Different applications have different options in their Help menus, but the commands listed here are pretty standard.

How **1.** To bring up a list of topics, press F1. (Alternatively, you can click on the Help menu (Alt H), and choose Help Index or Help Contents to get to the same point.) A list of available help topics will appear.

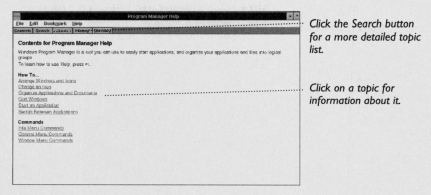

Click the Search button for a more detailed topic list.

Click on a topic for information about it.

2. When the Help window appears, click on the topic you want information about, and Windows will display a more detailed index of the topic, or help on that topic. If you don't see a topic that looks right, click on the Search button, and you'll get a box that looks something like this one:

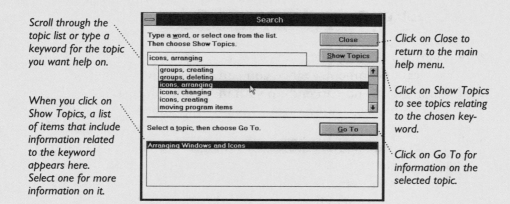

Scroll through the topic list or type a keyword for the topic you want help on.

When you click on Show Topics, a list of items that include information related to the keyword appears here. Select one for more information on it.

Click on Close to return to the main help menu.

Click on Show Topics to see topics relating to the chosen key-word.

Click on Go To for information on the selected topic.

3. In the Search dialog box, type a keyword for the topic you want help with in the Search field. As you type, Windows finds topics beginning with that word and displays them for you on the list. You can also scroll through the list of topics to look for a likely sounding subject and then click on the Show Topics button. A list of items that include information on the topic you chose will appear in the window at the bottom of the dialog box.

4. From the topic list at the bottom of the Help window, choose the item you want to read and click the Go To button. Windows will display Help text on that topic.

Notes • Help is displayed in a window, not in a dialog box, so you can keep it open at all times. To close Help, you use the window control commands described in the box "Using Wildcards in DOS Commands" on page 202.

Windows Cookbook

To Arrange Windows on the Desktop

Why Each Windows application can have several windows containing separate documents. Since you can also run more than one application, you can end up with many windows on your screen. It's less confusing if your windows are neatly arranged.

The Program Manager, the File Manager, and most applications include commands in a Windows menu that let you automatically arrange windows on screen. Most let you either "cascade" windows (set them to overlap) or "tile" them (fit them together like tiles on a wall.) You can also cascade or tile the main application windows on the screen.

Tiling windows arranges them in a regular grid on screen.

Cascading windows arranges them in an orderly stack.

How • In the Program Manager, File Manager, or many other applications, choose Cascade or Tile from the Windows menu (Alt W T or Alt W C) to rearrange the windows within the application. *Or...*

• To arrange the main application windows on the desktop, choose Switch To from the Window control icon at the top-left corner of any main program window (or double-click anywhere on the desktop outside of a window). The Task List window will come up. Click on either Tile or Cascade to rearrange the windows on screen.

To Close a Window

Why When you are done working with a window, you can close it to make room for others on screen. If the program is a main application window, closing the window will also close the program. Some programs let you have multiple document windows open at the same time. In that case, closing the window will only close that file.

How • Double-click on the window control menu icon at the top left of the window. *Or...*

• From the File menu, click on Close (if it's a file window inside an application) or Exit (if it's an application window).

To Move a Window

Why Sometimes you'll need to move a window to get to another window behind it on screen, or you will just want to arrange the windows to suit the way you work.

How Click on the title bar of the window, and without letting up the mouse button, drag the window to a new position. When it's where you want it, let up on the mouse button.

To Resize a Window

Why You can make windows bigger so that you can see more of their contents. You can make them smaller so that you can fit more windows on screen. You can even shrink them down to icon size so that they will be completely out of the way but still open.

How • To resize a window manually, move the pointer to the bottom corner of the window, where the pointer will turn into a two-headed arrow.

When you see the two-headed arrow, press the mouse button, and without letting it up, drag the corner of the window until the window is the size you want it.

• To enlarge the window to its maximum size, click the up arrow (the maximize button) at the top-right corner of the window. If it's an application window, it will fill the whole screen. If it's a file window, it will fill its application window.

• To turn the window into an icon at the bottom of the screen, click on the down arrow (the minimize button) at the top-left corner of the window. Once it's icon-size, you can just double-click on it to open it on screen again.

To Scroll a Window

Why Often, the entire contents of a window won't fit within the window frame on screen. You can scroll the window to see more of its contents.

How • If the window contains parts that you can't see on screen, the window will have a **scroll bar** that looks like this:

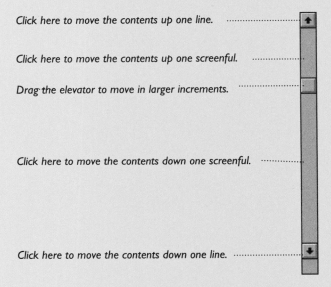

Click here to move the contents up one line.

Click here to move the contents up one screenful.

Drag the elevator to move in larger increments.

Click here to move the contents down one screenful.

Click here to move the contents down one line.

• You can click in the scroll bar to scroll the window's contents by different amounts. *Or...*

• You can scroll using the PageUp and PageDown keys to move the contents of the window one screenful at a time.

To Add a New Program to a Program Group

Why Most Windows programs will be installed into a program group when you install the program on your system. Once a program is in a program group, you can move or copy it to new program groups using the recipes "To Move a Program From One Program Group to Another" and "To Copy a Program to a New Program Group." Sometimes, however, you will have removed a program from every program group and want to reinstall it somewhere else.

This recipe is also useful for installing DOS programs into a Windows program group. Once you do that, you can run the DOS program just as you would run a Windows program—by double-clicking on its icon in the Program Manager.

How **1.** In the Program Manager, open the program group into which you want to install the new program.

2. Choose New from the Program Manager's File menu (Alt F N). A New Program Item dialog box will appear.

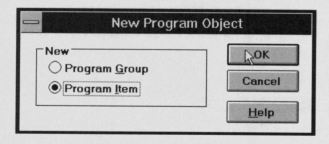

3. If it is not already chosen, click on the Program Item button and click OK or press Enter. The Program Properties dialog box will appear.

Windows Cookbook

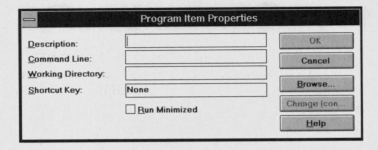

4. In the Description box, type in a brief description of the program (for example, "Scheduler"). Unlike in file names, you can include spaces, but you want this description to be brief because it will be used as the title for the program's icon.

5. Click on (or tab to) the Command Line box. This is the only box in this dialog box that you really have to fill out; the others are extra.

Now you've got two choices. If you know the full path and program name for the program you want to add, you can just type it here (for example, "C:\OFFICE\SCHEDULE.EXE").

You can save yourself the typing, and make sure you get the path right, by clicking on the Browse button. You'll get a Browse dialog box from which you can choose the program file you want to install.

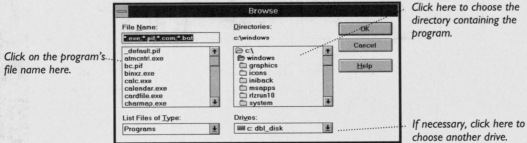

6. Once you've supplied the file name and path and you are back in the Program Item Properties dialog box, turn your attention to the Working Directory box. Here, you can specify a current directory that will be in effect while the program is running. If you want (or need) the program to have a particular current directory while it is running, click on (or Tab to) this box and type the path for the directory in the Working Directory box (for example, "C:\OFFICE"). Once again, you have the option of using the Browse button to save yourself the typing.

7. If you want to be able to run the program instantly by pressing a key combination, type a key (letter or number) in the Shortcut Key box. The key you type will be used along with the Ctrl and Alt keys to start up the program. For example, if you type S, you will be able to start the program by pressing Ctrl, Alt, and S all at once.

8. If you are installing a Windows program, the icon that comes with the program will be automatically assigned to it. If you're installing a DOS program, Windows will automatically assign a special, very boring "DOS program" icon. You can choose a new icon by clicking on the Change Icon button. The dialog box that appears will include several stock icons you can choose from. Most people choose one that suggests the kind of work the program does (for a scheduler, a calendar or datebook icon might be appropriate), but it's completely up to you.

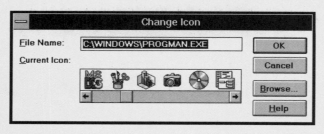

9. Now click on OK. The program icon will be installed in the program group.

Notes • Some DOS programs need special settings before they will run properly under Windows. These settings specify how the program uses the video display, memory, and other parts of the system. If you install a DOS program and it doesn't run properly, you may be able to get it to run correctly by setting up a **PIF** (program information file). See your program's user manual (or call the technical support line) if you need help.

To Copy a Program to a New Program Group

Why One program may be used for more than one kind of activity. For example, you might have separate program groups for business reports, correspondence, and creative writing. In that case, you want the icon for your word processor to appear in all three program groups so that you can start the program from whichever of the groups you are working in.

How **1.** In the Program Manager, find a program group that contains the icon for the program that you want to copy. (You may have to open or scroll the group window until the icon comes into view.)

2. Open the program window for the group to which you want to copy the program.

3. While holding down the Ctrl key, use the mouse to drag the program icon from the original group to the new group. Position the icon where you want it to be in the new group, and release the mouse button. The icon will now appear in both groups.

Notes • You can also copy a program icon into a new group by clicking on the icon with the mouse and then choosing Copy from the File menu. You will be prompted to select the destination group.

• You can drag a program icon onto the icon for a closed program group, and then release the mouse. The program will be copied to the new group, but you don't get to specify just where the new icon will appear.

To Create a New Program Group

Why Many people like to keep separate program groups for each kind of work they do. For example, say you buy a financial planning program and a spreadsheet and you want to use them together with other programs as part of a new Planning program group.

How **1.** In the Program Manager, choose New from the File menu (Alt F N). The New Program Object dialog box will appear.

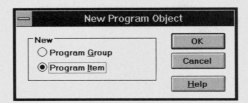

2. Click on the Program Group button.

3. Click on the OK button (or press Enter). The Program Group Properties dialog box will appear.

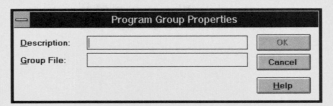

4. Click in the Description box and type in a brief description of the new program group (for example, "Financial Planning"). This description will become the new group's window name in the Program Manager. Just ignore the box labeled "Group File" (Windows will name the file automatically).

5. Choose the OK button (or press Enter). Windows creates your new group and displays its window.

6. Add the programs you want to include in the group using the recipes "To Copy a Program to a New Program Group" and "To Move a Program From One Program Group to Another."

7. Close the window and drag it into the position you want it in the Program Manager, or use the Tile or Cascade commands in the Windows menu to arrange all your windows neatly on screen.

To Go to DOS Without Quitting Windows

Why If you want to work at the DOS prompt for any reason, you can do so without quitting Windows. This allows you to return quickly to Windows when you are done, and you can even run the DOS interface in a window among your other programs.

How **1.** In the Program Manager, open the Main program group and find the DOS Prompt icon. In Windows 3.1, it looks like this:

MS-DOS
Prompt

Double-click on the icon.

2. The screen will change to a standard text screen with a DOS prompt. You can type whatever program names or commands you want at the DOS prompt, and they will operate as usual.

3. When you want to close your DOS session and return to Windows, type **EXIT** and press Enter at the DOS prompt.

If you want to return to Windows but leave DOS running, just press Alt-Tab to return to Windows. You can then switch back and forth between your DOS session and the other programs you have running.

Notes • You can run a DOS program without going to a DOS prompt. To find out how, see the "To Start a Program" recipe.

• You can find out more about switching between open programs with Alt-Tab and other methods in the "To Jump From One Program to Another" recipe.

• A few programs and DOS commands will not operate properly in a Windows DOS prompt session. Check your program's or DOS's user guide if you have problems.

To Jump From One Program to Another

Why   In Windows, you can have several programs open and running at once, each in its own window. However, just one window is "active" at any one time. (You can tell which one is active by looking at the menu bars—the active window's title bar is colored in. There are lots of methods you can use to quickly activate a different window or program.

How   • If any part of the window you want to activate is visible on screen, click anywhere in it. The program will come to the top of the stack and be ready to receive your commands. *Or...*

• Press Alt and hold it down while you press Tab. With each press of the Tab key, Windows will display a box with the name of one of the programs you are running in it. When you see the program you want, release the Tab key, and that program will be brought to the front and be ready for input. (This is an especially elegant method.) *Or...*

• Hold down the Alt key and press Escape repeatedly. This will also cycle through all the running programs, highlighting each program's window or icon in turn. Release the Escape key when you come to the program you want to work with. *Or...*

• Select Switch To from the Window Control menu. Then select the program you want to switch to from the Task List dialog box that appears and click OK (or just double-click on the program's name).

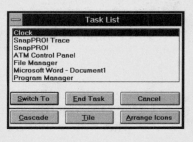

Notes   • You can also bring up the Task List by pressing Ctrl-Esc or by double-clicking on the desktop (the part of the screen outside any window, near the edge.)

To Move a Program From One Program Group to Another

Why Anytime you change the way you are organizing your work, you can move a program from one group to another. Perhaps you no longer use a program for a particular purpose, or you decide that the program fits better in a different program group. For example, you might have been using Windows Write in the Reports group, but you then buy a more powerful word processor, such as Microsoft Word. You decide to move Write to the Personal program group, where you will use it to write personal letters.

How 1. In the Program Manager, open the program group that contains the icon for the program you want to move (you may have to scroll the group window until the icon comes into view).

2. If the program group to which you want to move the program is not open on screen, double-click on its icon to open it.

3. Use the mouse to drag the program icon from the original group to the new group. Position the icon where you want it to be in the new group, and release the mouse button. The icon will now be in the new group and removed from the old one.

Notes • You can also move a program by clicking on it with the mouse and then choosing Move from the File menu. You will be prompted to select the destination group.

• You can drag a program icon onto the icon for a minimized program group, and then release the mouse. The program will be moved to the new group, but you don't get to specify just where the new icon will appear.

To Quit Windows

Why It's time to go to lunch—or go home. There's more to life than computers, you know.

How **1.** If you are running the DOS prompt, go to that window, type **EXIT** at the DOS prompt, and press Enter. That will close the DOS session.

2. In the Program Manager, choose Exit Windows from the File menu (Alt F X). A dialog box will appear, warning that this will end your Windows session.

3. To exit Windows, click the OK button (or press Enter). If you change your mind, click on Cancel.

Windows will quit, and you'll be returned to a regular DOS prompt. You can now turn off your PC.

Notes • You should always exit Windows in the way described here, rather than just shutting off your PC. An abrupt shutoff can waste disk space and could cause you to lose data in files that you have been working on.

• You can close the Program Manager window just as you would close any other window, by double-clicking on the window control icon, which is in the upper-left corner of the window.

• If you try to exit Windows while a program is running and you haven't saved all your changes, the program will warn you and give you a chance to save your work before quitting.

• You don't have to exit Windows to run a DOS program. See the "To Go to DOS Without Quitting Windows" recipe.

Windows Cookbook

To Remove a Program From a Program Group

Why You may have a program that you don't use any more, or that you've replaced with a later version. In that case, you will probably want to remove it from its program group.

How **1.** In the Program Manager, find the icon for the program you want to remove, and click on it.

2. Choose Delete from the Program Manager's File menu (Alt F D) or press the Del key.

3. Windows will show you a warning box asking you to confirm the deletion. If you want to delete the program, click on OK or press Enter. If you change your mind, click on Cancel.

The icon will disappear from the program group.

Notes • Removing a program icon from a program group doesn't actually remove the program's files from your hard disk. You will need to use the File Manager, DOS commands, or if there is one, your program's Uninstall feature, to do that.

• If the program is installed in several groups, you will need to delete it from each group separately. Deleting it from one won't delete it from the others.

To Remove a Program Group From the Program Manager

Why Many Windows programs create their own program group when you install them. If you remove or move the icon for the program, you may want to get rid of the program group. You may also want to delete program groups when you finish a project or otherwise reorganize your work.

How **1.** In the Program Manager, open the program group that you want to remove.

2. Click on the program group's title bar.

3. Choose Delete from the File menu (Alt F D) or press the Del key.

4. If the program group contains programs, Windows asks you whether you want to delete each one in turn. When it asks whether you want to delete the first program, click on Yes (or press Enter) to delete it. If you change your mind, click on Cancel. Choose Delete or press Del again and repeat the process for each program icon in the group.

5. When all the icons are gone from the group window, choose Delete again. This time Windows will ask you whether you want to delete the program group itself. Click on OK (or press Enter) to delete the group.

Notes • Remember, removing a program icon from your Program Manager doesn't actually remove the program's files from your hard disk. You will need to use the File Manager, DOS commands, or if there is one, your program's Uninstall feature, to do that.

To Run a DOS Program in a Window

Why Running a program in a window lets you see other programs at the same time and makes it easier to cut and paste data from one program to another. Windows programs automatically run in movable, sizable windows. You can also run many DOS programs in similar windows. (Some DOS programs cannot run in a window because of the way they use graphics. In that case, the program will warn you when you try to put it in a window.)

How **1.** Start the DOS program, either using the Run command in the Program Manager's File menu, or by double-clicking on its icon in the Program Manger, if it is installed in a program group. (See the recipes "To Start a Program" and "To Add a New Program to a Program Group" for more information.)

2. Once the program is running, press Alt-Enter. The DOS session will be put into a window that you can control like any other.

Notes • You can also set up your DOS programs to automatically run in Windows when you start them. The procedure is described in your Windows user guide.

• Windows must be running in 386 Enhanced mode with a VGA monitor in order to run DOS programs in Windows. Most 386 systems are automatically set up this way, so you probably don't need to worry about this.

To See a List of All the Programs that Are Currently Running

Why Since you can run many programs at a time with Windows, some program windows can get hidden under others. You may forget whether you're running a particular program.

How • Select Switch To from the Program Manager window's control menu. (This menu is shown as a small horizontal line in the upper-left corner of the window). *Or...*

• Hold down the Ctrl key while you press Esc. *Or...*

• Double-click on the desktop (the part of the screen outside any window, near the edge.)

When you do any of these actions, a Task List will appear, showing a list of all the programs that are currently running. You can now switch to a particular program by double-clicking on its title in the list, or you can close one of the programs by clicking on its title and then clicking the End Task button.

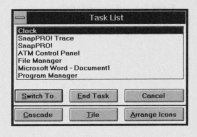

Windows Cookbook

To Start a Program

Why Before you can do any work with a program, you must "launch" it, or start it running. Windows gives you several methods to choose from. Most of the methods I'll describe here will work for both DOS and Windows programs.

How • If the program is installed in a program group in the Program Manager, double-click on the icon to start the program. *Or...*

    • Choose Run from the Program Manager's File menu (Alt F R). In the Run dialog box that appears, you can type the command that runs the program, just as you would on the DOS command line.

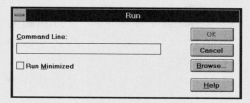

If you're not sure of the path or the file name, you can click on the Browse button to see a dialog box in which you can view the disk's directories and files.

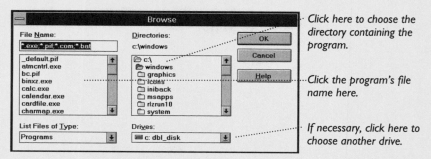

Click here to choose the directory containing the program.

Click the program's file name here.

If necessary, click here to choose another drive.

Or...

• You've even got a third choice: You can also run a program from the File Manager. If the File Manager isn't open, double-click on its icon in the Main program group. Then double-click on the folder in the directory list on the left. Double-click again on the program file you want to start.

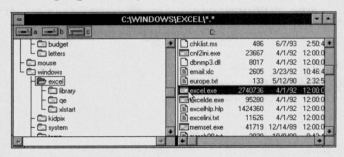

Notes • You can also run a Windows program by opening a file that is "associated" with that program. For more on that, see the recipe "To Open an Existing File."

• In Windows, you can run more than one program at a time, each in its own Window. To start up a new program, just repeat this procedure.

To Start a Program Automatically

Why Sometimes you will have programs that you want to use every time you start your computer—perhaps the Notepad or Calendar applications that come with Windows. To do that, you can use a special Windows program group that acts something like an AUTOEXEC.BAT file for Windows programs.

How **1.** In the Program Manager, locate the icon of the program that you want to start automatically. (Programs that come with Windows, such as Notepad and Calendar, are in the Accessories program group.)

2. Locate the program group called "StartUp." (This group is set up automatically when you install Windows 3.1.)

3. While holding down the Ctrl key, click on the program with the mouse and drag it to the StartUp program (either to the group's icon or to its window if the group is open). This will copy your program to the StartUp group. Next time you start Windows, the program will start automatically.

Notes • This recipe assumes that the program you want to add to the Startup group is already in another program group in your Program Manager. That's because in almost every case, the installation program for a Windows program will install the program in a program group. If for some reason the program you want to add to the StartUp group isn't already in a group, follow the recipe "To Add a New Program to a Program Group."

To Start Windows From DOS

Why Some systems that include Windows are set up so that Windows starts automatically when you turn on the computer. If yours isn't, you can easily start Windows from DOS.

How At the DOS prompt, type `WIN`, and press Enter:

```
C:\>win
```

Windows should start right up.

Notes • If you want Windows to run automatically when you start your PC, add these two lines to the end of your AUTOEXEC.BAT file:

```
cd \windows
win
```

(For more on changing your AUTOEXEC.BAT file, see the recipes "To Add a PATH Command to Your AUTOEXEC.BAT File" and "To Run a Program Automatically" in the DOS Cookbook.

To Copy Something From One Place to Another

Why You may have information in a document that you want to repeat someplace else—either in a new place in the same file or in another file entirely. You can do this easily in almost any Windows program.

How **1.** Select the text or object you want to copy.

2. Select Copy from the program's Edit menu (Ctrl-C). A copy of the selected material will be saved on the Windows **Clipboard**.

3. Now move to the location where you want to paste the material, and click the mouse at the new location to place the insertion point. This can be in the same document, in a document in a different window, or even in a document in a different application.

4. Select Paste (Ctrl-V) from the Edit menu of the window you're placing the material in.

Notes • Anything you place on the Clipboard with a Cut or Copy command stays there until you cut or copy something else. That means that you can paste the same material over and over again to different locations just by repeating the Paste command.

• The keyboard shortcuts I've given here should work in most Windows applications, but they may be different in the application you're using. If they don't work, pull down the Edit menu in your application and check the keyboard shortcut listed next to the commands there.

To Delete Something From a Document

Why Sometimes things just don't work out. Windows provides several ways to get rid of parts of a file you don't want anymore.

How **1.** Select the text or object you want to delete.

2. Select Cut from the Edit menu (Ctrl-X), or press the Del key, or press Backspace.

Notes • If you use the Cut command in the Edit menu or press Ctrl-X, the material you cut will be placed on the Windows Clipboard so it can be pasted somewhere else or pasted back in the same place if you made a mistake. If you press Backspace (or any other key), it just disappears. (You can recover if you immediately select Undo from the Edit menu.)

• The keyboard shortcuts I've given here should work in most Windows applications, but they may be different in the application you're using. If they don't work, pull down the Edit menu in your application and check the keyboard shortcuts listed next to the commands there.

To Move Something From One Place to Another

Why You may have information in a document that you want to move to a more appropriate place in the same document or to another document. For example, you might decide that an explanation would make more sense if one paragraph were moved so that it came before another.

How **1.** Select the text or object you want to move.

2. Select Cut (Ctrl-C or Shift-Del) from the program's Edit menu. The selected text will disappear from the document and be placed on Windows' Clipboard.

3. If necessary, activate the window that contains the file where you want to place the material, and click the mouse to place the insertion point where you want the text to be placed. This can be in a different window or even in a different application.

4. Select Paste (Ctrl-V or Ctrl-Ins) from the Edit menu in the destination window.

Notes • Anything you place on the Clipboard with a Cut or Copy command stays there until you cut or copy something else. That means that you can paste the same material over and over again to different locations by just repeating the Paste command.

• The keyboard shortcuts I've given here should work in most Windows applications, but they may be different in the application you're using. If they don't work, pull down the Edit menu in your application and check the keyboard shortcuts listed next to the commands there.

To Open an Existing File

Why Opening a file lets you work inside it: reading, adding, deleting, or changing its contents. To open a file, you need to first open the application that works with it. In many cases—if the file is "associated" with a particular application—you can open the file and the application at the same time.

How • If the application you use to work with the file is open, choose Open from the application's File menu (Alt F O). The Open dialog box will appear.

Type the name of the file here

...or select it from this list.

Select the directory the file is in here.

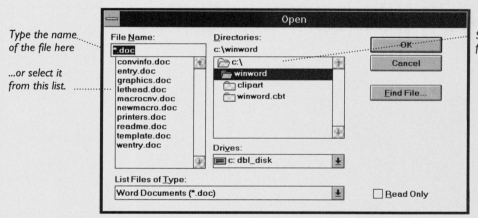

In the Open dialog box, click on the file name and click OK (or press Enter), or double-click on the file name.

• If the file is "associated" with an application, you can open it by double-clicking on its name in the File Manager.

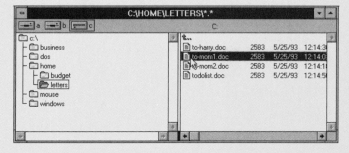

Windows Cookbook

You can open the File Manager by double-clicking on its icon in the Main program group. Then double-click on the folder that contains the file in the directory list on the left. Double-click again on the file you want to open.

Notes • Files are "associated" with applications by their file extensions. For example, text files with the .TXT extension are automatically associated with the Windows Notepad. Most applications automatically save their files with an extension that is associated with that application. See the recipe "To Associate a Document With an Application" for more information.

To Open a New File

Why Opening a new file gives you a blank workspace in which you can start work from scratch.

How **1.** Open the application that you will use to create the new document. (See the "To Start a Program" recipe.)

2. Choose New from the File menu (Alt F N).

3. The application will create a blank document. Some applications may ask you for some extra information (such as the name of a template or style to use) before the document is opened.

Notes • When a new document is opened, it is stored only in the computer's memory. As soon as you have done any work, you should choose Save from the File menu to save your work to disk (that procedure is described in the "To Save a File" recipe.)

To Print a File

Why Printing is like telling your computer to type out everything you've told it. It's handy to get a printout to check your work or to distribute it to others.

How **1.** If the file you want to print isn't open, open it using the instructions in the "To Open an Existing File" recipe.

2. Select Print from the File menu (Alt F P).

3. In the Print dialog box, select the range of pages you want to print and the orientation of the page, and click OK.

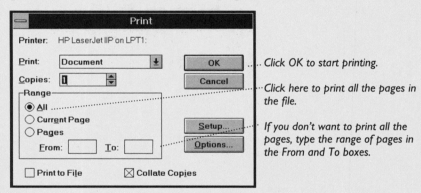

Click OK to start printing.

Click here to print all the pages in the file.

If you don't want to print all the pages, type the range of pages in the From and To boxes.

Notes • In order for the Print command to work, your printer must be attached, turned on, and installed correctly in Windows. If you have a problem, see your Windows documentation for information on installing a printer.

• Some applications have more elaborate print dialog boxes. If there are extra options, you will find instructions for using them in the program's user guide.

To Quit From a Program

Why In Windows, you can keep a program running in the background while you use other programs, but if you don't think you'll need a program again, it's a good idea to close it. That saves memory and display space and may speed up your computer.

How **1.** Choose Exit from the application's File menu (Alt F X), or double-click on the window control icon in the upper-left corner of the program's window.

2. If you have made changes in a file and have not yet saved them, the program will show you a dialog box and ask if you want to save the changes.

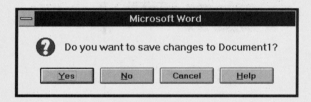

Click on Yes (or press Enter) to save changes and exit the program. Click on No if you want to exit the program but don't want to save the changes. Click on Cancel if you decide that you don't want to quit the program after all.

To Save a File

Why You should save files often so that your work is safely stored on disk. Until you save, your work is kept only in the computer's RAM (its short-term memory) and will disappear when you turn off the computer—or if the power is interrupted unexpectedly.

How 1. Choose Save from your application's File menu (Alt F S).

2. If this is the first time you've saved the file, a dialog box will appear asking you to name the file and choose the directory it should be saved in. Type the name, choose the directory, and click OK.

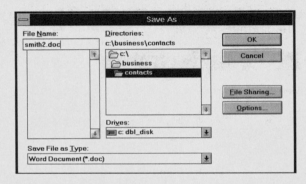

Notes • Some applications, especially word processors, let you set up an "automatic save" feature that will save your file at specified intervals of time (such as every ten minutes). Check your program's user guide to find out if this feature is available.

To Save a File Under a Different Name

Why If you have to create a document that is similar to one you've already created—a business letter that varies in only a few sentences from person to person, for example—you can open the original file, tailor it to the new use, and save it under a new name.

How **1.** With the file open on screen, choose Save As from the application's File menu (Alt F A).

2. A dialog box will appear asking you to name the file and choose the directory it should be saved in. Type the name, choose the directory, and click OK.

Type a name for the file here.

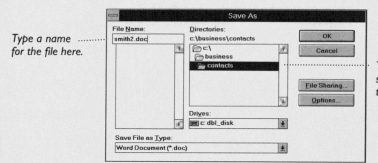

The directory the file will be saved in is the one open in the directory list.

After you click OK, notice that the file name in the title bar of the window changes to the new name. You've just created a new file on the disk and all further changes will be saved in that file.

Notes • When you choose Save As, the old document remains on disk, under its original name.

• If you try to save the file under a name that is already used in the directory you're saving in, Windows will display a dialog box asking you whether you want to write over or replace the other file. Usually you don't want to do this, so you should choose Cancel from the dialog box to back out of the operation, and then use Save As again, this time choosing a different name.

Windows Cookbook

To Undo What You Just Did

Why We all make mistakes from time to time. Fortunately, most Windows applications are very forgiving. If you've done something you regret, Windows gives you a way to reverse or "undo" the command you've just given or the text you've just typed or deleted.

How Select Undo from your application's Edit menu (Ctrl-Z).

Notes • Generally, Undo only works on the last action you took, although some programs offer a "multiple undo" feature that undoes each action, one at a time, starting with the last action. Undo cannot undo everything. If the Undo command is dimmed, the last action cannot be undone. You're stuck with it.

• You can "undo an undo" by giving the Undo command a second time.

• Ctrl-Z works in most applications. If it doesn't work in yours, check the Edit menu to see whether another keyboard shortcut is listed next to the Undo command.

To Change the Name of a File or Directory

Why There are many reasons why you might want to change the name of a file or directory. Perhaps you think of a name that better describes its purpose. Or perhaps a program gives the file an uninspiring default name like "FILE1.PIC," and you want to change the name to something you're more likely to remember.

How **1.** If the File Manager isn't already open, open it by going to the Program Manager, double-clicking on the Main program group, and then double-clicking on the File Manager icon.

2. In the File Manager, click on the name of the directory (in the directory list on the left) or file (in the file list on the right) you want to rename.

To see a particular subdirectory, you may need to double-click on the folder of the directory that contains it. When you click on the directory you want, the files it contains are displayed along the right side of the File Manager window.

3. Choose Rename from the File menu (Alt F N). You will see this dialog box:

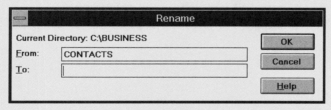

4. Type the new name in the To box and click OK (or press Enter).

Notes • Names of directories in Windows follow the same rules they do in DOS: They must have no more than eight characters, with no punctuation. And although most people don't use them, they can also have a three-character extension.

Windows Cookbook

• You can also rename a file while copying it to the same or another directory. See the "To Copy or Move a File..." recipes in this section.

• Some programs depend on a directory having the name it was given during installation. Be very cautious before renaming directories that contain programs. If you change the name of a directory in the path to a program file, you will have to tell Windows the new path before you can run the program from the Program Manager again. See the recipe "To Add a New Program to a Program Group."

To Copy a Floppy Disk

Why When you get a new software package, it's a good idea to make backup copies of all the original disks, put them in a safe place, and use the backups to install the software. You may also want to make extra copies of important archive or backup disks.

How **1.** If the File Manager isn't already open, open it by going to the Program Manager, double-clicking on the Main program group, and then double-clicking on the File Manager icon.

2. Select the Copy Disk command from the Disk Menu (Alt D C). You will see the Copy Disk dialog box.

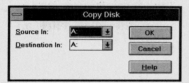

3. If you will be using a drive other than drive A: to make the copy, click on the Source box to change the drive letter to the one you will be using.

4. Click on OK (or press Enter). Windows will warn you that the copy operation will erase all data on the destination disk and ask you if you want to continue.

5. If that's OK with you, click on Yes. Windows will display a message asking you to place your source disk in drive A: (or B:, if you are working with that drive).

6. Insert the disk you want to copy in the drive, and press any key on the keyboard to signal that you're ready. Windows will begin to copy the disk, loading up as much data as it can store in free memory; it will then ask you to insert your destination disk.

7. Insert the disk you want to copy the first disk to (making sure you've got the right disk), and press any key. Windows will copy the information in memory onto the second disk and then ask for the first disk (the source disk) again to continue the process, if necessary.

8. Keep inserting the source disk and destination disk, as prompted by Windows, until the operation is complete. When it is, Windows will ask if you'd like to name the disk.

9. If you want to name the disk, type the name and click on OK. (You don't have to type a name if you don't want to.)

10. After you click on OK, Windows will ask if you'd like to copy another disk. If you want to copy another disk, click on Yes (or press Enter); otherwise click on No.

Notes • At setup, Windows took note of whether you had one floppy drive or two, and what sizes they were. The instructions above are for one floppy drive. If you have two floppy drives of the same size and capacity, put the source disk in drive A: and the copy in drive B: You won't need to keep inserting and taking out the different disks: Windows will do the switching between drives automatically. Note that this won't work if your disk drives are different sizes or capacities—you won't be able to copy a 3.5-inch disk to a 5.25-inch disk, for example.

To Copy or Move a File From a Floppy Disk to the Hard Disk

Why When someone hands you a floppy disk that contains files you want to use, you will probably want to copy the files on the floppy to your hard disk so you can work more easily with them. You'll also need to copy from a floppy to your hard disk when you are restoring an archive copy of a file.

How **1.** If the File Manager isn't already open, open it by going to the Program Manager, double-clicking on the Main program group, and then double-clicking on the File Manager icon.

2. In the File Manager, open a second directory window by choosing New Windows from the Windows menu (Alt W N). Then arrange the windows so that you can see both by dragging the title bar of the top window or by using the Tile or Cascade commands in the Windows menu to arrange them automatically.

3. Put the floppy disk containing the files in your disk drive.

4. In one of the directory windows, click on the icon representing your hard drive (usually C:); then click on the directory to which you want to copy the file. The file window will show a list of the files in that directory. Your File Manager Screen should now look something like this:

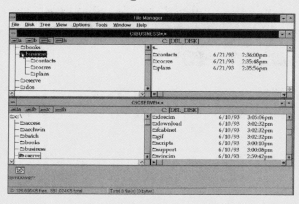

5. In the other directory window, click on the icon that represents the drive that contains the floppy disk (usually A: or B:).

6. To move the file, click on the file you want to move, and without letting up the mouse button, drag the file to the file list window or directory folder you want to move it to. Let up the mouse button when the destination window or folder is highlighted.

To copy the file, press the Ctrl key while you drag the file.

When you're copying, a plus sign appears in the icon as you drag it.

7. A dialog box will appear, asking you to confirm that you want to copy or move the file. Click on OK (or press Enter) to complete the copy, or click on Cancel if you decide not to make the copy.

Notes • You can also make copies by using the File Manager's Copy command. First select the file or files you want to copy. Choose Copy from the File menu (Alt F C). You will see the Copy dialog box. In the To box, type the path for the directory to which you want to copy the file(s), for example, "C:\BUSINESS\CORRES." You can also change the name of the file as you copy it with the Copy command.

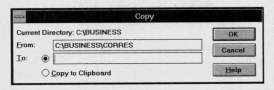

• If the destination directory has a file with the same name as the file you're copying, the File Manager will show you the name, length, and date of both files and ask you to confirm the copy. Check to make sure the file on your hard disk isn't a later version than the file you're copying from the floppy. Click on OK (or press Enter) if you want to continue the copy. Otherwise, click on Cancel, and the file won't be copied.

• If you want to copy more than one file at a time, just select all the files you want to copy before dragging them to the new disk or giving the Copy command. To select adjacent files, press Shift while you click on files after the first one. To select files that aren't adjacent, press Ctrl while you select additional files.

Windows Cookbook

To Copy or Move a File From One Directory to Another

Why You will probably move files between directories as you continually reorganize your work. Copying comes in handy when you find that a file you already have can serve a double purpose in a separate project.

How **1.** If the File Manager isn't already open, open it by going to the Program Manager, double-clicking on the Main program group, and then double-clicking on the File Manager icon.

2. In the File Manager, open a second directory window by choosing New Windows from the Windows menu (Alt W N). Then arrange the windows so that you can see both by dragging the title bar of the top window or by choosing Tile or Cascade from the Windows menu.

3. In one of the directory windows, click on the directory that contains the file you want to copy. In the file window you will see a listing of the files in the selected directory; make sure the file you want to copy is there. (You may need to scroll the windows to see it.)

4. In the other directory window, click on the directory into which you wish to copy the file. The file window will show a list of the files in that directory. Your File Manager Screen should now look something like this:

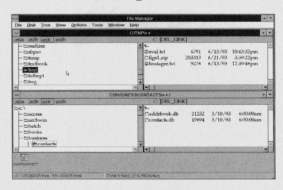

5. If you want to copy the file (keeping the original), hold down the Ctrl key and, with the mouse, click on the file you want to copy and, without letting up the mouse button, drag it to the file list or folder of the destination directory. Let up the mouse button when the destination window is highlighted.

If you want to move the file (deleting the original) rather than copying it, hold down the Shift key (rather than the Ctrl key) while dragging the files.

6. A dialog box will appear, asking you to confirm that you want to copy or move the file. Click on OK (or press Enter) to complete the copy, or click on Cancel if you decide not to make the copy.

Notes • You can also move or copy a file using the File Manager's Copy or Move command. First select the file you want to copy. Then choose Copy or Move from the File menu (Alt F C or Alt F M). Windows will display a dialog box. In the To box, type the path and file name for the new copy. You can give the new copy a different file name by typing the new name here.

• If the destination directory has a file with the same name as the file you're copying or moving, the File Manager will show you the name, length, and date of both files and ask you to confirm the copy. Check to make sure that the version in the directory to which you're copying isn't later than the version being copied. If you want to make the copy, click on OK (or press Enter). If you want to cancel the copy, click on Cancel.

• If you want to copy more than one file at a time, just select all the files before dragging them to the new directory or giving the Copy or Move command. To select adjacent files, press Shift while you click on files after the first one. To select files that aren't adjacent, press Ctrl while you select additional files.

To Copy or Move a File From the Hard Disk to a Floppy Disk

Why You can share files with colleagues by copying the files to a floppy disk and then giving them the disk. You may also want to make archive copies of seldom-used files on floppies and then delete the files from your hard disk to save space.

How **1.** If the File Manager isn't already open, open it by going to the Program Manager, double-clicking on the Main program group, and then double-clicking on the File Manager icon.

2. Put the floppy disk to which you will be copying the files in your disk drive. (If the disk isn't formatted, you'll have to format it. See the "To Format a Floppy Disk" recipe.)

3. In the File Manager's directory window, click on the icon representing your hard drive (usually C:), if that drive isn't already selected; then click on the directory that contains the files that you wish to copy. The file window will show a list of the files in that directory. Your File Manager screen should now look something like this:

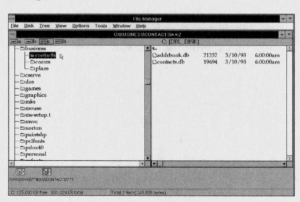

4. To copy the file, click on the file name, and without letting up the mouse button, drag the file to the icon for the floppy disk. Let up the mouse button when the icon is highlighted.

If you want to move the file, hold down the Shift key while you drag the file name.

5. A dialog box will appear, asking you to confirm that you want to copy or move the file. Click on OK (or press Enter) to complete the copy, or click on Cancel if you decide not to make the copy.

Notes • You can also move or copy a file using the File Manager's Copy or Move command. First select the file you want to copy. Then choose Copy or Move from the File menu (Alt F C or Alt F M). Windows will display a dialog box. In the To box, type the path and file name for the new copy. You can give the new copy a different file name by typing the new name here.

• If the destination directory has a file with the same name as the file you're copying or moving, the File Manager will show you the name, length, and date of both files and ask you to confirm the copy. Check to make sure that the version in the directory to which you're copying isn't later than the version being copied. If you want to make the copy, click on OK (or press Enter). If you want to cancel the copy, click on Cancel.

• If you want to copy more than one file at a time, just select all the files before dragging them to the new directory or giving the Copy or Move command. To select adjacent files, press Shift while you click on files after the first one. To select files that aren't adjacent, press Ctrl while you select additional files.

To Create a New Directory

Why Creating a new directory is like getting out a clean file folder to hold the paperwork for a new project. Giving each new project its own directory on your hard disk makes it easier to find the files you need to work with, and easier to make backup or archive copies of them later.

How **1.** If the File Manager isn't already open, open it by going to the Program Manager, double-clicking on the Main program group, and then double-clicking on the File Manager icon.

2. In the File Manager, choose Create Directory from the File menu (Alt F C). The Create Directory window will appear. The box gives the path of the current directory.

3. In the Name box, type the name of the directory you wish to create. (If you don't want the directory to be a subdirectory of the current directory, type a complete path, such as "C:\BUSINESS\CORRES").

4. Click OK or press Enter. The new directory will be created and will appear as a folder in the File Manager's directory list.

To Delete a Directory

Why If you are no longer working on a particular project, or you want to reorganize your hard disk, you can delete directories you no longer find useful.

How **1.** If the File Manager isn't already open, open it by going to the Program Manager, double-clicking on the Main program group, and then double-clicking on the File Manager icon.

2. In the File Manager, select the directory you want to delete by clicking on its folder in a directory list at the left of the File Manager window.

3. If you want to keep any of the files that are in the directory, move them to other directories or floppy disks using the "To Copy or Move a File..." recipes in this section.

4. Now choose Delete from the File menu (Alt F D). The Delete box will appear.

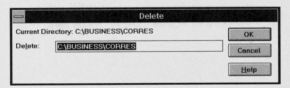

5. The path and directory name for the directory you've chosen will already be in the text box. Click on OK or press Enter to delete the directory.

6. A confirmation box will appear. Click on OK (or press Enter) to delete the directory. (If you change your mind, click on Cancel, and the directory won't be deleted.)

Windows Cookbook

7. If there are files in the directory that you want to delete, the File Manager will ask you to confirm that you want to delete the first file. Click on Yes (or press Enter), and you will be asked in turn to confirm the deletion of each file in the directory. If you click on "Yes to All," the remaining files will be deleted without asking for further confirmation, and then the directory will be deleted. Click on Cancel if you decide that you don't want to delete the files.

To Delete a File

Why Even a large hard drive can quickly fill up with files. If you don't delete files that you no longer need, you'll soon run out of room for the ones you do need.

How **1.** If the File Manager isn't already open, open it by going to the Program Manager, double-clicking on the Main program group, and then double-clicking on the File Manager icon.

2. In the File Manager's directory window, click on the directory containing the file you want to delete and then select the file by clicking on its name in the file list.

3. Choose Delete from the File menu (Alt F D) or press the Del key. You will be asked to confirm that you want to delete the file. Click on OK (or press Enter) to delete the file. If you change your mind, click on Cancel.

Notes • If you want to delete more than one file at a time, just select all the files before giving the Delete command. To select adjacent files, press Shift while you click on files after the first one. To select files that aren't adjacent, press Ctrl while you select additional files.

Windows Cookbook

To Restore a File that Has Been Deleted

Why Uh-oh! You've just deleted a file—and then remembered that you still need it. Don't despair. If you act quickly you can probably recover your deleted file. (If you don't have DOS 6.0, you'll need to go to the DOS prompt to do this, as described in the recipe "To Restore a File You've Deleted" in the DOS Cookbook.)

How **1.** Before you do anything else, open the Microsoft Tools program group in the Program Manager and double-click on the Undelete icon. The icon looks like this:

Once you've launched Undelete, you will see a window like this:

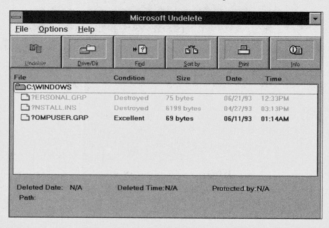

2. If the file you want to recover isn't in the current directory, click on the Drive/Dir button. In the Drive/Dir box, type in the directory that contained the deleted file.

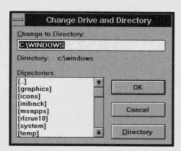

If you're not sure about the name or location of a deleted file, you can also click on the Find button in the Undelete window. This option lets you type in a file specification (such as *.* to search all of drive C:), some text to search for in the file (if it was a letter, for example, you can type the name of the addressee here), or you can select a Windows program group in which to search for the file.

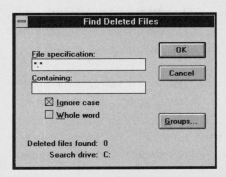

3. Once you've chosen the directory, click once on the name of the file you want to get back, and then click on the Undelete button.

4. DOS erases the first character of the file name when you delete a file, so a window will now ask you to type in the first character of the file name. (Usually you can figure this out from the context. If not, type any character you want.)

The file will be undeleted and restored to its place in the directory.

Notes • Undelete will not always be able to get your file back intact. If you have closed any programs or saved any files since you deleted the file, some parts of the file may not be available. Next to the file name in the Undelete list, the program lists the file's condition. If the condition of the file you want to restore is described as excellent or good, all or most of the file's data can probably be recovered. On the other hand, if the condition is listed as poor, your recovered file will probably be missing some data. In either case, open your file once you get it back and check it to make sure it's all there and in good shape.

• If the file you deleted was an application program file, the best approach is just to reinstall the program from your backup copies of the floppy disks it came on, rather than use Undelete. If the condition isn't described as excellent, and all clusters aren't available, there is no point in even trying to recover a program file.

To See a List of the Files and Directories on a Disk

Why You want to review the organization of your hard disk, or check on the location of some files. The File Manager makes it easy for you to browse the directories and files on even a large hard disk. This is particularly useful for doing your weekly housekeeping and for weeding unneeded files from your hard disk.

How 1. If the File Manager isn't already open, open it by going to the Program Manager, double-clicking on the Main program group, and then double-clicking on the File Manager icon.

2. In a File Manager directory window, click on the icon for the drive you want to search (if that drive isn't already selected).

3. The screen will show one or more directory windows, each with a directory list on the left and a file list on the right. The current directory is highlighted in the directory list, and its folder icon is open. The file list shows the files in the current directory.

4. You can view the directory list showing just one level of directories, or two levels, or any number of levels up to all of them.

You can "expand" the directory tree to show extra levels of directories in two ways:

• If you double-click on a directory folder symbol, the folders for any subdirectories will be shown indented to the right. Double-clicking again on the folder symbol "collapses" the subdirectories and hides them again. *Or...*

• You can choose commands from the Tree menu to expand all directories, just the current branch, or just the current directory, or to collapse each branch.

Windows Cookbook

To Associate a Document With an Application

Why   While you're working at your computer, you probably don't say to yourself, "Gee, time to run the word processor again." Instead, you probably say something like "OK, let's revise that memo." In other words, you think in terms of what document you want to work on, not what program you want to run.

Windows recognizes that you think this way, so it lets you set up things so you can work comfortably. When you "associate" a document with an application, you can just double-click on the name of the file in the File Manager to open it. That will also automatically open the application it is associated with. You don't have to open the application first and then open the document, as you otherwise would.

Most documents created by Windows programs are automatically associated with the program that created them. If you want to use a file extension other than the program's default extension, though, you'll have to associate the files manually.

How **1.** If the File Manager isn't already open, open it by going to the Program Manager, double-clicking on the Main program group, and then double-clicking on the File Manager icon.

2. In the File Manager, select the Associate command from the File menu (Alt F A). You'll see the Associate dialog box.

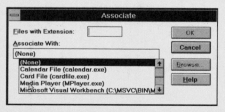

3. Files are associated with applications through their file extensions. In the Associate dialog box, type the extension you want to use for the associated files.

4. Now you need to select the program you want those files associated with. You can do this in any of three ways:

• You can click on the text field to see a drop-down list of the programs. (This list may not contain all the programs on your hard disk; it contains only those programs that already have files associated with them.) *Or...*

• You can click on the Browse button and search through your directories for the program. You'll get a Browse dialog box from which you can choose the program file you want to install.

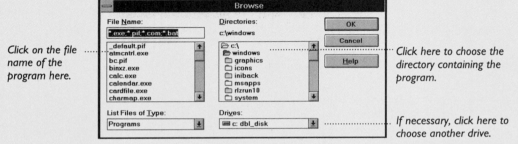

Click on the file name of the program here.

Click here to choose the directory containing the program.

If necessary, click here to choose another drive.

Or...

• You can type in the path and name of the application.

5. After you've supplied the program name, click OK (or press Enter) to finish up.

Notes • You can have more than one extension associated with an application. For example, you could associate the extensions .DOC, .RPT, and .LTR with your word processor.

• You can't, however, have the same extension associated with more than one application program. If you could, Windows wouldn't know which program you wanted to run when you clicked on the file.

To Back Up Your Hard Disk

Why It's a good idea (as you know) to keep current backup copies of all your work. If you work mostly on just one or two files, you can easily keep a backup version of them by using the File Manager to copy the files periodically to a floppy disk. (See the "To Copy or Move a File From the Hard Disk to a Floppy Disk" recipe.)

If, however, you work with a variety of files, or you work with programs that use a variety of files that are constantly updated, you can't count on remembering which files you have created or changed each day. You need a more systematic backup strategy. Many computer experts insist that you need to back up your entire hard disk once a week, if not more often. If you have DOS 6.0, you should have a group called Microsoft Tools that contains a program called Backup; you can use that program to back up your hard disk to floppies.

How **1.** Decide what you need to back up. You've probably noticed that many files seldom, if ever, change. If you organize your hard disk so that each application has a directory for its program files, and data files (documents) are in their own directories, you don't need to back up those tens of megabytes of program files. If something goes wrong, you can always reinstall the program from its installation disks, which you should have backup copies of.

2. In the Program Manager, double-click on the Microsoft Tools program group to open it, and then double-click on the Backup icon.

Backup

3. Backup will read the directories and files on your hard disk (this may take a few moments). The first time you run Backup, the program will check out your hardware (disk drives, processor, etc.) and test it to determine its most efficient use. Just follow the prompts and make selections when asked. Backup will make a small test backup and then compare the backed up files with the originals on your hard disk to ensure that it is making accurate backups.

4. When it's finished, note the five buttons just below the menu bar. These determine what "mode" Backup is working in. To back up files, click on the Backup button. The window will then look like this:

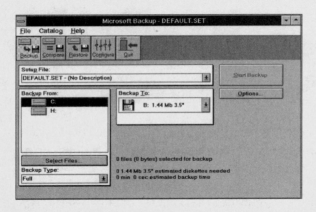

5. Make sure that you specify what drive you are backing up from and what drive you are backing up to. Normally the defaults, which specify backing up from drive C: to drive A:, will be fine, though you might want to back up to drive B: instead, if that is your 3.5-inch drive (3.5-inch disks hold a little more data than 5.25-inch disks do, and they're easier to store). If you need to change any of the options shown on this screen, just click on the highlighted area and a list of possible choices will open up.

6. Now specify which files you are going to back up. If you want to back up everything on the hard drive, double-click on the drive letter in the Backup From box.

7. If you just want to back up certain files, click on or select the Select Files button. You will see a screen that looks like this:

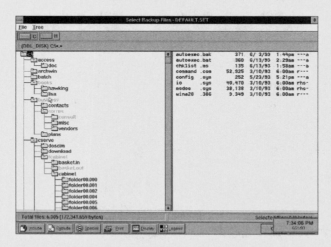

8. Select directories and files that you want to be backed up. Selecting works a little differently here than it does for most Windows programs:

• To view the files in a directory, click on the directory name. Click on the "folder" next to a directory name to show or hide any subdirectories. *Or...*

• To select all files in a directory, double-click on the directory name. *Or...*

• To select individual files in the file list for a directory, double-click on each file name, or drag the mouse over a series of file names to select all of them. (You don't need to Shift-Click.)

9. Another way to select files is to click on the Include button at the bottom of the file selection screen. You will see a dialog box like this:

This box lets you select all files that match a particular file name pattern, without your having to select them "by hand." First fill in the PATH specification with the directory from which you want to back up files. (If you do not want subdirectories of this directory to be included, click on the Include All Subdirectories box to uncheck it.)

10. Now type in a file specification using wildcards. For example, if you want all .DOC files in the specified directory (and subdirectories, if checked) to be backed up, type `*.DOC` in the File specification box. Click on or select the OK button to return to the Select Files screen. You can make more than one file-inclusion specification if you want, by repeatedly selecting the Include button. MSBACKUP keeps a list of all your inclusions and exclusions; you can review and edit them by selecting them from the Include/Exclude list at the bottom of the window. (For more on wildcards, see the box "Using Wildcards in DOS Commands" at the beginning of the DOS Cookbook.)

11. You can do any combination of manual or automatic file selections you want. You can also use the Exclude box, which works just like the Include box, except that it specifies a pattern for files that won't be backed up. A typical example would use the file pattern *.EXE to exclude all program files from the backup.

12. Once you've specified the files you want to back up, return to the main Backup screen by selecting the OK button. Note the message that tells you how many floppies you will need and approximately how long the backup process will take. If you have the time and enough disks, select Start Backup to begin the backup process. Backup will prompt you to insert disks, which need not be formatted, though they must be all of the same capacity.

Important Be sure to label your backup disks in order! Include the "backup catalog number" that MSBACKUP assigns you. You will need this if you have to restore files later.

Notes • If you have DOS 6.0, but you don't have the Microsoft Tools program group in your Program Manager, you can install it by rerunning the DOS 6.0 installation program. If you have DOS 5.0 and not 6.0, you can use DOS 5.0's Backup program, from DOS. See the "To Back Up Your Hard Disk" recipe in the DOS Cookbook for details.

• It can take some time to specify all your backup settings. Fortunately, Backup lets you save the current settings to a "setup file." To save the current settings, select Save Setup from the File menu in the main Backup screen.

Next time you back up, you can choose Open Setup to load a saved setup file. You can have several setup files for different backup needs, such as a full disk backup, a backup of just document files, or a backup of just a few key directories.

• Backup has lots of features that I can't cover here. Remember that you can always get lots of help while running Backup by pressing F1 after you've started running the program. (See the "To Get Help With a Windows Program or Command" recipe.)

• For later backups, you may want to go to the Backup Type list
and change the type of backup from full backup (the default) to
"incremental" backup. An incremental backup backs up just
those files that have been created or changed since the last full
or incremental backup. If you use this method, you end up with
a large set of floppies from the full backup, plus a series of sets
of just one or a few disks that reflect the changes made since
the last backup.

A "differential" backup is similar, except that each time it backs
up everything that's been changed since the last full backup.
With this method, you end up with your original full backup
disk set and one new set that gradually grows larger as more
files are changed.

To Change the Color Scheme of Your Monitor

Why This one is just for fun. Microsoft provides several different color schemes that you can use for your Windows display. The default choice is low-key and restful. If that's not your style, you've got some pretty wild alternatives to choose from. You can also choose higher-contrast schemes that make the windows easier to work with on a monochrome monitor.

How **1.** In the Program Manager, double-click on the Control Panel icon in the Main program group. The icon looks like this:

Control Panel

2. You will see the Control Panel window.

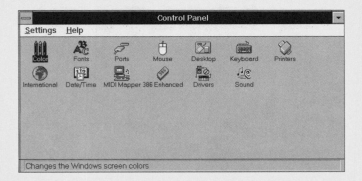

3. Now double-click on the Color icon. You will see this window:

The Color Window shows you an example of the current color scheme, showing what a window title, menu, and highlighted and background text look like.

4. To choose a different color scheme, click on the Color Schemes list box and select a scheme from the list by clicking on it. The display in the center of the Color window changes to reflect the new scheme. When you have found a scheme you like, press OK, and your scheme will take effect.

5. If you want to "fine tune" your color scheme or create a completely customized one, click on the Color Button. An additional window will appear.

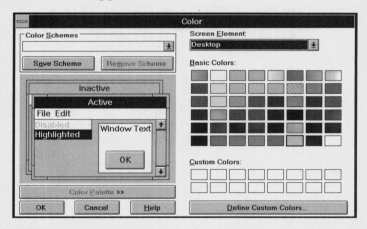

6. Select a screen element to work with from the list box at the top of the Color Palette window (for example, Window Background or Window Text). Then click on a color to choose it for that element, or click on Define Custom Colors to create the exact shade you want from the Custom Color Selector.

7. When you have defined colors for each Windows element, click on the Save Scheme button and type in a name under which to save your custom color scheme, Then click on OK, and your scheme will take effect.

Notes • If you're running Windows on a monochrome monitor, try the Monochrome color scheme. If you have a laptop, try the LCD option. They should provide the best contrast.

To Change the System Date and Time

Why Your PC has a battery-powered clock that keeps track of the date even when the machine is off. The system date is used to keep track of creation and modification dates for files, which are displayed in directory listings, so having the correct date and time is important. You will need to reset your system time at least twice a year, when the time changes to and from Daylight Savings Time.

How **1.** In the Program Manager, click on the Control Panel icon in the Main program group. The icon looks like this:

Control Panel

2. You will see the Control Panel window.

3. Now click on the Date/Time icon, and you will see this window:

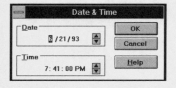

4. To change the date, click on the part of the date display you want to change (month, day, or year), and then either type in the correct number or click on the up and down buttons to the right of the date to increase or decrease the number.

Windows Cookbook

5. To change the time, click on the part of the time display you want to change (hours, minutes, seconds, AM, or PM), and then either type in the correct number or click on the up and down buttons to the right of the time to increase or decrease the number and toggle between AM and PM.

6. When you've finished, click on the OK button. If you decide not to change the settings after all, click on Cancel.

To Find Out What Version of Windows You Are Using

Why New versions of Windows come out periodically. If you get a new program, it might not run under the version you have. You can find out what version of Windows you're running and upgrade, if necessary.

How 1. In the Program Manager, choose About from the Help menu (Alt H A) You will see a little box like this:

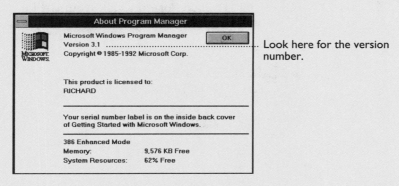

Look here for the version number.

2. Note the Windows version. In the example here, we're running Windows version 3.1.

To Format a Floppy Disk

Why Before you save anything on a new floppy disk, you must "format" it, which magnetizes it in a pattern DOS recognizes. Formatting is also a good way to erase an entire disk, when you want to reuse it for new information.

How **1.** Insert a new floppy disk in a disk drive.

2. In the File Manager, choose Format Disk from the Disk menu (Alt D F). Windows will display the Format dialog box shown here:

3. In the Format dialog box, choose the options you want.

• If you are formatting a low-density disk in a high-density drive, change the drive capacity.

• If you want the disk to have a descriptive label in its directory listings, type the text in the Label box.

• If you want to use the disk to boot (start) the system, click in the Make System Disk check box.

• If the disk is already formatted and you just want to wipe out its directories and files for a clean slate, click in the Quick Format check box.

4. When you've specified all your options, click OK (or press Enter).

Windows will display a box warning you that formatting will erase everything on the floppy disk.

5. When you're sure you have the right disk in the drive, click OK (or press Enter). Windows will display a box informing you of the progress of the formatting operation. When it's done, it will ask you if you'd like to format another.

6. Click on Yes if you want to format another disk; otherwise click on No.

Windows Cookbook

To Restore Files You Have Backed Up With the Backup Program

Why Your hard disk has crashed. The shop fixes it, but you have to restore all your files back to the disk from your backup copies. Or maybe things aren't quite that bad, but you've tried to use a particular file and you get a disk error message. It's time to restore it from the backups you made earlier. (Remember?)

How **1.** In the Program Manager, double-click on the Microsoft Tools program group, and then double-click on the Backup icon.

2. When you see the main Backup screen, click on the Restore button. The Restore screen shown here will appear:

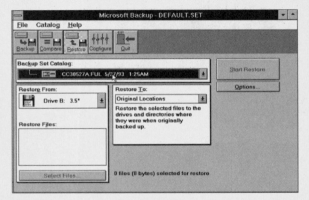

3. Click on the arrow at the right of the Backup Set Catalog box to see the drop-down list. Find the catalog number that matches the one that you've put on the label of the disk set from which you'll be restoring files (the one you wrote on your backup disks when you did the backup). Click on the catalog name or highlight it with the arrow keys and press Enter. (You could also just type it in.)

4. If the Restore From box doesn't show the drive that will contain your backup disks, click on the arrow next to the box and then click on the appropriate drive letter in the drop-down list.

5. If you want to restore all the files on your backup set, double-click on the drive letter under Restore From.

If you want to restore only certain files, click on the Select Files button. The Select Restore Files screen will appear:

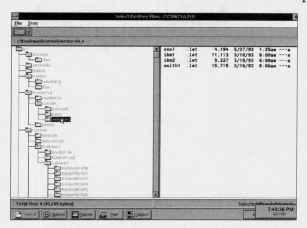

This screen works in much the same way as the one you used to select files to back up (described in the "To Back Up Your Hard Disk" recipe). If you want to restore only certain files in the directory, select the files to be restored from the file list window. Repeat until you have selected all the directories and files you want to restore.

6. Now choose a directory to which you want to restore files. By default, files will be restored to their original locations. If you want to restore the files to a different drive and/or directory, click on the arrow to the right of the Restore To box and choose Alternate Disk or Alternate Directory from the drop-down list. You will be asked to specify the particular directory and/or disk during the restore process.

Windows Cookbook

7. Click on the Options button. In the dialog box that appears, click on the options you want.

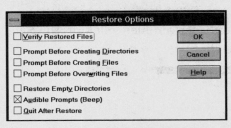

8. Choose the Start Restore button to begin restoring files. DOS will prompt you when it is time to insert a disk in the drive.

To See How Much Room Is Left on Your Hard Disk

Why Hard disks fill up surprisingly quickly. It's a good idea to check periodically to make sure your hard disk isn't getting too full. That way, you won't be surprised when your program won't let you save your files because there's no room.

How In the File Manager, click on the drive icon for your hard disk (usually C:). The bottom of the screen will show the drive letter, the amount of space free, the amount of space used, and the number of files and bytes in the current directory.

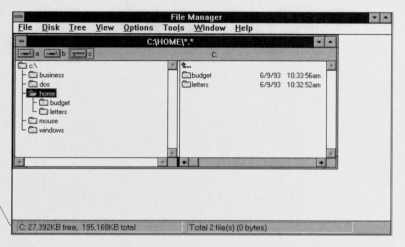

This number tells you how much hard disk space you have left.

Notes • If the File Manager tells you that you have less than 5 MB (5,000 K) left on your hard disk, it's time to do some housecleaning. Use the File Manager to review your directories and files, and delete or archive any files that you don't need.

Glossary

A

adapter See *expansion board*.

application program A piece of software that does a particular task, such as word processing, database management, or accounting.

ASCII Pronounced "as-key," it stands for American Standard Code for Information Interchange. It's another term for *plain text*, a file format that includes only alphabetic characters and no format information.

AUTOEXEC.BAT A special *batch file* that DOS runs automatically each time you start the computer. The AUTOEXEC.BAT file is usually used to automatically start up programs you use all the time, such as Windows.

B

backing up Creating copies of program and data files, in case the original is damaged.

batch file A DOS file that holds a list of *DOS commands*. When you type the name of a batch file at the *DOS prompt*, DOS executes all the commands listed in the file. All batch files end in the extension .BAT.

baud A term used to describe data-transmission speeds, especially for modems. Baud is often used to mean *bits per second* (bps).

BIOS Stands for "basic input/output system." A chip that determines how your computer works with peripherals and software.

bit The smallest unit of measurement for electronic data, a bit is one on or off signal. Eight bits make one *byte*.

bit-mapped graphics Graphics that are made up of an arrangement of tiny dots.

bits per second A measurement of data-transmission speeds, especially for modems. Abbreviated bps.

board See *expansion board.*

boot To start up the computer. The word is derived from the expression "to pull up by the bootstraps," because the computer uses information stored in its own memory to start itself up.

bps See *bits per second.*

bug An error in a computer program or system. It got its name when a moth was found on a tube in one of the first computers.

bus Pathways for moving data inside a computer. It's important to know what bus standard your computer uses so that you can buy compatible expansion boards. See also *EISA, ISA, Local Bus,* and *MCA.*

button A Windows program control that you click on with the mouse to activate.

byte Eight *bits.* A byte is enough information to convey a single alphabetic character in a file.

C

C prompt See *DOS prompt.*

cache memory A portion of memory set aside for temporary storage, generally used to speed up processing.

CAD See *computer aided design.*

card See *expansion board.*

cartridge drive A storage system that uses removable disk cartridges.

CD-ROM Stands for "compact disc, read-only memory." A technology used to store large amounts of information. CD-ROM discs look like the CDs you buy for a stereo system. They are about the same size as a floppy, but they hold much more information (about 600 megabytes).

They are used for distributing lots of information, such as graphics libraries or on-line reference works. The data on a CD-ROM is permanently etched and cannot be changed.

central processing unit The *chip* on a computer's *system board* that does the main processing. For PCs, these chips are of the Intel 80X86 family (80286, 80386, and 80486), as well as Intel's new Pentium processor. Abbreviated CPU.

CGA Stands for "Color Graphics Adapter." The original color graphics standard for PCs, now outmoded. See also *VGA* and *SVGA*.

check box In Windows, a program control that allows you to pick an option by clicking in a box next the the option name.

chip See *processor*.

click To press and release the *mouse button* once to select something on screen.

clip art Files containing ready-made pictures that you can buy on disk and use in your own work.

Clipboard In Windows, a temporary holding place for information you cut or copy from a document. Data from the last cut or copy is kept on the Clipboard so that you can paste it to a new location.

clone A computer that is not made by IBM but is *IBM-compatible*.

COM The designation for your computer's *serial ports*. The first serial port is referred to as COM1, the second as COM2, and so on. You use the name to tell setup programs where they can find peripherals, such as modems or mice, that are connected to the computer via serial ports.

COMMAND.COM A file that holds some of the information DOS needs to carry out the *boot* process.

communications software A kind of software that handles sending and receiving information between computers.

communications standards The languages that a communications program or modem understands.

computer aided design Using a computer for product design. Abbreviated CAD.

CONFIG.SYS A file stored in the *root directory* of your hard disk that DOS reads each time you start up your computer. It includes instructions for DOS about how to set up memory and other system configurations.

context-sensitive help On-line help that gives you information for the task you are in the middle of. For example, if you are using a particular dialog box in an application and call up help, a program that offered context-sensitive help would automatically bring up a help window pertaining to that dialog box.

CPU See *central processing unit.*

CRT Stands for "cathode ray tube." See *monitor.*

current directory When you issue a DOS command that applies to a file, this is where DOS assumes the file is located, unless you specify a different directory.

cursor The blinking line that shows your position on the computer's screen.

cursor keys On a keyboard, the keys, labeled with arrows, that move the cursor around the screen.

D

database Any collection of information, from a phone book to a company's inventory data. On a computer, you use a *database management program* to create and control databases.

database management program Software designed to handle large amounts of information on a computer.

desktop publishing Using a personal computer to lay out complex documents.

dialog box In Windows, a box from which you choose command options.

directory 1. A section on a hard disk, like a file folder in a file cabinet, in which you keep a related set of files. 2. A list of the files that are saved on a disk.

directory tree A depiction of the directory structure of a disk, so called because it branches from a root directory in a treelike, many-branched structure.

disk A magnetic surface on which information is written for permanent storage. Most PC users use internal *hard disks* to save the bulk of their data. *Floppy disks* are used to distribute files to others and to *back up* hard disk data.

disk cache An area in memory that's used to temporarily store information from the disk drive. Its use speeds up operations because the computer can access memory faster than it can access the *disk*.

disk drive The mechanism that reads information from a *disk*.

disk drive name The name assigned by DOS to each of a computer's drives. The first floppy drive is drive A:, the second is drive B:, the first hard disk is drive C:, and so on.

display See *monitor*.

display adapter An *expansion board* that translates data into video information for a monitor.

DOS Stands for "disk operating system." It is the *operating system* used by most IBM-compatible PCs.

DOS command Commands you type on the DOS command line (at the C> prompt).

DOS command line See *DOS prompt*.

DOS prompt The line DOS displays when it's waiting for a DOS command. On most computers it will be some variation of C:\>. (The letter, in this case C, names the current disk drive.)

DOS Shell A program that comes with DOS 5.0 (and later versions of DOS) that provides a simpler *interface* for DOS.

dot matrix printer A type of *printer* that creates images using a multipin print head. The most inexpensive printers use a 9-pin print head; the best use a 24-pin print head.

dot pitch A measure of the closeness of the tiny red, green, and blue dots that make up each *pixel* on a color monitor.

double-click To press and release the *mouse button* twice in quick succession.

double-density One of two densities for floppy disks. (The other is referred to as *high-density*.) A double-density 3.5-inch disk holds 720 kilobytes of data. A double-density 5.25-inch disk holds 360 kilobytes.

dragging A mouse action that consists of moving the mouse with the mouse button pressed down, usually in order to move an object or select a string of text on screen.

drawing program A program that creates *object-based graphics*, that is, creates pictures from collections of individual geometric shapes.

drive A: A PC's first floppy drive.

drive B: A PC's second floppy drive.

drive C: A PC's hard drive.

driver A small program that runs peripheral hardware. Drivers are usually loaded into memory via the *CONFIG.SYS* file.

drop-down list In Windows, a list showing options for a *field* that appears when you click an arrow next to the field.

E

e-mail See *electronic mail*.

EISA Stands for "extended industry-standard architecture." A hardware standard that determines what kind of *expansion boards* you can use in your computer. An EISA computer can use EISA or *ISA* boards.

electronic mail A method of posting messages over a *network* or via a *modem*. The addressee receives the message almost instantaneously.

error message A message displayed by a piece of software to inform you that something has gone wrong. Error messages are sometimes in the form of codes that you must look up in the software manual or report to a technician.

error-correction protocol A communications standard used by modems to make sure that information has been transferred correctly.

expansion board Boards that add processors to your *system board* to add extra functions to your computer. You add expansion boards via your computer's *expansion slots.*

expansion slot A place set aside on your computer's *system board* where you can attach *expansion boards* to add extra functions to your computer.

F

fax modem A modem that has the capability of sending and receiving faxes to and from regular fax machines or other computers with fax modems.

field 1. A place in a *dialog box* into which you add information. 2. One area of information in a *database.*

file A collection of data with a name attached, saved on a computer's disk.

file extension Three characters following a period at the end of a *file name.* The file extension usually indicates the *file format.*

file format The kind of data a file holds. Any *application program* can read and save only certain file formats. The file format is usually indicated by the file's *file extension.*

File Manager The area in Windows from which you can view, delete, copy, open, and otherwise manipulate files. You open the File Manager by double-clicking on its icon in the *Program Manager.*

file name The name assigned to a file. A file name can be up to eight characters long, with a three-character *file extension.*

flat-file database A database management system that can work with information from only one file at a time. Cf. *relational database.*

floppy disk A portable disk consisting of a floppy mylar disk enclosed in a pliable or hard shell.

floppy disk drive The mechanism in a PC that reads data from and saves data to floppy disks.

font A collection of characters in a certain type style.

format *1.* To prepare a floppy disk to hold information, via the DOS command FORMAT. *2.* The kind of information saved in a file. *3.* To add design information to a document.

freeware See *public domain software.*

function keys A set of keys on a PC keyboard, usually labeled F1, F2, and so on, which can be programmed to carry out special commands.

G

gigabyte About a billion *bytes* or a thousand *megabytes* of data (1,073,741,824 bytes). Abbreviated GB.

H

handshake A process in which two modems establish the speed and *protocols* to be used during a connection.

hard disk A storage device, either internal or external to a computer's system unit, that holds large amounts of data.

hardware The physical components of a computer system. Cf. *software.*

high-density One of two densities for floppy disks. (The other is referred to as *double-density.*) A high-density 3.5-inch disk holds 1.4 megabytes of data. A high-density 5.25-inch disk holds 720 kilobytes.

I

IBM compatible 1. A PC that works with any software or hardware that is designed for an IBM personal computer. 2. As an adjective, software or hardware that works with such computers.

icon In Windows, a small picture that represents a file, a program, or a command.

ink jet printer A type of printer that creates images on the page with controlled spurts of ink. See also *laser printer* and *dot matrix printer*.

insertion point In Windows, an *I*-shaped indicator, similar to a cursor, that shows where any text you type will be inserted. You place the insertion point by pointing to the desired location with the mouse and clicking the mouse button.

integrated program A program that combines features of several application programs in one, usually word processing, spreadsheet, database, graphics, and communications.

interface The rules by which a piece of software communicates with you and you with it. Each piece of software has its own interface, although Windows programs generally have similar interfaces.

interlacing For monitors, a method of drawing an image on screen in which only every other line of information is drawn in each pass. Non-interlaced monitors have a more stable image.

ISA Stands for "industry-standard architecture." A hardware standard that determines what kind of *expansion boards* you can use in your computer. An ISA computer can use only ISA boards.

J K

keyboard The typewriterlike mechanism you use to input text and give commands.

kilobyte 1024 *bytes*. Abbreviated K or KB.

L

laptop PC A small, usually battery-powered PC that combines the *keyboard, monitor,* and *system unit* into a single, portable unit. The term usually refers to portable PCs that weigh between six and ten pounds. Cf. *notebook PC.*

laser printer A type of printer that writes images onto paper using a laser beam, similar to the mechanism used for a copy machine. Generally, laser printers provide the highest-quality images available from a desktop printer.

Local Bus A hardware standard that determines what kind of *expansion boards* you can use in your computer. A Local Bus computer can use only Local Bus boards.

LPT The PC's designation for *parallel ports.* The first parallel port is LPT1, the second is LPT2, and so on. You use the name to tell setup programs where they can find printers and other peripherals that are connected to the computer via those ports.

M

Macintosh A type of personal computer made by Apple Computer. Macintoshes use a different operating system and run different application software than do IBM-compatible PCs. They use an interface similar to Windows.

macro A command that activates a series of actions or types a preset string of characters. Many applications include a macro capability. You can also buy special programs that let you add macros to a number of different applications.

math coprocessor A *processor*, specially designed for speedy math calculations, that is added to the *system board* of some computers.

MCA Stands for "Micro Channel Architecture." A hardware standard that determines what kind of *expansion boards* you can use in your computer. MCA computers can use only MCA boards.

megabyte About a million bytes (1,048,576, to be exact). Abbreviated MB.

megahertz A measurement of processor speeds. Abbreviated MHz.

memory The place where a computer keeps programs and files when they are in use. Also called *random access memory* (RAM). Cf. *storage*.

menu A list of commands displayed by a program from which you choose the command you want to give next.

menu bar In Windows programs, the list of menu names that ranges across the top of an application's main window.

Microsoft Windows An operating environment that adds an easy-to-use *interface* and other features to DOS.

modem A device that *mo*dulates computer data into signals that can be carried over phone lines, and *dem*odulates data it receives from other modems over phone lines into a form readable by the computer. Modems work with communications software to let you retrieve data from distant computers.

monitor The televisionlike screen on which programs display information. Also called CRT or *display*.

motherboard See *system board*.

mouse A device that allows you to easily give commands and select items on screen.

mouse button A control on the top of a mouse that you click in order to activate a command.

mouse pad A pad used under a mouse to make its movements more smooth.

mouse port A socket on the back of some computers that is designed specifically for plugging a mouse into.

MS-DOS Stands for "Microsoft disk operating system." The standard *operating system* for *IBM-compatible* PCs.

multiscan monitor A monitor designed to work with a variety of graphics adapters.

N

network A collection of personal computers that are wired together so that users of each one can share files and *electronic mail*.

notebook PC An especially small, battery-operated PC, typically weighing between four and seven pounds.

O

object-based graphics Graphics created from collections of individual geometric shapes that can be manipulated separately. See also *drawing program*.

on-line help Information about a piece of software that you can call up on your computer's screen. For Windows programs, you can almost always get on-line help by pressing the F1 key. See also *context-sensitive help*.

on-line bulletin board A service that allows computer users with modems to post and retrieve electronic messages for a special-interest community. Sometimes known as a "BBS" (bulletin board service).

on-line service A service, available by subscription, that offers such features as *electronic mail*, libraries containing all types of information, *shareware* and *public domain software*, and on-line forums on which you can chat via your keyboard with other subscribers. You access on-line services with a *modem* and *communications software*.

operating system The software that takes care of basic system activities, such as reading from and saving to disk, so that application software can focus on doing its own particular tasks. For PCs, the standard operating system is MS-DOS.

optical disc A storage device that can hold large amounts of data and is less vulnerable than other types of storage to harm, but is somewhat slower than a hard disk.

P

painting program Graphics software that creates *bit-mapped graphics*, which create a picture by assembling tiny black-and-white or color dots.

parallel port A connector used to attach printers and other devices to the computer.

path A string of directory names that tells DOS where to locate to a particular file or directory. A path has three parts: the disk drive name, the list of directories that leads to the designated file or directory, and finally, the file name, if appropriate. The directory names are separated by backslash characters (\). If you don't specify a path, DOS assumes the file is in the *current directory*.

PC Stands for *personal computer*, but usually refers more specifically to an *IBM-compatible* personal computer.

PC comptible See *IBM compatible*.

PC-DOS IBM's version of *DOS*. It's virtually identical to *MS-DOS*.

PCL A language used by Hewlett-Packard and HP-compatible laser printers. Stands for Printer Control Language.

PCMCIA card A type of *expansion board* made for laptop computers.

peripheral Hardware, such as a *modem* or *printer*, that you use with a computer.

personal computer Any computer made to be used by a single person.

personal information manager A kind of database program designed to be used for names, addresses, and scheduling information. Often abbreviated PIM.

PIF Stands for "program information file." A file used with Windows programs that determines how the program is configured.

piracy Illegally copying someone else's software, rather than buying your own copy.

pixel Short for "picture element." On a monitor, one pixel is a single dot of light out of all the dots that make up an image.

plain text See *ASCII*.

pointer An on-screen indicator that shows the movements of a *mouse*.

port A connector used to attach devices to the computer. See also *parallel port* and *serial port*.

PostScript A language created by Adobe Systems, commonly used in desktop publishing applications and high-end laser printers.

printer A device that puts text or pictures on paper.

processor A circuit in a computer that processes information. Processors are attached to the *system board* or to add-on *expansion boards*. See also *central processing unit* and *coprocessor*.

program file A file that holds program code. In DOS, program files end with the extension .EXE, .COM, or .BAT.

program group In Windows, a set of programs grouped under a single name and displayed as an icon in the *Program Manager*.

Program Manager The area in Windows from which you start programs.

prompt A signal presented by a piece of software when it needs information from you.

protocol A standard method of communication agreed upon by software manufacturers so that data can be transferred between *modems*.

public domain software Software that its creators give out freely, without asking for payment. Also called *freeware*. Public domain software is available from *on-line services*, *user groups*, and companies that sell compendiums of programs. See also *shareware*.

pull-down menu A *menu*, such as those used by Windows, that drops from the top of the screen when a user selects it.

Q R

radio button In Windows, a program control that lets you pick on option from a set of options by clicking on a round button next to the option name.

RAM See *memory*.

random access memory See *memory*.

READ.ME file A text file distributed along with many software programs that informs the user of any important information the software publishers have that didn't make it into the user's manual.

reboot To turn off your computer and start it again, or to press the Ctrl, Alt, and Del keys simultaneously to restart it. It's what you do when a computer freezes up. Many computers also provide a reset button that reboots the computer without turning off the power.

relational database A database management program that is able to work with data from more than one file at a time. Cf. *flat-file database*.

resolution A measure of how many pieces of information are in a particular area in a visual representation. On printers, resolution is measured in dots per inch; on monitors, it is measured by the number of pixels on the screen. The higher the number, the sharper the image.

RGB Stands for "red, green, blue," the primary colors used by a computer monitor to create an entire spectrum of colors. Sometimes people refer to a color monitor as an RGB monitor.

root directory The top-level directory in a h*ard disk*'s *directory structure*. All directories you create on your hard disk are subdirectories of the root directory.

RS-232 port A term often used to refer to a *serial port*.

S

scanner A device that translates a graphic image into a computer-readable file.

screen shield A detachable plate that can be added to a *monitor* to reduce glare and, in some cases, radiation from the monitor.

scroll bar In Windows, a control that appears whenever a window contains more than it can show at one time. You can scroll the window's contents by clicking in the scroll bar.

serial port A connector used to attach *peripherals* to the computer. Usually the serial ports are used for *mice* and *modems,* while parallel ports are used by *printers.*

shareware Software that is distributed for free but that you are asked to pay for if you keep using it after an initial trial period. Shareware is usually distributed over *on-line services* and by *user groups* and can be freely copied among friends and co-workers. See also *public domain software.*

SIMM Stands for "single in-line memory module." A device, designed to plug easily into your computer's *system board,* that holds memory chips.

slot See *expansion slot.*

software Computer programs. Cf. *hardware.*

sound board An expansion board that increases the sound capabilities of your computer. Used with games, educational software, and music applications.

spreadsheet A type of *application program* designed for working with numbers. A spreadsheet's *interface* is patterned after an accountant's worksheet, with the data arranged in rows and columns.

storage Where you keep files not currently in use. It usually refers to a computer's hard disk. Cf. *memory.*

subdirectory A directory that rests inside another directory on a disk.

Super VGA A graphics standard that supplies color resolution at 800 by 600 *pixels* or 1024 by 768 pixels, depending on the software. (VGA stands for "Virtual Graphics Adapter.")

surge protector A device that a computer plugs into that protects the computer from electrical surges. (The surge protector itself plugs into an electrical wall outlet.)

SVGA See *Super VGA.*

system board The main board in the computer's *system unit* that holds the *central processing unit, memory,* and other circuitry.

system disk A disk that holds the DOS files that a PC uses to *boot* from.

system unit The box that holds the computer's workings, including the *system board* and *disk drives*.

T

tape cartridge A storage device, usually used for backing up hard drives, that stores data on magnetic tape.

text box In Windows, a box into which you type information.

text editor A simple word processor that creates text in ASCII format. Text editors are generally used to work with program files, such as AUTOEXEC.BAT, that must be in pure text format.

trackball A device, consisting of a rotating ball embedded in a base, that can be used instead of a mouse.

TrueType A type standard used by *Microsoft Windows* to control the look of type on screen and in printed output.

U

user group A group of computer users who band together to offer each other help with computer problems and other computer-related services.

utility A piece of software that carries out a special function, such as checking for viruses or backing up your hard disk.

V

vertical refresh rate Describes the number of times per second that a monitor's screen is redrawn from top to bottom, measured in Hertz (Hz). The higher the number, the less flicker on screen. A refresh rate of 72 Hz is considered good for SVGA monitors.

VGA Stands for "Virtual Graphics Array." A graphics standard that offers 640- by 480-pixel color resolution. It is the current minimum standard for color monitors.

virus Software designed to cause damage to computers or files. Viruses generally enter your computer system via files you receive on floppy disks or over networks. They can be guarded against with a virus-detection program.

W X Y Z

wildcard A symbol used in DOS commands that can stand for unknown characters in a file name. The DOS wildcard symbols are * (which stands for any number of characters) and ? (which stands for a single character).

window A frame on the computer's screen that contains a file, an application, or a group of icons.

word processor A type of *application program* that enables users to write, edit, and format text and, often, incorporate graphics.

workstation Another word for *personal computer*. Usually it refers to especially powerful PCs.

wrist rest A soft pad that sits in front of a keyboard to support your wrists as you type to guard against wrist injuries associated with extensive keyboard use.

workstaion Another word for personal computer. Typically, it refers to especially powerful PCs. It also refers to PCs that are connected to a *network*.

write-protecting Using a device on a floppy disk to ensure that nothing can be saved to the disk.

WYSIWYG Pronounced "wizzy-wig." Stands for "what you see is what you get." Used to refer to programs that can display a document on screen exactly as it will be printed.

Index

cursor, 9
cursor keys, 55
cutting and pasting
    in Windows, 300

D

damaged files
    recovering, 240-242
data bus
    See bus
database management programs, 120,
    141–147, 164
DATE command, 255
dBase IV (Borland), 142, 145
DBLSPACE command, 236
DEL (delete) command, 215
Del (Delete) key, 55
deleting
    directories, 213–214, 321–322
    files, 215, 323
    in Windows documents, 299
    programs from program groups, 290
Dell Computer, 30
DELTREE (delete tree) command, 213–214
densities (of floppy disks), 106
Design Your Own Home series
    (Abracadata), 158
DeskJet printers (Hewlett-Packard), 64, 66
desks, 86
desktop presentation software, 156–157
desktop publishing, 120
dialog boxes, 268–269
DIR (directory) command
    finding a file with, 216–217
    checking whether a file is present with,
      218
    listing files in a directory with, 220
    checking disk space with, 231
directories, 97–100
    creating, 212, 320
    deleting, 213–214, 321–322
    listing files in, 216–217, 327
    moving between, 100, 207
    organizing, 101–102
    renaming in Windows, 309–310
directory tree, 100
    viewing, 222
disk cache, 36

disk drives
    names of, 99
    See also floppy disk drives; hard disks
disk space
    creating, 236–237
    See also compression software
DISKCOPY command, 234–235
display adapters, 48
displays
    See monitors
DOS, 8, 9
    finding out what version you're using,
      259
    going to from Windows, 286
    using, 9–10, 198
    utility programs in, 167, 169
DOS commands
    batch files and, 94
    controlling the output of, 223
    parameters in, 199
    paths in, 200
    using, 10, 198, 201
    wildcards in, 202
    See also individual commands
DOS prompt, 9, 89, 198
    and the current directory, 201, 207
DOS Shell, 10, 89
dot matrix printers, 60, 64–65, 67
    color, 66
dot pitch (of monitors), 52
double-clicking, 14
DoubleSpace program, 41, 169
    using, 236–237
dragging (as a mouse command), 14
drawing software, 150–152, 164
drivers, 95, 253
drop-down lists (in Windows), 269
Dvorak's Guide to PC Games, 176

E

e-mail
    See electronic mail
Eclipse Fax (Eclipse), 73
EDIT program, 135, 249–250, 251–252,
    253–254, 257–258
Egghead Software, 125, 127
EISA (bus), 47

multimedia presentations, 156
multiscan monitors, 48

N

naming
    directories, 99, 309
    files, 91–92, 209, 309
New York Times Crossword Puzzle (SWFTE), 181
Norton Anti-Virus (Symantec), 169
Norton Backup (Symantec), 110
Norton Utilities (Symantec), 114, 167
notebook computers, 28
    See also laptop computers
Num Lock (Number Lock) key, 55
number pad
    See numeric keypad
numeric keypad, 55

O

object-based graphics, 150
    See also drawing software
OCR (optical character recognition), 69
Office Layout (Autodesk), 158
Okidata printers, 65
Okna Desktop Set (Okna), 147
on-line services, 20, 68–69, 75, 160, 170
    and modem speed, 70
    faxing via, 72
on-line help, 15
    in DOS, 198, 203–205
    in Windows, 272–273
opening files in Windows, 301–302, 303
operating system, 9
    See also DOS
Operation Neptune (The Learning Company), 189
optical character recognition , 69
optical discs, 45
options (in DOS commands), 199
OS/2, 10

P

PageMaker (Aldus), 134
painting software, 152, 154–155
PaintJet printers (Hewlett-Packard), 66
Panasonic printers, 65
Paradox (Borland), 142, 144–145

parallel ports, 46
    plugging a printer into, 82
PATH command, 200, 206, 249–250
paths, 97–100
    in DOS commands, 200
Pause/Break key, 54
PC -SIG, 126
PC Brands computers, 30
PC compatible, 7–8
PC/Computing, 19
PC Connection, 126
PC Magazine, 19
PC Novice, 19
PC Paintbrush V+ (Z-Soft), 149, 155
PC Today, 19
PC Tools (Central Point Software), 114, 167, 168
PC World, 19
PC Write, 131
PC Zone, 126
PC-File (ButtonWare), 142, 145
PCL (Printer Control Language), 63
PCMCIA cards, 28
.PCX files, 154, 155
Pentium processor, 9, 35
peripherals, 46
Personal Tax Edge (Parsons Technology), 173
personal information managers, 142, 145–147
Persuasion (Aldus), 156
PFS: First Choice (Spinnaker), 165
photo retouching, 155
PhotoFinish (Z-Soft), 154, 156
Photoshop (Adobe), 156
PhotoStyler (Aldus), 156
PIF files, 282
PIMs
    See personal information managers
piracy, 128–129
pixels
    See monitors, resolution
PKUNZIP (PKWARE), 170
PKWARE
    PKUNZIP, 170
    PKZIP, 170
PKZIP (PKWARE), 170
Playroom (Broderbund), 184, 185